Ethnicity, Nationalism, and Minority Rights

This interdisciplinary collection addresses the position of minorities in democratic societies, with a particular focus on minority rights and recognition. For the first time, it brings together leading international authorities on ethnicity, nationalism, and minority rights from both social and political theory, with the specific aim of fostering further debate between the disciplines. In their introduction, the editors explore the ways in which politics and sociology can complement each other in unraveling the many contradictory aspects of these complex phenomena. Topics addressed include the constructed nature of ethnicity, its relation to class and to "new racism," different forms of nationalism, self-determination, and indigenous politics, the politics of recognition versus the politics of redistribution, and the reemergence of cosmopolitanism. This book is essential reading for all those involved in the study of ethnicity, nationalism, and minority rights.

STEPHEN MAY is Professor of Education at the University of Waikato, New Zealand and a Senior Research Fellow in the Centre for the Study of Ethnicity and Citizenship at the University of Bristol.

TARIQ MODOOD is Professor of Sociology, Politics, and Public Policy and the founding Director of the Centre for the Study of Ethnicity and Citizenship at the University of Bristol.

JUDITH SQUIRES is a Senior Lecturer in the Department of Politics and a member of the Centre for the Study of Ethnicity and Citizenship at the University of Bristol.

Ethnicity, Nationalism, and Minority Rights

Edited by

Stephen May, Tariq Modood, and Judith Squires

CAMBRIDGE
UNIVERSITY PRESS

CAMBRIDGE UNIVERSITY PRESS
Cambridge, New York, Melbourne, Madrid, Cape Town, Singapore,
São Paulo, Delhi, Dubai, Tokyo, Mexico City

Cambridge University Press
The Edinburgh Building, Cambridge CB2 8RU, UK

Published in the United States of America by Cambridge University Press, New York

www.cambridge.org
Information on this title: www.cambridge.org/9780521603171

First published 2004

A catalogue record for this publication is available from the British Library

Library of Congress Cataloguing in Publication data
Ethnicity, nationalism, and minority rights / edited by Stephen May, Tariq
Modood, and Judith Squires.
  p. cm.
Includes bibliographical references and index.
ISBN 0 521 84229 8 – ISBN 0 521 60317 X (pb.)
1. Ethnicity. 2. Human rights. 3. Minorities – Civil rights. 4. Indigenous
peoples – Civil rights. 5. Nationalism. 6. Self-determination, National.
I. May, Stephen. II. Modood, Tariq. III. Squires, Judith.
GN495.6.E8934 2004
305.8 – dc22   2004045703

ISBN 978-0-521-84229-7 Hardback
ISBN 978-0-521-60317-1 Paperback

Contents

Part III.   New directions

Preface

Like many publications, this one has had a long gestation. The idea for it has emerged, over time, from a number of closely related ventures with which we have been centrally involved.

The first of these was a major conference, Nationalism, Identity and Minority Rights, organised by the three of us, at the University of Bristol in September 1999. The conference had two principal aims. The first was to achieve a critical nexus between the disciplines of sociology and politics with respect to debates on ethnicity, nationalism, and identity politics. The second key aim of the conference was to achieve an international perspective on these issues, drawing from as wide a variety of social and political contexts as possible. In both respects, the conference was regarded as a major success. Key commentators from within sociology and politics, as well as other related disciplines such as anthropology, cultural studies, and education, contributed to the conference. The internationalism of the conference was represented both by the range of contexts discussed, and by the participants themselves, who came from thirty-seven countries.

At the conference, the Centre for the Study of Ethnicity and Citizenship, situated within the Sociology Department at the University of Bristol, and with Tariq Modood as its Director, was also launched. The Centre has subsequently become a key UK contributor to funded research in these areas.

Also closely associated with the centre has been the establishment in 2001 of the international journal, *Ethnicities*, edited by Stephen May and Tariq Modood. The journal's aims reflect those of the conference – to promote a critical dialectic between sociology and politics, and related disciplines, in relation to ethnicity, nationalism and identity politics. A related objective of the journal is to examine the complex interconnections between culture and structure with respect to the mobilisation of ethnicity, other social movements, and the implications of such mobilisations for modern nation-states. In this sense, it aims specifically to bring together the more 'traditional' materialist emphases and concerns of race and ethnicity studies, with the wider theoretical debates on the (re)construction of democratic societies.

And it is this last concern that we want to revisit in more detail and in more depth in this edited collection. In order to do this, we have again brought together many of the leading academic commentators in social and political theory to discuss explicitly these issues and their interconnections. In so doing, we hope to show what each discipline can offer the other in terms of continuing to build our understanding, and explication, of the complex phenomena that are ethnicity, nationalism, and minority rights, along with their individual and collective impact on modern nation-states.

This is, we believe, crucially important if academic debates on these issues are to continue to move forward. However, there is also of course much more at stake here as well. After all, *how* the politics of ethnicity, nationalism, and minority rights are enacted and outworked in the social and political contexts in which many of us live invariably has enormous, and sometimes very damaging, consequences for those whom it directly affects. This makes the effective study of ethnicity, nationalism, and minority rights all the more urgent.

In bringing this edited collection to print – and sometimes we did wonder if it would ever actually make it – we are enormously grateful to our contributors, who persisted with us and this project over what ended up being a much longer timeframe that we had ever anticipated. We would also like to thank the anonymous readers commissioned by CUP for their highly apposite and constructive comments on the original proposal and the first draft of the manuscript – the end result is significantly enhanced by these interventions.

To our colleagues and erstwhile colleagues in the Sociology and Politics Department at the University of Bristol, many thanks for providing the stimulating intellectual and collegial environment that allowed this work to develop. And finally to Sarah Caro at CUP, for her outstanding editorial support and advocacy throughout. It was she who encouraged us to persist with this edited collection, when we ourselves were at times not so sure. We hope that you will agree that the end result was worth it.

Stephen May, Tariq Modood and Judith Squires
May 2004

Contributors

ROGERS BRUBAKER is Professor of Sociology, UCLA. He has written widely on social theory, immigration, citizenship, and nationalism. His publications include *Citizenship and Nationhood in France and Germany* (1992) and *Nationalism Reframed: Nationhood and the National Question in the New Europe* (1996). *Ethnicity without Groups* is forthcoming.

CRAIG CALHOUN is Professor of Sociology and History at the Department of Sociology, New York University. He is also Director of the Center for Applied Research in Social Science. His publications include: *Neither Gods Nor Emperors: Students and the Struggle for Democracy in China* (1994), *Critical Social Theory: Culture, History and the Challenge of Difference* (1995), *Nationalism* (1997). *The Oxford Dictionary of the Social Sciences* is forthcoming.

PATRICIA HILL COLLINS is Chair of and Charles Phelps Taft Professor of Sociology within the Department of African American Studies at the University of Cincinnati. Much of her research and scholarship has dealt primarily with issues of race, gender, social class, and nation specifically relating to African American women. Her publications include *Black Feminist Thought: Knowledge, Consciousness, and the Politics of Empowerment* (1990); *Fighting Words: Black Women and the Search for Justice* (1998) and *Black Sexual Politics* (2003).

THOMAS HYLLAND ERIKSEN is Professor of Social Anthropology at the University of Oslo. He has written widely on nationalism, ethnicity, tribalism, (multi)cultural identity, creolization, and globalization. His publications include *Ethnicity and Nationalism: Anthropological Perspectives* (1993), *Tyranny of the Moment* (2001) and *Between Universalism and Relativism: A Critique of the UNESCO Concept of Culture* (2001).

WILL KYMLICKA is the Canada Research Chair in Political Philosophy in the Department of Philosophy, Queen's University Ontario and a visiting professor in the Nationalism Studies program at the Central European University in Budapest. His publications include *Liberalism,*

Community, and Culture (1989), *Contemporary Political Philosophy* (1990; 2nd edition 2002), *Multicultural Citizenship* (1995), *Finding Our Way: Rethinking Ethnocultural Relations in Canada* (1998), and *Politics in the Vernacular: Nationalism, Multiculturalism and Citizenship* (2001).

STEPHEN MAY is Professor of Education at the University of Waikato, New Zealand, and a Senior Research Fellow in the Centre for the Study of Ethnicity and Citizenship, University of Bristol. His research interests include the sociologies of language and education, ethnicity, nationalism, multiculturalism, and indigenous rights. Major recent publications include *Critical Multiculturalism* (1999), *Indigenous Community-based Education* (1999), *Language and Minority Rights: Ethnicity, Nationalism and the Politics of Language* (2001), and *Ethnonational Identities* with S. Fenton (2002). He is a founding editor of the international and interdisciplinary journal, *Ethnicities*.

TARIQ MODOOD is Professor of Sociology, Politics and Public Policy and the founding Director of the Centre for the Study of Ethnicity and Citizenship at the University of Bristol. He is a joint founding editor of the journal *Ethnicities*. His publications include *Not Easy Being British* (1992), (co-author) *Ethnic Minorities in Britain: Diversity and Disadvantage* (1997), and *Multicultural Politics: Racism, Ethnicity and Muslims in Britain* (2005); he has also co-edited *Debating Cultural Hybridity* (1997), *The Politics of Multiculturalism in the New Europe* (1997) and *Ethnicity, Social Mobility and Public Policy in the US and UK* (2004).

T. K. OOMMEN, recently retired from Jawaharlal Nehru University, and former President of the International Sociological Association, has published 18 books and over 100 articles on ethnicity and related topics. His recent books include: *Citizenship, Nationality and Ethnicity* (1997), *Equality, Identity and Pluralism* (2002), *Nation, Civil Society and Social Movements* (2004).

BHIKHU PAREKH is Centennial Professor at the London School of Economics. A leading interpreter of the history of political theory, he has written books on Bentham, Marx, and Gandhi. His most recent writings have been on the dilemmas of policy in multiethnic Britain and the political theories and principles that should guide thinking on these issues. His recent publications include *Rethinking Multiculturalism: Cultural Diversity and Political Theory* (2000), *Gandhi: A Very Short Introduction* (2001).

JAN NEDERVEEN PIETERSE is Professor of Sociology, University of Illinois Urbana-Champaign. He has written widely on global futures, the interaction of modernities, development theory, and social theory. His publications include *Empire and Emancipation: Power and Liberation on a World Scale* (1990), *White on Black: Images of Africa and Blacks in Western Popular Culture* (1992), and *World Orders in the Making: Humanitarian Intervention and Beyond* (ed.) (1998).

JUDITH SQUIRES is Senior Lecturer in the Department of Politics, University of Bristol. Her research focuses on contemporary political theories of democracy and citizenship, feminist political theory, and politics of gender. Her publications include *Women in Parliament: A Comparative Analysis* (2001), *Gender in Political Theory* (1999), *Feminisms: A Reader* (ed.) (1997), *Cultural Readings of Imperialism: Reflections on the Work of Edward Said* (ed.) (1997), *Principled Positions: Post Modernism in the Rediscovery of Value* (ed.) (1993).

IRIS MARION YOUNG is Professor of Political Science at the University of Chicago. She is affiliated with the Gender Studies Center and the Human Rights program. Her research interests are in contemporary political theory, feminist social theory, and normative analysis of public policy. Her books include *Justice and the Politics of Difference* (1990), *Throwing Like a Girl and Other Essays in Feminist Philosophy and Social Theory* (1990), *Intersecting Voices: Dilemmas of Gender, Political Philosophy, and Policy* (1997), and *Inclusion and Democracy* (2000).

NIRA YUVAL-DAVIS is Professor in the School of Cultural and Innovation Studies University of East London. Her research interests are in the social and political dynamics of the Zionist settler project and the ways it has affected gender, ethnic, national, and class divisions in Israel/Palestine. Her publications include *Racialized Boundaries* (1992, with F. Anthias), *Unsettling Settler Societies* (ed. with D. Stasiulis, 1995), *Gender and Nation* (1997) and *Women, Citizenship and Difference* (ed. with P. Werbner, 1999).

1 Ethnicity, nationalism, and minority rights: charting the disciplinary debates

Stephen May, Tariq Modood, and Judith Squires

Introduction

This edited collection aims to bring together key perspectives and debates in social and political theory on ethnicity, nationalism, and minority rights. This is important because, despite the rapidly burgeoning literature on these topics in recent years within both fields, their discussion continues to be largely situated – we would say, constrained – within their respective disciplinary traditions.

One of the interesting features of the way disciplines develop is how they reflect their own distinctive starting-points and dynamics. For example, a generation ago, social theory was strongly committed to the Marxian proposition that the point of theory is not merely to understand the world but to contribute to changing it. Those in sociology who were not Marxists were more likely to favor a social democratic, "social engineering" approach (Popper, Kalakowski) rather than a systemic change but, interestingly, were also more likely to be working on more substantive fields within sociology. Nevertheless, it was a feature of sociology that it was organized by the idea of contemporary relevance and so, despite differing views of how contemporary relevance was to be demonstrated, theorists could not afford to become too remote from substantive studies.

This was not the case in political theory. Around the middle of the twentieth century, Anglophone political philosophy seemed to have retreated into linguistic analysis and the death of political theory was regularly announced until, in the 1970s, Rawls relaunched a liberal normative political philosophy. Political theory then became less introspective about the possibility of theorizing and more concerned to build a systematic view of the world. But this "view" was spun out of abstract, universal propositions with no reference to the empirical, merely some hypothetical, sketchy cases to illustrate a logical distinction. Hence, as political theory gained in confidence and purpose, a chasm grew between political theory and the empirical study of politics.

As political theory was gaining in confidence, however, the epochal dis-illusionment with Marxism in most of its manifestations meant the oppo-site was happening in social theory. Echoing previous declarations of the death of political theory, social theorists who declared the "end of grand narratives" met little resistance from their colleagues. Moreover, social theory – and indeed, several humanistic disciplines such as anthropol-ogy, geography, and literary criticism – became extremely self-reflexive and skeptical of what their disciplines, or any other disciplines, could say about one's own or another's society. Concerns were increasingly expressed about how any such analysis invariably involved particularistic and sometimes oppressive assumptions, masquerading as universalistic truths about human nature, reason, or modernity.

Meanwhile, to complete the symmetry, as political philosophy has come to actively pursue the justification of principles, postmodern social studies has defined its object of study as discourse and representation rather than true propositions about society. So, for many inquirers it is sufficient to study how Asian women are represented in Western media without having to take a view as to whether those representations are true or what kind of corrections would be required to render them true.

Given this broad characterization of the contrasting dominant trends within social and political theory, it is no surprise that each kind of theory has engaged with issues of ethnicity, nationalism, and minority rights in different ways, though these engagements too have influenced the devel-opments within the respective disciplines.

In political theory, for example, the analysis of ethnic and ethnonational movements has tended to concentrate on the sociopolitical implications that such movements have for liberal democratic nation-states. In recent years, the development of political theory has thus provided us with rich and varied discussions concerning the actual and potential consequences for modern nation-states of ethnic and ethnonational claims. Such dis-cussions have ranged from orthodox defenses of liberalism and liberal democracy to alternative communitarian, consociational, and "politics of difference" conceptions of the nation-state. Questions of ethnicity, nationalism, and identity politics have been usefully explored in relation to fundamental normative concepts such as equality, liberty, democracy, and justice. At times the constitutional implications of these discussions for nation-states have been elaborated but the key thrust has been to (re)define key normative concepts.

Sociology, with its interest in society as a whole rather than in political institutions, took a much earlier interest in questions of "difference" and "identity politics." In social theory, this has been expressed principally via the dominance of social constructivist accounts of ethnic and national identity, focusing in particular on the constructedness and malleability of identities. These discussions provide an important dimension often missing in political theory analysis. Indeed, the latter has, more often than not, simply assumed the nature of ethnicity and nationalism as given, with less emphasis placed on the constructedness of social groups and more on the social and political consequences of group claims. In contrast, constructivist social theory accounts tend to reject any solidary notion of groups, emphasize the complex and cross-cutting identities at play in the postmodern world and, from this, articulate and explore the consequences of a more fluid (and contested) politics of identity and representation.

These debates, which also link in with anthropological discussions of culture and ethnicity, thus highlight the complex, and at times constructed and contradictory interconnections between identity claims, their political mobilization, and their social and political consequences. Along with related discussions in cultural studies, feminist studies, and some strands of political philosophy, these debates also explore issues to do with postmodernity, postcoloniality and globalization, and their influence upon articulations of ethnicity, racisms, gender identities, and other forms of social and cultural identity and politics in the postmodern world (see, for example, Said 1978; Benhabib 1992; Hall 2000).

A successful exchange between the disciplines should thus facilitate an analysis of wider theoretical debates, and their potential consequences for the (re)construction of democratic societies, in conjunction with their practical articulation in particular social and political contexts. This dual emphasis on the theoretical and practical consequences of ethnic, nationalist and wider identity claims is conspicuously underrepresented in extant literature in the area, where we tend to see theoretically sophisticated and empirically grounded analyses of ethnicity and nationalism, but seldom in the same publication. This collection aims also to redress this all too common disjuncture. Before exploring the potential interconnections between social and political theory further, however, we want to turn to a more detailed discussion of what each discipline has contributed thus far to the debates on ethnicity, nationalism and minority rights.

Political theory goes multicultural

Political theorists have, in recent years, addressed questions of ethnicity and minority rights with increasing gusto, even heatedness (see, for example, Kymlicka 1995; Kymlicka and Norman 1999; Joppke and Lukes 1999; Barry 2000; Parekh 2000; Kelly 2002). The particular locus of much of this discussion has centered on the merits, or otherwise, of multiculturalism as public (state) policy.

The emergence of ethnicity and minority rights on the political theory mainstream agenda can be traced back to Rawls' writing on pluralism and consensus as the essence of liberal democratic thinking (see, especially, 1971). This work generated a huge literature, much of which focused subsequently on what has come to be termed the liberal-communitarian divide. On the one hand were those who would prioritize the choice and autonomy of the individual (Dworkin 1977; Gutmann 1985). On the other hand were those who argued that a broader communal socialization in a historically rooted culture was necessary to enable the preconditions of such individualism (Sandel 1982; Raz 1986; Taylor 1994).

In the early 1990s the liberal-communitarian controversy transformed into a more particular debate about how to accommodate cultural and ethnic claims onto a broadly liberal political theory. Will Kymlicka's (1989) *Liberalism, Community and Culture* was a significant text in making this shift. This debate between liberals and communitarians soon evolved into a discussion about liberal western values in relation to non-western traditions, minorities and immigrants (Kymlicka 1999a; Okin 1999; Nussbaum 1999).

Political theorists have consequently focused their reflections on the kinds of demands made by minority cultures on the state. These demands have been categorized into three broad types (Kymlicka 1995). First, there are rights to do with government, including special representation rights, devolution and national self-determination. Second, there are rights that seek to accommodate a variety of distinct cultural practices within larger states. These include both exemption rights and cultural rights, which give special assistance to a disadvantaged minority, such as affirmative action programs. Third, there is a category of demands that are not rights claims, but pertain to the issue of collective esteem. This "becomes a matter for public policy when the symbolism of flags, currencies, names, public holidays, national anthems, public funds for cultural activities and the content of school curricula bear on a minority's fragile presence in the public political culture" (Seglow 2002: 158). This typology of the demands made by minority groups upon the state structures the debate within political theory, with theorists arguing for and against the normative desirability of the state granting the rights demanded and giving the recognition claimed. Yet, notwithstanding the heated nature of debate within political theory (see Barry 2000; Kelly 2002), the debate is very clearly framed in a manner which excludes as much as it illuminates.

Multicultural practices tend to be viewed, within political theory debates, through a rather liberal normative lens. Much of this literature therefore remains entrapped within the disciplinary confines of political theory. For example, in *Multicultural Citizenship* (1995), Kymlicka draws an analytic distinction between national minorities and ethnic groups. The point of this distinction is to justify his hierarchy of cultural rights: while national minorities merit rights to special representation and devolved self-government, ethnic groups deserve only rights to help them integrate on terms that are fair. The nature of this distinction is a product of the normative analytic framework, requiring one to legislate, in a categorical way, when a culture qualifies for minority rights and when it does not. Yet the nature of culture and the nature of groups do not tidily fall into categorical distinctions, thus vitiating the aim of being relevant to real world dilemmas and challenges.

Young's work represents another significant shift within this liberal theory framework. Offering an explicit critique of Rawls, Young captured the thrust of US-centered radical multiculturalism, which challenged an important blind-spot in mainstream liberal thinking: the inescapable effects of power, domination, and historical oppression on the political and personal chances of true participation for minority and ethnic groups. Her theory brought back to center stage a sociological concern with the effects of substantive inequality on people's ability to choose, and a political scientist's awareness of the pervasiveness of power. Yet, Young's *Justice and the Politics of Difference* (1990) remains bound by its context. Any attempt at a systematic analysis of cultural assimilation as a form of oppression undertaken within Western Europe, for example, would not have failed to include religion as a significant category. This raises the broader issue of the extent to which the central theoretical concepts of North American philosophy are informed by an experience that is different to that of Europe, and the degree to which an uncritical application of the former to the latter is highly damaging. Moreover, attempts such as hers and James Tully's, which try to integrate a constructivist account of social groups into their recommendations for group representation (Young 1990, 2000; Tully 1995) are open to a further criticism. Their normative commitment to group representation has led critics to charge them with holding a "billiard-ball concept of cultures" (Barry 2000). Whether it is possible to square a recognition of the "overlap, interaction and continuous renegotiation and transformation of cultures by their members" (Tully 2002: 104) with group representation is a contested issue (see Squires 2002; Tully 2002; Barry 2002; Owen 2003). This is a vitally important debate, and one which requires all the theoretical resources available within both social and political theory.

Another limitation of the dominant political theory approach to questions of minority rights lies with the level of abstraction at which the debate is usually conducted, and the rather cavalier approach to empirical reality. There has been an internal shift within political theory, away from hypothetical armchair examples to the recognition that "practical reason" involves a sustained engagement with real examples taken from everyday political and social issues (Favell and Modood 2003). However, the introduction of favored – often highly selective – multicultural dilemmas into a predominately abstract analytical debate has still tended to proceed without much sensitivity to or awareness of the complexity of the social and political situations discussed. The principal limitation attendant upon this approach is clearly that empirical cases are inevitably employed as *illustrations* for a general theoretical point. The risk is then that facts will be selected and presented in such a way that they fit a preconceived normative judgment. Certainly, "thick descriptions" of social and political contexts, to employ Clifford Geertz's phrase, remain relatively rare in political theory and this militates against the efficacy of asserting normative principles in the first place.

Be that as it may, the shift towards a more applied political theory is still a significant one. The evolution of Will Kymlicka's work is a case in point. His *Liberalism, Community and Culture* (1989), though representing a significant intellectual shift, was still a predominantly abstract Oxford philosophy text, focusing on Dworkin and Taylor. *Multicultural Citizenship* (1995), however, was something very different, discussing the applied history of liberal principles on minorities, and wanting to engage with specific, contemporary hard cases. Unusually, it demonstrated awareness (in both sociological and legal terms) of the complexity of the actual issues surrounding the Native-American population in liberal Canada, an awareness that was extended in his next book (1998) to a broader discussion of Canadian multiculturalism (see also, Carens 2000). More recently still, Kymlicka has explored questions and concerns about the comparability and appropriateness of his model of minority rights to Eastern and Central Europe (Kymlicka and Opalski 2002; see also this volume), picking up on a comparative trend already well established by sociologists of ethnicity and nationalism such as Rogers Brubaker (1992, 1996).

This comparative engagement within political theory debates on multiculturalism is highly promising, and long overdue, not least in questioning and opening up for debate the normative ascendancy of North American philosophy in such debates and its applicability, or otherwise, to other national and regional contexts. This latter feature can be further illustrated, again in relation to Kymlicka's work, with respect to specific differences between North America and Britain.

What people in Britain call multiculturalism (for example, the provision of halal meat in hospitals or the marking of Diwali by a school holiday), Kymlicka calls "polyethnicity" (Kymlicka 1995). He makes a sharp distinction here between a state incorporating, perhaps by treaty or conquest, a part or whole of a nation, and the presence of loose associations of individuals and families, with some connections based on origins, who have entered the state not as a nation but as voluntary migrants. This may be helpful for conceiving of immigration-derived polyethnicity in the USA and Canada, but it is less helpful for Britain. British "polyethnicity" is a legacy of empire; most migrants came from states that had been incorporated into the British Empire in ways not dissimilar to the incorporations of "nations" in Canada and the USA. These states contributed to Britain's economic development and to its superpower status; some migrants were ex-servicemen, with many others having relatives who had risked or given their lives for Britain. For the West Indians, England was the "mother country"; for the children of the Raj, the Queen was the head of the British Commonwealth and the migrants were subjects of the Crown with, albeit circumscribed by increasingly restrictive legislation, free rights of entry, settlement, and indeed British citizenship. It is thus difficult to apply Kymlicka's framework without severing, or making a mockery of, the connection between the "new British" and old Britain (Modood 2005).

While we have used Kymlicka's work as a prominent example of the growing trend towards comparative engagement in political theory, he is of course not the only political theorist so engaged. Bhikhu Parekh's *Rethinking Multiculturalism* (2000) further develops the tradition of applied political theory, showing a sociological sensitivity to practice and context. Parekh is a leading exponent of grounding political philosophy through discussion of real multicultural dilemmas. What is particularly significant is that Parekh's book, and the string of articles that preceded it, draw deeply upon policy challenges that have arisen in non-North American polities, especially Britain. While this makes his theoretical work particularly relevant to British policy thinking – most evident in the report of the Commission on the Future of Multi-Ethnic Britain, which he chaired (CMEB 2000) – it also raises a further methodological issue. Neither normative political theory nor postpositivist social theory offer a sustained engagement with the kinds of methodologies basic to other social science disciplines, stressing the need for empiricist comparative approaches before any generalizations can be drawn.

The significance of such contextual theorizing points towards the need to negotiate yet another disciplinary boundary: it signals the strength gained by theorizing that interacts with the comparative methodology of mainstream political and social sciences. Interestingly, Kymlicka's comparative evaluation (in this volume) of Western and Eastern and Central European state responses to minority claims represents precisely this strength, indicating a further development in his own methodological framework.

Contextual political theory could draw on the work already developed within political science in this regard. There is now a large and important comparative literature on the national regimes and institutions shaping the sociopolitical context, and how they facilitate or impede the integration of immigrants and the second generation. Initially led by some North Americans (especially Brubaker 1992), this approach has focused much more on European states than the political theory literature has to date. This literature concentrates on the ideological aspects of citizenship and nationalism, exploring ways in which ethnic conceptions of citizenship have their own distinctive characteristics in different countries. Some countries see the migrants as temporary; others insist on assimilation and actively promote naturalization; yet others are more tolerant of group difference but valorize some forms of group, e.g. "racial," more than other kinds e.g. religious. Thus different countries can be said to have different "philosophies of integration" (Joppke 1996; Favell 1998). Such comparative work shows how political frameworks have developed in different countries, and explains why legislation, institutions and policies have emerged in different countries, and why different kinds and intensities of migrant mobilization have occurred. They also show how these factors have shaped the self-proclaimed identities and political strategies of migrant ethnic groups (Kastoryano 1998, 2002; Koopmans and Statham 2000).

Multiculturalism in social theory

The discipline of political theory has shaped and constrained reflections on ethnicity and minority rights by political theorists in very specific ways. Exactly the same can be said for social theory.

A principal feature of relevant social theory has been the dominance of constructivist accounts of ethnic and national identit*ies*, with a deliberate emphasis here on the plural. Many social and cultural theorists have argued that groups do not have the unitary character that political theorists and others assume, and that culture needs to be analyzed as an interactive process rather than a fixed set of properties (Gilroy 1987; Hall 1992a). The central idea is that ethnic identities are not pure or static but change in new circumstances or by sharing social space with other heritages and influences. Blackness, for example, is necessarily a syncretic identity, for it has historically grown alongside, in interaction with and influenced by dominant and dissenting European or white cultural forms (Gilroy 1993). This lack of pure identities means that minority groups are not homogeneous and cannot be represented through formal group structures.

This broad constructivist consensus of identity – now itself under increasing challenge (of which more later) – can be traced to Barth's influential *Ethnic Groups and Boundaries* (1969). Barth's principal argument here is that ethnicity is *not* some bundle of unchanging cultural traits – the "cultural stuff" of ethnicity, as he calls it – that can simply be examined and enumerated in order to determine differences between ethnic groups. Rather, ethnic groups are situationally defined in relationship to their social interactions with other groups, and the boundaries established and maintained between them as a result of these interactions.

Acknowledging that ethnicity is a social and cultural construction in this way allowed social theorists to explore its articulation with other social forces and the various, or multiple, manifestations, that may result. In so doing, the way in which ethnicity is deliberately employed – or mobilized – in specific contexts also becomes central, as do the particular ends pursued in the process of mobilization. Put another way, if ethnicity is primarily an aspect of social relationships, then it can best be analyzed through the various uses to which individuals and/or groups put it.

Such a view also presupposes the fluidity or malleability of ethnicity. In effect, the origin, content, and form of ethnicity are all open to negotiation, reflecting the creative choices of individuals and groups as they define themselves and others in ethnic ways (Nagel 1994). Mobilizing particular identities will also depend, to a large extent, on the audience(s) being addressed. As Joane Nagel observes, a "chosen ethnic identity is determined by the individual's perception of its meaning to different audiences, its salience in different social contexts, and its utility in different settings" (1994: 155).

Relatedly, these various identities may overlap with, or cross-cut other social identities. For example, one may be a woman, a Muslim, a Bangladeshi, a Bengali speaker, an Asian, working class, a Londoner, English, an English speaker, and British, all at the same time. However, which of these identities predominates in any given circumstance, and how they interact with each other, will depend on the context, the audience and the ongoing balance between the internal definition and external ascription of social identities discussed earlier. This complex dialectic also suggests that there will be significant *intra*ethnic differences evident within any given ethnic group. The varying confluence of ethnicity, language, class, religion and gender will result in a full repertoire of social identifications and trajectories among individual members of a particular ethnic group. In this light, it also needs to be constantly borne in mind that ethnic, linguistic, class, religious and gender groups are themselves not solidary groups but have their own broad-based internal divisions.

Following from this, we have seen the articulation and development of the related notion of hybridity, most notably in the work of key social theorists such as Stuart Hall, Homi Bhabha, and Paul Gilroy, among others. Hall's (1992b) discussion of "new ethnicities," Bhabha's (1994) celebration of creolization and subaltern voices from the margin, and Gilroy's (1993) discussion of a Black Atlantic – a hybridized, diasporic black counterculture – all foreground the transgressive potential of cultural hybridity. Hybridity is viewed as being able to subvert categorical oppositions and essentialist ideological movements – particularly, ethnicity and nationalism – and to provide, in so doing, a basis for cultural reflexivity and change (Werbner 1997).

Within the discourses of hybridity, and of postmodernism more broadly, the new social agents are plural – multiple agents forged and engaged in a variety of struggles and social movements. In line with postmodernism's rejection of totalizing metanarratives, exponents of hybridity emphasize the contingent, the complex and the contested aspects of identity formation. Multiple, shifting and, at times, nonsynchronous identities are the norm for individuals.

Conversely, postmodernist commentators reject any forms of "rooted" identity based on ethnicity and nationality. Rooted identities such as these are branded with the negative characteristics of essentialism, closure, and conflict. Instead, postmodernist commentators such as Bhabha (1994) argue that it is the "inter" and "in-between," the liminal "third space" of translation, which carries the burden of the meaning(s) of culture in this postmodern, postcolonial world. Others have described this process as one of "border crossing" (see Anzaldúa 1987; Rosaldo 1989; Giroux 1992; di Leonardo 1994). In his more recent work, Gilroy (2000) identifies the bonds of racial solidarity as one of the biggest obstacles to moving forward towards what he describes as a new "planetary humanism," one that is predicated on hybridity, but also allied to the principle of universalism.

The dominance of constructivist and postmodernist understandings of identity within social theory poses a particular challenge to the politics of multiculturalism and, by extension, political theory debates on the various rights attributable to minority groups. The challenge is this: how can multiculturalism, based as it is on a notion of group-based rights, avoid lapsing into reification and essentialism? In effect, how can it account for postmodernist understandings of voice, agency, and the malleable and multiple aspects of identity formation without solidifying corporate identities? Indeed, in light of the almost *de rigueur* dismissal of any articulation of group-based identity as essentialist – a totalizing discourse that excludes and silences as much as it includes and empowers – how can multiculturalism's advocacy of group-based identities be viewed as anything other than irredeemably *passé*?

This is perhaps the central and ongoing challenge that constructivist social theory presents for political theory, and not only for proponents of multiculturalism. After all, critics of multiculturalism (see, e.g. Schlesinger 1992; Barry 2000) often adopt essentialist and closed constructions of (national) identity – treating traditional constructions of the nation-state with almost quasi-ontological status – in order to foreclose the possibility of a fluid, changing and dynamic public culture, or at least a more equally negotiated one (May 2003). This approach invariably involves the "projection" of nationalism onto "others" and the "naturalization" of one's own, a process best described by Billig's notion of "banal nationalism." The result, conveniently, is that majoritarian forms of nationalism "not only [cease] to be nationalism . . . [they cease] to be a problem for investigation" (1995: 17). Consequently, protagonists on both sides of the multicultural debate are challenged by constructivist social theory's insistence on the ongoing malleability and fluidity of identity.

However, constructivist social theory has itself become the subject of increasing critical examination of late. The result is the nascent reemergence of the "cultural stuff" of ethnicity, alongside an acknowledgment of its situatedness and multiplicity (Jenkins 1997; Smaje 1997; May 2001). A principal criticism here is that constructivist accounts overemphasize the possibilities of individual agency and underestimate, or even simply ignore, the wider structural constraints within which ethnic "choices" are made.

For example, the range of choices available to particular individuals and groups varies widely. A white American may have a wide range of ethnic options from which to choose on the basis of their ancestry. An African American, in contrast, is confronted with essentially one ethnic choice – black – irrespective of any preferred ethnic (or, for that matter, other) alternatives they might wish to employ. As Nagel observes:

the extent to which ethnicity can be freely constructed by individuals or groups is quite narrow when compulsory ethnic categories are imposed by others. Such limits on ethnic identification can be official or unofficial. In either case, externally enforced ethnic boundaries can be powerful determinants of both the content and meaning of particular ethnicities. (1994: 156)

The above example also suggests that the different ethnic choices available to majority and minority group members are a product of *unequal* power relations in the wider society. In particular, it is the differing location(s) of particular ethnic groups within the nation-state that shapes and constrains the ethnic options available to them – a point more clearly acknowledged by political theorists like Kymlicka.

Meanwhile, hybridity theory also has its limits. For example, the heterogeneous, hybrid, and plural identities so enamored of hybridity theorists are assumed by them to be somehow unique to the (post)modern world, replacing the homogeneous, bounded identities of the past (particularly, ethnicity, and nationalism). But this is simply wrong, or at the very least bad history. Cultural mixture and adaptation have been features of all societies, in all historical periods, as Lévi Strauss (1994) has rightly argued. Thus, the historicist model adopted by hybridity theorists – of closed to open, absolutist to relativist, static to dynamic – is simply implausible (Jenkins 1997). It is also highly modernist in its teleological view of "progress." And, perhaps most ironically, in assuming that heterogeneous identities have now replaced previously bounded and homogeneous ones, hybridity theory ends up treating cultures as complex wholes. This perpetuates an essentialist conception of culture rather than subverting it (Friedman 1997; Wicker 1997). The juxtaposition of purity/hybridity, authenticity/mixture – so central to hybridity theory – is thus fundamentally misconceived because contrary to its stated intentions it actually museumizes culture as "a thing" (Werbner 1997; see also Caglar 1997; Modood 1998).

And if this were not enough, it is also abundantly clear that there is considerable disparity between the intellectual celebration of hybridity (whatever its merits) and the reality of the postmodern world. This world *is* increasingly one of fractured, and fracturing, identities. But these identities are generally *not* hybrid; just the opposite, in fact. Nation-states are facing a plethora of ethnic, regional, and other social and cultural minority demands, many of which are couched in singular, collectivist terms. The tendency to rootedness and to boundary maintenance (often expressed via ethnicity) thus militates against ecumenism, and these tendencies are generated and reinforced by the real fragmentation occurring within and between nation-states in a global era (Friedman 1997). Given this, as Jonathan Friedman asserts, the valorization of hybridization is largely self-referential and self-congratulatory:

hybrids, and hybridisation theorists, are products of a group that self-identifies and/or identifies the world in such terms, not as a result of ethnographic understanding, but as an act of self-definition – indeed, of self-essentialising – which becomes definition for others via the forces of socialisation inherent in the structures of power that such groups occupy: intellectuals close to the media; the media intelligentsia itself; in a sense, all those [and, one might add, *only* those] who can afford a cosmopolitan identity. (1997: 81)

Ahmad (1995), in a similarly scathing critique, argues that articulations of hybridity fail to address adequately the social and political continuities and transformations that underpin individual and collective action in the real world. In that world, he argues, political agency is "constituted not in flux or displacement but in given historical locations." Moreover, it is sustained by a coherent "sense of place, of belonging, of some stable commitment to one's class or gender or nation" (1995: 16, 14).

In short, hybridity theory might sound like a good idea, but it is not in the end consonant with many people's individual and collective experiences. This disjuncture also holds true with social constructivist accounts of ethnicity more generally. After all, there is something strange going on when theorists proclaim that ethnicity is "invented" and set out to "decentre" it, while at the same time the news is full of ethnic cleansing and genocide (Levine 1999). Consequently, we need to explain more adequately why ethnicity does seem to continue to mean something to so many people. Perhaps more importantly, we also need to be able to explain why when ethnicity matters, it can really matter (Jenkins 1997).

Political theorists have a clear role to play here. Certain dominant strands of social theory appear to manifest an idealistic preoccupation with culture at the expense of broader material and structural concerns and focus on articulations of hybridity devoid of any sustained evaluation of social and political continuities. The weaknesses of social theory, in other words, are precisely the strengths of political theory and political science, and vice versa. Political theory, with its focus on the institutions of the state, provides an important counterbalance to the cultural focus of social theory. There are, we suggest, real benefits to be had from interdisciplinary research in this regard.

Social and political theory: beyond boundaries?

One area in which both social and political theorists are developing their ideas in tandem can be found in debates about cosmopolitanism, which has emerged as an influential new ideal amongst both groups of theorists in recent years. Reacting against state-centered politics and attempting to engage with the positive potential of the forces of globalization, cosmopolitan theorists offer a vision of global citizenship characterized by cultural diversity. David Held, Andrew Linklater, Craig Calhoun, and Nira Yuval-Davis, for example, all see new forms of political community as immanent within the current international states-system (Held 1999; Linklater 1998; Yuval-Davis 1999; Calhoun 2003).

Both Held and Linklater suggest that the dual processes of globalization and fragmentation are eroding traditional conceptions of community and reducing the significance of national boundaries, which allows a move beyond a pluralist society of states to a postsovereign era of cosmopolitan democracy. The key features of cosmopolitan democracy are usually characterized as a form of universalism complemented by a greater sensitivity to difference.

Indicators of the emergence of this postsovereign era are taken to include the growth of a body of international law, the increased role of international organizations, the emergence of transnational networks and social movements, and – of course – the increasing centrality of non-territorial networks of exchange (in industry and banking, information and communication, travel and culture). The further development of a cosmopolitan democracy will entail addressing the democratic deficit faced by these international organizations, increasing popular control of these organizations, devolving power downwards to substate political communities, and cultivating solidarities amongst groups that transcend state boundaries (Linklater 1998). This is a process of "double democratization": the deepening of democracy within a national community and the extension of democratic forms and processes across territorial borders (Held 2003).

One striking feature of much of the cosmopolitan literature within political theory, however, is its focus on the potentialities of the international and its description of a world as it may eventually look at various stages of cosmopolitan democratization. Notable by its absence is any sustained attempt to explicate the processes that people and groups will have to go through in order to achieve this. As Held himself notes: "Cosmopolitan democracy requires the accountability of experts and politicians, but how this can be achieved has still to be imagined and tested" (Held 2003).

Perhaps unsurprisingly, social and political theorists (even those who share an enthusiasm for the project) have tended to imagine the emergence of cosmopolitan democracy in rather different ways. Held, for example, stresses that "new institutions and mechanisms of accountability need to be established" (Held 1999: 106). Craig Calhoun, by contrast, suggests in this volume that longstanding solidarities and relations between groups will need to be developed via communication in the public sphere. These two approaches are not incompatible, indeed they could complement one another – and the project of imagining a truly compelling cosmopolitan democracy will surely need to draw on the resources of both political and social theory in this regard. For there are many who are skeptical about the cosmopolitan project, doubting the extent to which capital mobility erodes state sovereignty, that a sense of belonging to a community can extend beyond national boundaries, and that transnational organizations can be made democratic in any meaningful sense (see Kymlicka 1999b: 112–26). For these skeptics democratic citizenship remains firmly national, even if moral principles are cosmopolitan in their scope.

Wherever one stands on these questions, it is clear that the debate is an interdisciplinary one, engaging social and political theorists to an equal degree, which is perhaps symptomatic of a broader trend toward not only shared concerns but also genuine dialogue between social and political theorists.

Structure of the book

In order to begin to address these interdisciplinary issues and concerns, we have gathered together, in this collection, many of the leading social and political theorists of ethnicity and nationalism. They were asked to address the issues of ethnicity, nationalism, and minority rights from the perspective of their own disciplinary conventions and preoccupations. The results are indicative of broader patterns of disciplinary differences, but also point to possible areas of synthesis and overlap, and – more importantly – potential areas of future research, taking the insights of one discipline into the framework of another.

To this end, we have organized the book in three sections. Part I focuses on ethnicity and ethnic groups. Part II focuses on state responses to ethnic minority claims. Part III focuses on forward-looking theoretical and practical developments, which draw on new understandings of both ethnicity and the state.

The essays in Part I all engage with the concept of ethnicity, and reflect on the way in which the notion of ethnic groups frames contemporary debates about minority claims on the state, both theoretical and practical.

Jan Nederveen Pieterse, in "Ethnicities and multiculturalisms: politics of boundaries," offers a typology of different understandings of both ethnicity and multiculturalism. He argues that the different approaches to ethnicity and multiculturalism can best be understood as different negotiations of group boundaries. He then uses these typologies to explore the ways in which ethnicities relate to multiculturalisms.

Rogers Brubaker, in "Ethnicity without groups," reflects that the term "group" would appear to be a core concept for most social science disciplines, and yet the concept has remained curiously unscrutinized. He addresses one problematic consequence of taking groups for granted: the tendency to take discrete, sharply differentiated, internally homogeneous and externally bounded groups as basic constituents of social life, chief protagonists of social conflicts and fundamental units of social analysis. In contrast, Brubaker suggests that ethnic conflict, or what he calls ethnically framed conflict, need not, and should not, be understood as conflict between ethnic groups. Such framing, he argues, may be a key mechanism through which groupness is constructed.

Thomas Hylland Eriksen, in "Ethnicity, class, and the 1999 Mauritian riots," notes that much recent work on ethnicity has tended to focus on self-identification, discourses of exclusion and issues of cultural identity; while the philosophical debate on group identity and human rights has concentrated on tensions between cultural pluralism and social cohesion. Eriksen shows the limitations of both sets of approaches, via an analysis of recent events in Mauritius, an Indian Ocean island-state famous for its ethnic complexity, combined with a healthy democracy and a considerable economic growth rate. His analysis shows that cultural identity and the right to difference are not scarce resources in Mauritius, which has pursued a very pluralistic and multiculturalist model of nationbuilding since independence. Rather, it is the foundation of ethnicity in kinship-based networks that has created mounting discontent among Creoles. The perceived growing gulf between Creoles and Hindus is an outcome of social practices where informal social networks influence decisions and practices in the public sphere. Such social practices, Eriksen claims, are more important for the maintenance of ethnicity than discursive constructions.

Patricia Hill Collins, in "Black nationalism and African American ethnicity: the case of Afrocentrism as civil religion," reflects on the extent to which many African Americans use the core ideas of Black Nationalism in order to negotiate the dilemmas they face in negotiating the fluid structures of the "new" racism. She suggests that Black Nationalism's main ideas of self-definition, self-determination and self-reliance resonate with the experiences of large numbers of African Americans and that many use these ideas in crafting an ethnic identity. This process of constructing African American ethnicity using Black Nationalism's overlapping, cross-cutting, and conflicting systems of meaning requires one to evaluate it as a civil religion rather than a political paradigm. Being "logical" by using the criteria of Western theory simply misses the point of how people use ideas to construct meaning in everyday life.

The essays in Part II take a different approach. Rather than focusing on the nature of ethnicity, they concentrate on the nature of the state, and the ways in which it does and should respond to ethnic claims.

T. K. Oommen, in "New nationalisms and collective rights: the case of South Asia," suggests that the notion of the nation-state is inherently tension-prone because the constituent elements pull in two different directions. While the state is wedded to the creation of a uniform, homogenous citizenship, the nation is basically diversifying. Oommen explores the implications of this tension in relation to South Asian states.

He suggests that in the postcolonial South Asian era different types of nationalism emerged, from state-sponsored nationalism to sovereign state-seeking nationalism. Between these polar types one finds both "nations" (which seek limited political autonomy and cultural identity within the federal polity) and "ethnies" (which insist on preserving their cultural specificity without seeking any political status).

Will Kymlicka, in "Justice and security in the accommodation of minority nationalism," reflects that while the challenge of minority nationalism arises in all parts of the globe, the state's response to it varies tremendously from region to region. He compares the accommodation of minority nationalism in two regions: the Western democracies and the postcommunist countries of Eastern and Central Europe (ECE) and notes that the response to minority nationalism in these two regions is very different: in the West there is a trend towards accepting the legitimacy of minority nationalism, whereas in the ECE minority nationalism is often viewed as illegitimate. Kymlicka suggests that one important explanation for the difference between these approaches lies in the fact that in the West minority rights claims are assessed primarily in terms of justice, while in the ECE they are primarily assessed in term of security.

Iris Marion Young, in "Two concepts of self-determination," examines two interpretations of a principle of the self-determination of peoples. The traditional interpretation of self-determination in international law equates it with sovereign independence, where the self-determining entity claims a right of nonintervention and noninterference. Drawing on the theory of freedom as nondomination, Young offers a second conception of self-determination as nondomination. She argues that peoples can be self-determining only if the relations in which they stand to others are nondominating. She illustrates here arguments in relation to the claims of indigenous peoples for greater self-determination.

The essays in Part III are characterized by an attempt to reflect on contemporary developments, which highlight the significance of the theoretical debates in the other two parts.

Bhikhu Parekh argues, in "Redistribution or recognition?: a misguided debate," that the criticisms of a politics of recognition forwarded by socialists and social democrats in the name of a politics of redisribution are exaggerated. He suggests that the two forms of politics stress different but complementary aspects of equality. Moreover, the two politics give each other depth and energy. Accordingly, a well-considered theory of justice needs to address both.

Nira Yuval-Davis, in "Borders, boundaries, and the politics of belonging," explores questions relating to a politics of belonging, and the relationship between belonging and constructions of boundaries and borders.

She suggests that neither debates about citizenship nor those about identity entirely capture the notion of belonging, which invokes sociologies of emotions and power. Central to the politics of belonging is the process of constructing boundaries between those who belong and those who do not. Yuval-Davis applies these issues to recent debates about British citizenship in order to show just how central notions of belonging are to the process of inclusion or exclusion from the nation-state.

And finally, Craig Calhoun in "Is it time to be postnational?," explores the applicability, and limits, of cosmopolitanism – both as social theory and practice – in light of recent political events, most notably the terrorist bombings of the Twin Towers in New York on September 11, 2001. As he argues, these current events highlight the ongoing tension between the recognition of fluidity in identity choices and the very real consequences attendant upon the mobilization of political movements predicated, at least ostensibly, on singular, often monolithic identities.

Fostering interdisciplinarity

In reading this collection, you will find that the social theorists here tend to focus on ethnicity and ethnic groups, and on the plural, variegated nature of such groups. That said, there are also significant differences of approach and emphasis. While Brubaker's argument against the validity of groups represents the contemporary reaction against an earlier over-essentializing trend in the study of ethnicity, other social theorists continue to find ethnicity in the world. Whilst ethnicity is shown to have tremendous political implications – for solidarity as well as division – it is taken to be not reducible to the political. Indeed, it is in an important sense pre- or extrapolitical. Thus for Oommen, ethnies are sociocultural group formations which are not intrinsically political but may develop state-seeking and nationbuilding aspirations if they get anchored to a specific territory and have a common language. For Eriksen, ethnic groups are social structures and networks that can represent significant concentrations of power even when they seem to be politically self-effacing. Whilst for Calhoun, the presence of ethnic and religious groups, their ability to reproduce themselves in changed circumstances and command the allegiance of new generations by offering meaningful lives, is a reality that thoroughly restricts the pertinence of cosmopolitanism.

The political theorists, by contrast, focus on ways in which the claims of ethnic minorities require a retheorization and restructuring of the nation-state. Their central preoccupation is with the normative legitimacy of the state and their methodological approach is analytical. These theorists all engage with the notion of the state, offering normative recommendations regarding state formation and state policies.

In this sense, these political theorists reveal several of the distinctive traits of their discipline: the adoption of a normative approach and an analytical methodology, and a preoccupation with the function and form of the state. Yet they also show themselves to be particularly attuned to the insights and approaches of sociology, particularly with respect to balancing the view of cultural groups as sociopolitical actors, which may bear rights and have needs that need to be institutionally accommodated, with the wider discussions within social theory about hybridity. They also increasingly share with social theorists a critique of a certain political science approach to ethnic conflict, which takes ethnic identity for granted, and seeks to explain only the outbreak of conflict.

The political theorists included in this collection thus represent a political theory strengthened – to varying degrees – by the insights of sociological analysis, empirical engagement, and comparative evaluation. What makes their work still distinctively political theory, notwithstanding these various engagements with other methodological concerns, is the normative focus on the state. Political theorists are always *thinking for the state*; they are state-centered by definition (Favell and Modood 2003). This way of thinking, however, may miss many of the true sources of multiculturalism in Western liberal societies, which are multicultural not only because the state legislates for these practices, with positive rights, entitlements and policy frameworks, but also because of what it does not do. Many western liberal states became multicultural by default: because of the *laissez faire* attitude of the state toward cultural or market-led mechanisms that would have been very difficult to legislate for in terms of the state-centered logic of rights or citizenship (see CMEB 2000 on "multicultural drift"). However methodologically broad political theory becomes, there is still a need for it to draw on other disciplinary approaches.

And yet, social theorists should not undervalue the distinctive attributes of normative political theory either. Fully rounded engagement with ethnicity and minority rights requires an emphasis on the dynamic, cultural dimensions of identity and their complex interpellation with other forms of identity. But it also requires a focus on the state, and normative reflection on the consequences of minority rights' claims. The way forward for social and political theory here lies in the further exploration of these various interconnections. We hope this volume makes a useful start.

REFERENCES

Ahmad, A. (1995) "The politics of literary postcoloniality." *Race and Class* 36 (3): 1–20.

Anzaldúa, G. (1987) *Borderlands/La Frontera: The New Mestiza*. San Francisco, CA: Aunt Lute Books.

Barry, B. (2000) *Culture and Equality*. Cambridge: Polity Press.

(2002) Second thoughts – and some first thoughts revived. In P. Kelly (ed.), *Multiculturalism Reconsidered: Culture and Equality and its Critics.* Cambridge: Polity Press, pp. 204–38.

Barth, F. (1969) *Ethnic Groups and Boundaries: The Social Organization of Culture Difference.* Boston, MA: Little, Brown and Co.

Benhabib, S. (1992) *Situating the Self: Gender, Community and Postmodernism in Contemporary Ethics.* New York: Routledge.

Bhabha, H. (1994) *The Location of Culture.* London: Routledge.

Billig, M. (1995) *Banal Nationalism.* London: Sage.

Brubaker, R. (1992) *Citizenship and Nationhood in France and Germany.* Cambridge, MA: Harvard University Press.

(1996) *Nationalism Reframed: Nationhood and the National Question in the New Europe.* Cambridge: Cambridge University Press.

Caglar, A. (1997) "Hyphenated identities and the limits of culture." In T. Modood, and P. Werbner (eds.), *The Politics of Multiculturalism in the New Europe: Racism, Identity and Community.* London: Zed Books, pp. 169–85.

Calhoun, C. (2003) "'Belonging' in the cosmopolitan imaginary." *Ethnicities* 3 (4): 531–53.

Carens, J. (2000) *Culture, Citizenship and Community: A Contextual Exploration of Justice as Evenhandedness.* Oxford: Oxford University Press.

CMEB (Commission on Multi-Ethnic Britain) (2000) *The Future of Multi-Ethnic Britain.* London: Profile Books.

di Leonardo, M. (1994) "White ethnicities, identity politics, and baby bear's chair." *Social Text* 41: 5–33.

Dworkin, R. (1977) *Taking Rights Seriously.* London: Duckworth.

(1985) *A Matter of Principle.* Cambridge, MA: Harvard University Press.

Favell, A. (1998) *Philosophies of Integration. Immigration and the Idea of Citizenship in France and Britain.* Basingstoke: Macmillan.

Favell, A. and T. Modood (2003) "The philosophy of multiculturalism: the theory and practice of normative political theory." In A. Finlayson (ed.), *Contemporary Political Thought: A Reader and Guide.* Edinburgh: Edinburgh University Press, pp. 484–95.

Friedman, J. (1997) "Global crises, the struggle for identity and intellectual porkbarrelling: cosmopolitans versus locals, ethnics and nationals in an era of de-hegemonisation." In P. Werbner, and T. Modood (eds.), *Debating Cultural Hybridity: Multicultural Identities and the Politics of Antiracism.* London: Zed Books, pp. 70–89.

Gilroy, P. (1987) *There Ain't No Black in the Union Jack.* London: Hutchinson.

(1993) *The Black Atlantic: Modernity and Double Consciousness.* London: Verso.

(2000) *Between Camps.* London: Penguin.

Giroux, H. (1992) *Border Crossings.* London: Routledge.

Gutmann, A. (1985) "Communitarian critics of liberalism." *Philosophy and Public Affairs* 14 (3): 308–22.

Hall, S. (1992a) "The questions of cultural identity." In S. Hall, D. Held, and T. McGrew (eds.), *Modernity and its Futures.* Cambridge: Polity Press, pp. 274–325.

(1992b) "New ethnicities." In J. Donald and A. Rattansi (eds.), *"Race", Culture and Difference*. London: Sage, pp. 252–59.

(2000) "Conclusion: the multi-cultural question." In B. Hesse (ed.), *Un/settled Multiculturalisms*. London: Zed Books, pp. 209–41.

Held, D. (1999) "The transformation of political community: rethinking democracy in the context of globalization." In Ian Shapiro and Casiano Hacker-Cordon (eds.), *Democracy's Edges*. Cambridge: Cambridge University Press, pp. 84–111.

(2003) "What is globalization?" Available at: <www.opendemocracy.org>

Jenkins, R. (1997) *Rethinking Ethnicity: Arguments and Explorations*. London: Sage.

Joppke, C. (1996) "Multiculturalism and immigration: a comparison of the United States, Germany, and Great Britain." *Theory and Society* 25: 449–500.

Joppke, C. and S. Lukes (eds.) (1999) *Multicultural Questions*. Oxford: Oxford University Press.

Kastoryano, R. (ed.) (1998) *Quelle identité pour l'Europe? Le multiculturalisme à l'épreuve*. Paris: Presses de Science Po.

(2002) *Negotiating Identities: States and Immigrants in France and Germany*. Princeton and Oxford: Princeton University Press.

Kelly. P. (ed.) (2002) *Multiculturalism Reconsidered: Culture and Equality and its Critics*. Cambridge: Polity Press.

Koopmans, R. and P. Statham (eds.) (2000) *Challenging Immigration and Ethnic Relations Politics*, Oxford: Oxford University Press.

Kymlicka, W. (1989) *Liberalism, Community and Culture*. Oxford: Clarendon Press.

(1995) *Multicultural Citizenship*. Oxford: Oxford University Press.

(1998) *Finding Our Way: Rethinking Ethnocultural Relations in Canada*. Toronto: Oxford University Press.

(1999a) "Comments on Shachar and Spinner-Halev: an update from the multiculturalism wars." In C. Joppke, and S. Lukes (eds.), *Multicultural Questions*. Oxford: Oxford University Press, pp. 112–29.

(1999b) "Citizenship in an era of globalization: commentary on Held." In Ian Shapiro and Casiano Hacker-Cordon (eds.), *Democracy's Edges*. Cambridge: Cambridge University Press, pp. 112–26.

Kymlicka W. and W. Norman (1999) *Citizenship in Diverse Societies*. Oxford: Oxford University Press.

Kymlicka, W. and M. Opalski (eds.) (2002) *Can Liberal Pluralism Be Exported? Western Political Theory and Ethnic Relations in Eastern Europe*. New York: Oxford University Press.

Levine, H. (1999) "Reconstructing ethnicity." *Journal of the Royal Anthropological Institute* 5: 165–80.

Lévi Strauss, C. (1994) "Anthropology, race, and politics: a conversation with Didier Eribon." In R. Borofsky (ed.), *Assessing Cultural Anthropology*. New York: McGraw Hill, pp. 420–29.

Linklater, A. (1998) *The Transformation of Political Community: Ethical Foundations of a Post-Westphalian Era*. Cambridge: Polity Press.

May, S. (2001) *Language and Minority Rights: Ethnicity, Nationalism and the Politics of Language.* London and New York: Longman.

    (2003) "Misconceiving minority language rights: implications for liberal political theory." In W. Kymlicka and A. Patten (eds.), *Language Rights and Political Theory.* Oxford: Oxford University Press, pp. 123–52.

Modood, T. (1998) "Anti-essentialism, multiculturalism and the 'recognition' of religious groups." *Journal of Political Philosophy* 6: 378–99.

    (2005) Multicultural Politics: Racism, Ethnicity and Muslims in Britain. Minneapolis and Edinburgh: Minnesota University Press and Edinburgh University Press.

Nagel, J. (1994) "Constructing ethnicity: creating and recreating ethnic identity and culture." *Social Problems* 41: 152–76.

Nussbaum, M. (1999) *Sex and Social Justice.* New York: Oxford University Press.

Okin, S. (1999) *Is Multiculturalism Bad for Women?* Princeton: Princeton University Press.

Owen, D. (2003) "Culture, equality and polemic." *Economy and Society* 32 (2): 325–40.

Parekh, B. (2000) *Rethinking Multiculturalism.* Basingstoke: Macmillan.

Rawls, J. (1971) *A Theory of Justice.* Oxford: Oxford University Press.

Raz, J. (1986) *The Morality of Freedom.* Oxford: Oxford University Press.

Rosaldo, R. (1989) *Culture and Truth.* London: Routledge.

Said, E. (1978) *Orientalism.* London: Penguin.

Sandel. M. (1982) *Liberalism and the Limits of Justice.* Cambridge: Cambridge University Press.

Schlesinger, A. (1992) *The Disuniting of America: Reflections on a Multicultural Society.* New York: W. W. Norton and Co.

Seglow, J. (2002) "Multiculturalism." In R. Bellamy and A. Mason (eds.), *Political Concepts.* Manchester: Manchester University Press, pp. 156–68.

Smaje, C. (1997) "Not just a social construct: theorising race and ethnicity." *Sociology* 31: 307–27.

Squires, J. (2002) "Culture, equality and diversity." In P. Kelly (ed.), *Multiculturalism Reconsidered: Culture and Equality and its Critics.* Cambridge: Polity Press, pp. 114–32.

Taylor, C. (1994) "The politics of recognition." In A. Gutmann (ed.), *Multiculturalism: Examining the Politics of Recognition.* Princeton: Princeton University Press, pp. 25–73.

Tully, J. (1995) *Strange Multiplicity.* Cambridge: Cambridge University Press.

    (2002) "The illiberal liberal." In P. Kelly (ed.), *Multiculturalism Reconsidered: Culture and Equality and its Critics.* Cambridge: Polity Press, pp. 102–13.

Waldron, J. (1995) "Minority cultures and the cosmopolitan alternative. In W. Kymlicka (ed.), *The Rights of Minority Cultures.* Oxford: Oxford University Press, pp. 93–119.

Werbner, P. (1997) "Introduction: the dialectics of cultural hybridity." In P. Werbner, and T. Modood (eds.), *Debating Cultural Hybridity: Multicultural Identities and the Politics of Antiracism.* London: Zed Books, pp. 1–26.

Wicker, H.-R. (1997) "From complex culture to cultural complexity." In
P. Werbner, and T. Modood (eds.), *Debating Cultural Hybridity: Multicul-
tural Identities and the Politics of Antiracism*. London: Zed Books, pp. 29–45.
Young, I. (1990) *Justice and the Politics of Difference*. Princeton: Princeton
University Press.
(2000) *Democracy and Inclusion*. Princeton: Princeton University Press.
Yuval-Davis, N. (1999) "Multilayered citizenship in the age of 'Glocalization'."
International Feminist Journal of Politics 1 (1): 119–36.

Part I

Ethnicity and ethnic groups

2 Ethnicities and multiculturalisms: politics of boundaries

Jan Nederveen Pieterse

How far have ethnic studies advanced past the finding that ethnicity is constructed, not primordial? While the "decolonization of ethnicity" is still under way, at times the stream of ethnic studies seems to add up to little more than a series of vignettes. Ethnicity is still talked about in a generalizing fashion, as if in each contribution the sociology of ethnicity has to be reinvented again and again. But what if we unpack ethnicity by means of a typology and taxonomy of ethnicities, and thus bring the sociology of ethnicity to the foreground and bring finesse and method into the discussion? This is the aim of the first chapter.[1]

The second aim of this chapter is to twin the ethnicity discussion with the discussion on multiculturalism – combining and contrasting discourses of ethnicity and multiculturalism. Multiculturalism, like ethnicity, is a moving target – an ongoing cultural flux and an institutional arrangement, a target of criticism or a reform platform. Ethnicity is a contemporary vocabulary for various notions of group boundaries; multiculturalism, likewise, is a discourse that negotiates group boundaries. Thus both ethnicity and multiculturalism address the underlying theme of the politics and discourse of group boundaries. Group boundaries, a fundamental theme in anthropology and social science, now come back in various guises, such as the "spatial turn" that takes us beyond notions of borderlessness and nomadism, and reterritorialization, border matters, border theory, border consciousness, and so forth (cf. Nederveen Pieterse 2002).

This discussion first problematizes ethnicity and the notion of "ethnic conflict." Next I spell out four major varieties of ethnicity and consider each from the point of view of domination and emancipation. Ethnicities arise from different ways of drawing group boundaries; what sets diverse notions of multiculturalism apart also derives from different ways of drawing group boundaries. Notions of identity, difference, and inter-group relations interact to produce diverse angles on how group boundaries come about and decompose. In the closing section I consider how ethnicities relate to multiculturalisms and merge the two discourses.

27

The disease model and the emancipation model

Let us consider two diametrically opposite positions in relation to "ethnicity" – the disease model and the emancipation model. One is familiar, the other less so, but both are readily understandable. "To use a pessimistic but apt metaphor, ethnic conflict may be less like a common cold and more like AIDS – difficult to catch, but devastating once infected" (Lake 1995: 3). Here the focus is on ethnic conflict, the metaphor is that of disease, and the implied process is one of inevitable disaster. This is a common doomsday scenario of ethnic politics. The sequel argument is that there are hundreds of peoples in the world and about as many conflicts and civil wars to come. This is a commonplace view: ethnicity is an evil politics stalking the Enlightenment world of growing modernization. This point of view has been common in media representations and particularly prominent (but not exclusively) in American sources, such as Moynihan (1992) and Kaplan (2000). A radically different view holds: "recognizing rather than denying ethnicity holds the key to democratizing the state and development" (Salih 1999: 3).

In this view, ethnic politics is an emancipatory politics. Ethnicity is grassroots politics and a vehicle of vernacular democratization. The emphasis is on the state and development politics, and ethnicity is viewed as a means toward democratization. This revisionist position relates to wider concerns such as the reconciliation between traditional and modern institutions and whether modernization is indigenous or imported.[2]

There are other views, such as that the importance of ethnicity is being exaggerated,[3] but from the viewpoint of analyzing cultural politics these two diametrically opposite views, ethnicity as curse or as emancipation, are among the most significant positions. Much is at stake in these perspectives. The first implies a blank check for external intervention in local conflicts, while the rationale is profoundly pessimistic, i.e., conflict management without hope. The second opens the way to vernacular empowerment and endogenous politics, but in the process raises several problems.

These views leave us between a rock and a hard place. The first does not problematize nation-state politics, does not problematize the domination that has usually given rise to ethnic mobilization in the first place. It presents conventional politics, which is part of the problem, as the solution and thus in the name of conflict resolution offers more of the same. It addresses symptoms, not causes. At best it promises containment of the disease, not remedy. The second view does address state domination but does not reckon with the problem of domination-within-domination. Since the problem of state domination is familiar enough and widely discussed, it is the second problem of domination-within-domination that needs focusing on. This means a double take or multifocus look at ethnicity. That ethnic politics shows features of both domination and emancipation at the same time, has been argued before (Nederveen Pieterse 1997a); now we go further into specifics.

If we seek to impose conditions on state action (as in various frameworks for collective rights and multiculturalism), should ethnic groups have carte blanche? While political discourse devotes much attention to the state, the politics of ethnicity is not talked about as much (cf. Rupesinghe and Tishkov 1996).

In relation to African politics, at times state and ethnic politics are combined. Thus, in one view, African polities have increasingly become kleptocracies and ethnicity is decentralized kleptocracy, in which ethnic conflict often serves as way to settle Mafia-like struggles (Bayart *et al.* 1999). According to a markedly different view, Africa works and works precisely through neotraditional institutions of redistribution via ethnic and kinship networks (Chabal *et al.* 1999).

These issues can be addressed from various points of view. An angle taken here is that of collective learning and reflexivity. The point of collective learning as a perspective is not to suggest some ideal standard, model, or end state, but to focus on the ongoing process and to view it as a social learning process, the objective of which is learning itself rather than some kind of "end of history" settlement.[4] Since learning is contextual, the question is which approaches are most conducive to collective learning in particular contexts.

An obvious question is if we seek collective reflexivity in relation to the state and public sphere (as in notions of reflexive modernity), what about reflexivity at the level of ethnic groups? Can we then view ethnic politics as an exercise in collective learning, in multiple directions – within and between ethnic groups, in their interaction with other social forces, in relation to the state and institutional change, and ultimately, at the international level? This implies a notion of reflexive ethnicity, and in fact multiculturalism can be viewed as precisely a politics of reflexive ethnicity.

Reflexive ethnicity and parallel universes

The first consideration is to problematize ethnicity itself. Is the terminology of ethnicity appropriate at all? Does it belong to an era that is past? Does terminology matter? Are we walking into the twenty-first century burdened with nineteenth-century terminology? Is discourse itself a sign of the times or a badge of identity, a passport or green card to labor in discursive worlds? In that case, which one to chose, and perhaps more important, how do they interrelate? To which ethnicity do the two arguments spelled out above apply? Do we inhabit parallel universes in which what is a problem in one setting pops up as a solution in another?

In academic discourse, in anthropology and sociology, perspectives on ethnicity have in recent years been increasingly problematizing and open-ended (e.g. Jenkins 1999). Ethnicity fades into race, nationalism, multiculturalism, identity politics, community. Its significance and dynamics are circumstantial, conjunctural, contingent. Early discussions of ethnicity in comparative politics and political science followed the political modernization paradigm in which all differences would lead to national integration and nationbuilding. Since the 1970s the awareness grew that modernization can also increase the salience of ethnicity and by the 1990s the focus had shifted to ethnic conflict. In most of these discussions ethnicity is presented as an independent variable. Yet, according to Rupert Taylor (1999: 121), what ultimately remains unresolved is where ethnicity comes from and what it actually is.

There is no need to rehearse the large and growing literature on this score (see e.g. Bulmer and Solomos 1999) except to make some key points. (1) There is no point or advantage to naturalizing, essentializing, or reifying ethnicity. There is nothing "natural" about ethnicity. Ethnicity need not be considered as a primary affiliation with given territorial or other claims.[5] (2) The term recalls the colonial era and the prejudices of colonial anthropology. One option is to discard the term ethnicity and opt instead for the plain language of cultural difference (cf. Nederveen Pieterse 1997). On the one hand, despite the constructivist turn, "ethnicity" bears the stamp of essentialist thinking; on the other, it works as a way to connect with the literature, and "culture" invites problems too. It might be preferable to speak of cultural politics or culturally inflected politics, in contrast to class, interest, and ideological politics, for all "ethnicity" ultimately comes down to some form of cultural difference – such as nationality, nationalism, language, religion, region, community, kinship, clan, caste; all of which, along with "race," are themselves cultural constructs. However, similar problems as in relation to ethnicity apply to "culture," which cannot be settled here.[6] A neat distinction between interest politics and cultural or ethnic politics is not tenable either, because interest too is culturally constructed, mediated, and articulated (as in class consciousness), so ultimately these distinctions do not hold; which is not to suggest that class dissolves into culture but merely that it cannot exist outside culture.

While the "thingness" of ethnicity is bracketed and questioned in social science and considered unresolved in political science, in policy discourse, for instance in the context of "humanitarian intervention," fixed assumptions and closed, narrow understandings of ethnicity tend to prevail.[7] "Managing ethnic conflict" has become another cottage industry. But, in fact, what are "ethnic conflicts"?

> ❏ Hypothesis: When politics is upfront we speak of political conflict. When politics is opaque we say ethnic conflict.

Do we refer to conflicts in Kosovo and East Timor as ethnic conflicts? They are generally perceived as questions of nationalism in which ethnic groups play some part. What about Sierra Leone and Liberia? Political conflict refers to conflict among interest groups; these may be partly defined in cultural terms, but that does not necessarily alter the basic make-up of the situation. The visibility and transparency of "politics," however, is also a function of social distance and political conditions, including channels of information. Up close or as locals we would know of the political interests that are at stake. On the other hand, locals may be hoodwinked too, for instance through the monopolization of media. Thus the conflict in Rwanda was a political conflict among rival regional interest groups which largely involved Hutus; but for political reasons it was presented in Rwandese state-sponsored media as an ethnic conflict (Uvin 1999). Let us note the gradual changes in perceptions of distant conflicts when through continued reporting and analysis the conflicts become less distant. Conflicts in Sierra Leone in the 1990s were originally represented and perceived as ethnic or tribal fury, but gradually the stakeholders' interests became more visible: control over diamond mining and trade, warlords and gang warfare, small arms traffic and support for warring factions in neighboring countries.

> ❏ Hypothesis: Majority politics are designated "political" and minority politics are termed "ethnic," i.e. ethnicity is minority nationalism.

The war waged by the Tamil insurgents in Sri Lanka is perceived as an ethnic or ethnonationalist struggle while Sinhala majority politics is tacitly treated as ordinary national politics. Yet, if we step into the minutiae of the situation we may find Sinhala majority politics every bit as "ethnic" and steeped in prejudice and cultural bias as Tamil politics.[8] This illustrates the tenuous and biased distinction between nationalism and ethnicity, which privileges and naturalizes majority interests and politics, as a bias inherent in the terminology of ethnicity.

> ❏ Hypothesis: Nationalism refers to urban nationalism, while rural nationalism is often termed ethnicity.

According to Ramet (1996: 76), "the nationalist movement which made rapid gains after the death of Yugoslav President Josip Broz Tito in May 1980, and which came into its own in 1987, relies above all on rural support and is, in essence, a profoundly rural phenomenon. To say this is also to suggest that Milosevic's ascent to power represented the victory of the Serbian countryside over the city." She distinguishes between urban nationalism and rural nationalism, which is "more ethnic" (1996: 72). Among all of Yugoslavia's (former) provinces Serbia has by far the greatest percentage of the population engaged in agriculture (27.6 percent) (1996: 75). The conflict in Bosnia has been termed "urbicide" or a revenge of the countryside of predominantly rural Bosnian Serbs against predominantly urban Bosnian Moslems (Denitch 1994; Humphrey 1997).

❏ Ethnicity is relational

Chinese food eaten by Chinese in a Chinese restaurant overseas is food (a particular type of food, a regional food, etc.); the same food eaten by non-Chinese in the same restaurant becomes "ethnic food."

These points suggest that "ethnicity" fades and interest comes to the foreground as a function of growing knowledge of the situation, that is, what may underlie the distinction is the difference between a local optics and long-distance optics. Second, the term "ethnicity" may be a function of majority–minority relations. Third, "ethnicity" may be a function of perceived rural–urban differences. Fourth, "ethnicity" is relational and contextual. In Dwyer's words (1996: 4), "Ethnicity is a product of contact, not of isolation." Since ethnicity is relational it necessitates the scrutiny of relationships; and since social relations change over time this gives rise to different types of ethnicity.

Ethnicities

Reflexivity begins by opening up ethnicity, unpacking its "thingness," viewing ethnicity as process and showing diversity underneath the label. While discussions of ethnicity often proceed as if there is only one type, ethnicity varies across a wide range in terms of salience, intensity, and meaning. Ethnicity can be unpacked by distinguishing four types which may be viewed as snapshots of ethnicity as a moving target.[9]

1. *Domination ethnicity.* Considering that the term "ethnicity" itself is a discourse of domination and the distinction between nation and ethnicity is tenuous, if nationalism takes the form of monocultural control it may be considered a form of ethnicity, or ethnocracy. Ethnic mobilization is often a reaction to the imposition of a monocultural regime and discriminatory treatment or regional uneven development.

2. *Enclosure ethnicity*. This exists in three varieties of dormant ethnicity, cultural confinement, and inward-looking ethnicity, which all share a restriction of mobility and space. This may be an existing condition (dormant ethnicity), involuntary (imposed) or voluntary (self-chosen).[10]

- Dormant or latent ethnicity exists in an isolated group or where intergroup contacts have no or little salience, as in the case of the classic "primitive isolates" of anthropology.
- Cultural confinement occurs as a consequence of conquest (Amerindians in the Andes driven up the mountains by the encroaching Hispanic conquests and latifundios) or external imposition (the Jews confined to ghettos, the segregation of African Americans under the Jim Crow laws, the Bantustans in Apartheid South Africa).
- Inward-looking ethnicity refers to self-chosen segregation or dissociation as a strategy of building inner-group strength. Delinking itself can be a strategy of competition or preparation for competition. A mild variety is "buy black, vote black" and a stronger version is the Nation of Islam.

3. *Competition ethnicity*. Competition with the state or other cultural formations in relation to state power, resources, and development. This is the major problem zone of ethnic relations.

4. *Optional ethnicity*. Low-intensity ethnicity is light, volitional, and fluid, as in the case of ethnic entrepreneurs, symbolic ethnicity, ethnic chic, and shopping for identity (Waters 1990).

The question that arises next is how these varieties relate to one another, in other words the dynamics of ethnicity and the shift from one mode to another. A simple account is that nationalism awakens dormant ethnicity, imposes "minority" status or enclosure ethnicity, and over time enclosure ethnicity tends toward competition ethnicity. Competition ethnicity, in turn, over time tends toward the widening of choices of cultural affiliation because competition itself involves and generates the accumulation of crosscultural capital, which eventually may lead to optional ethnicity.

What is the status of this sequence – is it a likely or a necessary process, i.e. is teleology involved? Even if this sequence is widely observed, it does not mean it is universal. Under which conditions does this process apply? And how long does it take to unfold and what determines its pace? Is there only forward or also backward movement?

Experience and research suggest that these dynamics occur, but the instances where they do *not* occur, even though they may be relatively few, are precisely those that call for explanation. For instance, Sinhala Buddhist chauvinism in Sri Lanka has been maintaining its hold over a

Table 2.1 *Ethnicities*

Ethnicities	Variants	Keywords	Dynamics
Domination	Nationalism	Ethnocracy, chauvinism, monocultural regime	Engenders enclosure and/or competition
Enclosure	• Dormant, latent • Confinement, ghetto • Inward-looking, self-chosen	Low mobility, monocultural	Tends towards competition over time
Competition	Patronage. Survival	Mobile, bicultural Competition over niches, political and development resources	Tends towards optional ethnicity over time
Optional	Symbolic, low-intensity ethnicity Hybridity	Bicultural, multicultural Agency, ambivalence, opportunism Multiple identity	Beyond or after ethnicity

long period and continues to inform government policies and popular attitudes, thus reproducing the conditions in which Tamil nationalism can persist, resulting in a situation of ethnic gridlock. With these provisos, these dynamics have heuristic value, also in showing up counter instances. For a *précis* see Table 2.1.

Domination-within-domination

If we assume that cultural differences are not problematic *per se*, then the main factor that makes cultural differences salient and problematic is if and how they intersect with power relations. This too needs to be considered in process form. Each variety of ethnicity then represents features of both domination and emancipation in different relational contexts. Thus the classic problem of domination-within-domination takes different forms across the varieties of ethnicity sketched above.

1. Nationalism may be emancipatory in relation to colonialism and external domination but turns into domination when it takes the form of internal colonialism, xenophobia, and chauvinism, imposes a monocultural regime and practices suppression and discrimination of minorities and deliberate uneven development across regions. An example is the double role of Kemalism in Turkey: emancipatory in

relation to foreign powers and repressive in relation to minorities such as Armenians, Kurds, and Alevites.

2. (a) In dormant ethnicity, cultural difference is latent and not a political factor. (b) Cultural confinement often involves a chain effect in which the dominated reproduce domination within their own circles. Group membership is involuntary, internal differences are suppressed, group boundaries are rigid, individual choice is restricted and "passing" into another group is prohibited or discouraged. (c) Similar constraints apply to self-segregation (e.g. on the Nation of Islam, see Marable 1998).

3. Competition ethnicity stretches across a range of culturally inflected politics that is too wide for comfortable generalizations. Unity is strength and therefore there may be a tendency toward suppressing internal differences. Competition means seeking advantage in relation to other ethnic groups, which may lead to differences being played up. The vast legacy of "ethnic jokes" is a mild reminder of this pattern. However, interethnic cooperation or rainbow coalitions can also be a competition strategy, such as the Jewish–black coalition in 1960s American politics.

4. Optional ethnicity may be emancipatory by widening mobility and identity options, in effect to post-ethnicity. In optional ethnicity domination may relate to the self rather than others. Thus "passing" or adopting chameleon identities for the sake of mobility or gain can lead to alienation. An example is the practice of skin bleaching that is widespread across South Asia, the Middle East, parts of Africa, Latin America, and the Caribbean and among immigrants in the West. Such politics of complexion includes "passing" in the United States, "browning" in Jamaica and the saying that "money whitens" in Brazil.

Table 2.2 gives a *précis* of the ambivalent politics of ethnicity on the argument that to each variety of ethnicity there is a dimension of domination and of emancipation in different relational settings.

Since ethnicity is relational it always involves interrelations among ethnic groups who are each not merely different but also different types of ethnicity. They are not merely different ethnic groups but different ethnic strata occupying different class positions. An example is the distinction between "race" and "ethnicity" in the United States, which Mary Waters (1996: 238) draws as follows:

European ethnic groups are generally composed of voluntary migrants and their descendants who chose to come to the United States. Those defined racially, such as blacks, Native Americans, Mexicans in the South-West, and Puerto Ricans, have generally been incorporated into the United States historically through conquest or the forced migration of slaves.

Table 2.2 *Politics of ethnicities*

Ethnicities	Domination	Emancipation
Nationalism	Monocultural control, internal colonialism, oppression of minorities, xenophobia Regional hegemonism	Self-determination Anti-imperialism, anti-regional hegemonism, anti-racism
Enclosure	Cultural exclusivism Suppression of internal differences (gender, class)	Self-determination, autonomy, dignity
Competition	Suppression of internal differences while seeking advantage over other ethnic groups	Collective struggle for improvement
Optional	Alienation, inauthenticity, posturing	Individual or collective improvement, agency, fluidity, multiple identity, play

Considering that mobility is a function of power, dominant groups and individuals are per definition more mobile than subalterns; they can choose to identify ethnic or postethnic, to identify "white," to shop for identity, to identify as liberal or humanist, or to step outside the framework altogether and identify as world citizen. For "white ethnics" then, according to Waters (1996: 23–24), "ethnicity itself takes on certain individual and positive connotations. The process and content of symbolic ethnicity then make it increasingly difficult for white ethnics to sympathize with, or understand, the experience of a non-symbolic ethnicity, the experience of racial minorities in the United States."

Another way of phrasing this is that since ethnicity is relational it implies multiculturality of one sort or other. "Ethnicity" and "multiculturalism" then are two ways of describing the same situation.[11] Next, since ethnicity is always plural and implies ethnicities (for no ethnicity exists alone), to ethnicity there is always a reflexive moment (the exception is dormant ethnicity, which is non-ethnicity or the absence of ethnic consciousness): ethnic consciousness implies awareness of other ethnicities. In a similar vein, multiculturalism implies multiculturalisms (for different ethnicities hold different views on the nature of their interrelations). This brings us to the question of multiculturalisms.

Multiculturalisms

To contextualize multiculturalism, let's consider first what it is not and what kind of thinking preceded it. Earlier views essentialized cultural

Table 2.3 *Responses to group differences*

Responses	Keywords	Examples
Status differences	Ascribed status	Caste, estates, helots, slavery, colonial colour bar, Apartheid
Relative autonomy	Different populations can practice their religion and culture	Ottoman millet system
Segregation	Territorial confinement (and different legal status)	Ghettos, reservations, Jim Crow laws, Bantustans
Assimilation	Convergence toward a given center	Conversion. Melting pot, nineteenth-century *mestizaje*
Migration	Population transfer (forced or voluntary)	Pogroms, ethnic cleansing
Genocide		Armenians, Shoah

difference. To give one example, in the Romantic take on nations of Herder and de Maistre, each nation and people possesses its own genius and soul. In this view, the units of cultural difference are peoples; difference is typically expressed in language and other components of folk culture, and if boundaries do not naturally exist, state policy should strive to make them coincide.

But what if different peoples do coexist within the same polity as a consequence of migration, conquest, colonialism, or decolonization? Classic responses have been to institute status differentials (such as slavery, the caste system, and medieval estates), to provide relative autonomy within an overarching tribute-paying or imperial social formation (as in the Ottoman millet system), and assimilation. Other options are territorial segregation, population transfer, and genocide. Assimilation has been a major strategy to control difference, for instance the compulsory conversion of Jews and Moors in the wake of the Reconquest of the Iberian Peninsula. A familiar version of assimilation is the American melting pot. In Latin America *mestizaje* served as a hegemonic ideology of "whitening" and "Europeanization." These are forms of monoculturalism, or nationalism framed by a cultural hegemony and center of gravity, which in the United States for a long time used to be WASP hegemony. Group boundaries are taken to be fluid except those of the dominant group: all groups are expected to gradually melt and converge on the center, the cultural identity of Americanism, which itself was not supposed to change. A *précis* of classic responses to cultural difference is in Table 2.3.

An early perspective on the coexistence of cultural groups is plural society, a notion coined by Furnivall (1939, 1956) to describe the situation in the Dutch East Indies and colonial Burma. In the Dutch East Indies different populations (Muslims, Chinese, Dutch, and a scattering of Arabs) allegedly coexisted without mingling; they interacted only in the marketplace and thus made up a plural economy.[12] The idea of plural society has later been applied to other social formations such as the Caribbean, the American South, and the Philippines, and criticized in the process (Hollander *et al.* 1966). In England too, multiculturalism and the way in which cultural difference was recognized was originally patterned on the colonial experience (Ali 1992: 104). So the limitations of "plural society" are relevant to the further discussion:

- Group differences are treated as permanent.
- It ignores group intermarriage and intermingling. (Thus many Chinese in Java and elsewhere in Southeast Asia became integrated over time and intermarried with the indigenous population, giving rise to Mestizo groups; in the Malay world they were called "peranakan Chinese" in contrast to Chinese newcomers. The Dutch included newcomers from the Netherlands and the Indo-Dutch, who had been living in the East for generations, intermarried with locals, and developed a mixed colonial culture ["tempo dulu"]. An in-between group of lower status was "Indos," the offspring of relations between locals and the Dutch, who assimilated within the native population. The native population in turn consisted of many different groups and strata.)
- It ignores varieties within groups.
- It ignores or downplays status differences between groups within the colonial power hierarchy.
- It echoes late-colonial fictions on the separation between population groups (which had developed in the mid-nineteenth century in reaction to ideas of "race" imported from Europe) and gives a view "from above" rather than accurately describing intergroup relations.

Another approach to the coexistence of different cultural groups is *pillarization*, which derives from the settlement achieved in the wake of the *Kulturkampf* in the Netherlands. Pillarization was the Dutch mode of cultural pluralism from the 1910s to the 1970s. Pillarization refers to the history of cultural difference within the nation along religious lines – among Catholics, Protestants, and the non-church affiliated. Equal rights in terms of state support for education were granted to Catholics only by 1917. Government funding of schools founded by religious organizations established the system of pillarization, also known as the "silver strings" between the state and Christian denominations. Over time it gave rise to different trade unions, universities, newspapers, and broadcasting for

Protestants, Catholics, and the nonchurch affiliated, including socialists and liberals (Goudsblom 1967; Knippenberg and de Pater 1988). At a later stage this served as a model for multiculturalism.

In the 1980s there was talk of the return of pillarization in regard to immigrants. Pillarization seemed a logical mode in which to incorporate the newcomers. Thus Christian Democrats spoke of "emancipation within one's own circle," just as sixty years earlier this applied to Catholics and Protestants who each received state subsidies for their schools and denominational institutions. There are, however, differences between denominational and multicultural pillarization. The religious pillars communicated among one another at the top, together their elites constituted a roof over the pillarized society. But the mini-pillars of the newcomers with their low socioeconomic status do not reach that high. This truncated mini-pillarization did involve subsidies for immigrant institutions. The second difference was the timing; multicultural pillarization set in when religious pillarization was past, in an urbanized and secularized society in which denominational differences were becoming a background rumor. In the course of the 1980s the pillarization model gave way to greater emphasis on integration, advocated by social democrats and liberals. In the 1990s this takes the form of emphasis on learning the language, courses in "citizenship skills," and plans for immigrant employment schemes with a reporting system for companies. (Nederveen Pieterse 1997b: 192–93)

The Dutch political scientist Arend Lijphart was inspired both by Furnivall's work on plural society and the Dutch policy of pillarization, which he combined in the prescriptive model of *consociationalism* (1975, 1977). In what is technically known as "ethnic conflict regulation," consociationalism or powersharing is now still the leading model (Taylor 1999). The main objections to consociationalism are fairly familiar:

- It reworks the "plural society" and "pillarization" models.
- It does not sufficiently problematize "ethnicity" or group boundaries.
- The hybrids, the in-betweens are overlooked.
- It promotes patronage and clientelist politics.
- It produces static multiculturalism, as a mosaic of ghettos.
- New "mini-pillars" do not reach to the roof.

In this context, the proposal for accommodating ethnicity in African politics mentioned at the beginning does not really go beyond consociationalism. It represents an advance on conventional approaches to democracy in Africa that leave cultural difference out of the equation (an example is Wiseman 1997) and incorporates alternative development perspectives. The multilevel distribution of authority, as in Ethiopian ethnic federalism (state autonomy at federal levels and ethnic organization at local and regional levels) matches the classic pillarization and consociationalism approaches. But there are no safeguards in this approach against patronage politics, or against ethnic rivalry spilling over political watersheds and contaminating or taking over higher levels of governance, resulting in ethnic polarization and ethnocracy. If local and regional power bases become ethnic vote banks, state autonomy is at risk. If this approach went together with participatory democracy and therefore decentralization, it would clash with the strict separation between levels of authority required by pillarization. Accordingly, the emancipation model of ethnicity *tout court* leads to recycling patronage politics, a classic predicament in African politics (e.g. Shaw 1986).

Experiences in the North involving immigration and minorities dominate the discussion of multiculturalism while experiences in the South are usually discussed under headings such as ethnic segmentation or communalism. Since what is at stake in multiculturalism is the redefinition of citizenship it is not surprising that the leading discourse on multiculturalism is normative political theory. Political theory and its inquiries into the citizenship rights and entitlements of latecomers to a polity hold policy implications, while sociology and cultural studies tend to play interpretative and critical roles. Combining ethnicities and multiculturalisms may serve to combine experiences and perspectives North and South and thus place discussions of multiculturalism on a wider canvas.[13]

Conceptions of multiculturalism generally derive from several sources:

- colonial societies (such as plural society);
- settlements of the Kulturkampf in European countries (such as pillarization);
- combinations of both (consociationalism);
- North American adaptations to changing demography and cultural hegemony (United States, Canada);
- and corporate marketing strategies (such as ethnomarketing).

The various notions of multiculturalism reflect these lineages. Multiculturalism on the model of pillarization is a static, conservative archipelago of cultural groups or communities, a mosaic of ghettos. Peter McLaren (1995: 120–32) distinguishes conservative, liberal, left-liberal and critical or resistance multiculturalism. Hollinger (1995) contrasts pluralist multiculturalism, in which groups are permanent, enduring, and the subject of group rights,[14] and cosmopolitan multiculturalism, which involves shifting group boundaries, multiple affiliations, and hybrid identities, and is based on individual rights. If cultures are viewed as porous and interpenetrating, rather than as billiard balls, interculturalism would be a better term (Bernasconi 1998).

A familiar line of criticism dismisses multiculturalism as the cultural wallpaper of late capitalism (Jameson 1991; Zizek 1997), as the "bourgeois eclecticism" of corporate or consumerist multiculturalism *à la* Benetton (Martin 1998). A related notion is hegemonic multiculturalism *à la* the WTO (Matustík 1998). These forms of "managed multiculturalism" come in corporate and administrative varieties and reflect a "standard pluralism that not only leaves groups constituted as givens but entrenches the boundaries fixing group demarcations as unalterable" (Goldberg 1994: 7). The problem, however, is not that these forms of multiculturalism are managed *per se* (citizenship implies a relationship to the state and therefore some form of "management" or institutionalized settlement); the problem is on what terms they are managed. The multiculturalism = late capitalism view overlooks that cultural differences matter also prior to capitalism, recognizes but one variety of multiculturalism and one variety of capitalism, "late capitalism," and by assuming that "identity can wait" reproduces class reductionism.[15]

These forms of "multiculturalism from above" do not address power relations and if we accept that multiculturalism is about the renegotiation of hierarchies and power relations in postimperial and postcolonial settings, these managerial multiculturalisms miss the point. Alternative options are critical, transformative (Chicago Cultural Studies Group 1994; Martin 1998; May 1999) or revolutionary multiculturalism (McLaren 1997). This view has been criticized for being "culturalist" and requiring stronger political economy (McLennan 2001), which may be valid, although it echoes the points made in critical multiculturalism itself; the work of critique is never finished. Critical multiculturalism is critical, first, in that it does not treat cultural differences as givens but problematizes them as differences-in-relation; and second, it is critical in that by incorporating class analysis and emphasizing relations of power, access to citizenship, and citizenship rights, it brings politics back into the babble of diversity.

Table 2.4 presents a schema of different multiculturalisms. The boxes are not mutually exclusive. This sample of views originates mostly from North America. The axes on which they are constructed include perspectives on difference (McLaren) and the nature of group boundaries and notions of rights (Hollinger, Kymlicka).

What underlie these varieties of multiculturalism are assumptions concerning identity and group boundaries and the nature of the state and citizenship. A general backdrop to understandings of multiculturalism is the liberal state. All multiculturalisms above, except the plural society model, assume common citizenship and therefore a commitment to individual rights while ignoring noncitizens. In this general sense they are

Table 2.4 *Multiculturalisms*

Multiculturalism	Keywords	Related notions
Conservative	Groups and differences are enduring Group rights	Plural society, pillarization, consociationalism Pluralist multiculturalism (Hollinger)
Liberal	A natural equality underlies differences; inequality indicates lack of opportunity	Diversity Corporate, ludic, consumerist multiculturalism (Benneton)
Left-liberal	Differences are viewed as "essence"	Positionality, standpoint theory, identity politics "Strategic essentialism" (Spivak). "Show one's identity papers before dialogue can begin" (McLaren)
Critical, transformative	Differences in relation (McLaren)	Resistance multiculturalism
Fluid (Kymlicka)	Shifting group boundaries, multiple or hybrid identities, individual rights	Cosmopolitan multiculturalism, interculturalism

all liberal multiculturalisms: liberalism plus recognition of cultural differences. Liberalism is pluralism, which in multiculturalism is stretched to cultural pluralism (Kukathas 1998). A further assumption is a secure polity that has the capacity to guarantee and enforce citizenship rights.

The question is how individual rights and collective rights interrelate. Equality and difference is an old question, also in relation to gender. In North America a classic friction runs between the politics of recognition and those of redistribution (Fraser 1998). In an exchange with Iris Young (1998), Nancy Fraser argues that these are not reducible to one another and that the cultural left and the ideological left are divided. Young argues for a coalition politics that bridges these differences and Fraser responds that in reality such differences are being reproduced within these politics. Canadian multiculturalism is more fluid than United States multiculturalism. This debate calls to mind William Julius Wilson's plea to shift toward economic criteria for entitlement, to shift from "race" to class. Thus another way of phrasing this is that what is at issue is the need to strengthen the welfare state. In Europe, the friction between recognition and redistribution is tempered by the welfare state. In most European Union countries the recognition of collective rights based on cultural difference assumes fixed group boundaries, but since citizenship generally provides more basic entitlements than the residual US welfare state (or workfare state), the pressure for group affiliation and identification is reduced.

This is where notions of identity come in and where the varieties of multiculturalism meet with the varieties of ethnicity discussed earlier, as twin sets of assumptions concerning identity and group boundaries. Consider, for instance, Will Kymlicka's views in relation to "American multiculturalism":

the appropriate form of multiculturalism must be fluid in conception of groups and group boundaries (new groups may emerge, older groups may coalesce or disappear); voluntary in its conception of group affiliation (individuals should be free to decide whether and how to affiliate with their community of descent); and nonexclusive in its conception of group identity (being a member of one group does not preclude identification with another, or with the larger American nation). (1998: 73)

This adds up to the following conditions for intergroup relations: fluid group boundaries, voluntary group affiliation, and multiple identification. These ideas would go a long way in addressing the question of domination-within-domination, but in the process they raise several problems. In essence, this treats ethnicity as if it is optional, while the realities it refers to are probably conditions of competition ethnicity. If the stipulated conditions would indeed exist there would be no need for ethnic competition. The emphasis on individual choice in Kymlicka's view may be specific to North American conditions. In a sense it begs the question: if individual choice indeed exists as a viable option, what is the problem? In addition, if cultural identity is understood to be a matter of individual agency it clashes with the allocation of group rights, which assumes ascribed status.

Also, the perspective is from the outside, from the point of view of the state and multiculturalism, not from the point of view of the groups. The problem is how is this to be institutionalized? Collective rights may be granted to right past discrimination and disadvantage, but once granted they rigidify group boundaries – how else to know who are entitled? Thus the side effect of some remedies is that they sustain or aggravate the problem of difference. There is a clash between collective rights and fluid group boundaries: collective rights turn group membership into an ascribed status, not a voluntary choice. In addition, collective rights foster ethnic organization and hence patronage. To the extent that this approach is relevant to multiethnicity it does not settle the question of multinational societies and indigenous peoples, such as Native Americans. Here again, if collective rights are granted (such as tax exemption, welfare benefits, and free crossborder traffic) group membership is an ascribed status, not a voluntary choice.

A related problem is the question of hybrids and in-betweens. Nationalism (dominant culture, ethnocracy) and ethnic mobilization have both been highly visible and usually the field is seen as the friction between these two. But what about the in-betweens who are "neither and both," who belong in neither camp or in both (Nederveen Pieterse 2004)?

For instance, in the United States, demographers speak of a silent explosion in the number of mixed-race people. Between 1960 and 1990, the number of interracial married couples went from 150,000 to more than 1.1 million, and the number of interracial children of course leaps accordingly. "Since 1970, the number of mixed-race children in the United States has quadrupled. And there are six times as many intermarriages today as there were in 1960" (Etzioni 1997). Thus Etzioni and others propose, in addition to the choice of sixteen racial categories that the Census Bureau offers Americans, a new "multiracial" category. This idea has been infuriating to some African American leaders who regard it as undermining black solidarity. "African-American leaders also object to a multiracial category because race data are used to enforce civil rights legislation in employment, voting rights, housing and mortgage lending, health care services and educational opportunities" (1997). The proponents argue that this category – and a "category of 'multiethnic' origin, which most Americans might wish to check" – would help soften the racial and ethnic divisions that now run through American society. Amid ample controversy, the 2000 US Census for the first time offered Americans the option of multiple identification. This is but one example of the clash between the allocation of collective rights and the idea of multiple identity and fluid group boundaries.

If we juxtapose the varieties of ethnicity and of multiculturalism the problems become apparent. Domination ethnicity (monocultural nationalism) correlates with the suppression of difference through assimilation policies. Enclosure ethnicity suppresses differences through territorial segregation, often accompanied by ascribing a different legal status to different groups.

Liberal citizenship forecloses both these options. Here the real problem zone is competition ethnicity. Liberal multiculturalism sidesteps the question of competition by viewing inequality as lack of opportunity, thereby denying the problem of difference itself: a cultural division of labor that privileges some groups. Left-liberal multiculturalism recognizes this problem but in the process reifies and essentializes identities, so that what is a solution in one sphere (recognizing difference)

Table 2.5 *Ethnicities and multiculturalisms*

Ethnicities	Intergroup relations	Multiculturalisms
Domination	Assimilation	No (monoculturalism)
Enclosure	Segregation	No (apartheid)
Competition	Bicultural rivalries	Liberal, left-liberal, critical
Optional	Hybridity, postethnicity	Fluid, cosmopolitan

becomes a problem in another (reifying difference). Fluid and cosmopolitan multiculturalism, on the other hand, sidestep the problem of competition by treating ethnic identity as if it is optional already. That is, they
mix up what might be the likely outcome over time (ethnic identity as
choice) with the ongoing process (competition on the basis of identities).
Table 2.5 gives an overview combining ethnicities and multiculturalisms.

Coda

We can leave assimilation and hegemony out of the equation since they
are essentially variations on monoculturalism. Multiculturalism concerns
the redefinition of citizenship, and in effect the renegotiation of hierarchy,
in societies where the composition of the population and/or the political balance of power has been changing. North America and Europe
dominate in the discussion on multiculturalism, but of course changing
demography and shifting cultural hegemony are conditions that pertain
throughout the world.

In these situations what matters is neither pure and uncontested hierarchy nor enclosure (with reified or fixed cultural boundaries) nor optional
identities (shopping for identity, ethnic chic, ethnicity lite, confetti culture), but the in-between zone of differences in relation, the zone where
similarities between groups are sufficient to enable them to engage in
competition for the same resources, while falling short of convergence
upon sameness of identity or degree of mobility. It follows that in the
realities of culturally inscribed inequality, of the multiculturalisms discussed above only critical multiculturalism is a pertinent option – on the
understanding that as a critical perspective it poses more questions than it
provides answers; but the questions are pertinent. Collective learning as
a contextual process involves the awareness that each settlement is provi-
sional, contextual, temporary. A settlement should have in-built provisos
that avoid unnecessary closure and make it open to amendment. Standard pluralism shuffles stereotypes while fluid or cosmopolitan pluralism

overlooks stereotypes, assumes liquidity of identity and thus serves as a cure for which there is no ailment.

NOTES

1. An earlier version of this chapter was presented at the conference *Nationalism, Identity and Minority Rights*, University of Bristol, 1999. Thanks to Emin Adas, Stephen May, and a reviewer for comments.
2. For instance, the historian Ernest Wamba-dia-Wamba who long argued against the "imperial state" in Africa as a colonial imposition (1991) later became a spokesperson of the rebels in Eastern Congo.
3. For instance, according to Algis Prazauskas (1998: 2), "In the modern world, ethnic nationalism looks larger than life mainly because it has received wide coverage in the mass media and the lion's share of ethnopolitical research deals with secessionist movements and regions of ethnic strife rather than with progress of national integration in much larger areas."
4. Social learning is a salient theme in fields such as organization theory, social movements, industrial districts, research methodology, and development studies (cf. Nederveen Pieterse 2001b).
5. "Most rural Africa is still largely divided into ethnic territories (homelands) or enclaves inhabited by one or more dominant ethnic group. . . . Ethnic (or primary) affiliations still provide the basis on which individuals and groups gain access to land" (Salih 1999: 8).
6. One problem is the blurring of the distinction between "culture" and "cultures" or "cultural groups," discussed in Nederveen Pieterse 2004.
7. An example is Lake 1995; a discussion is Nederveen Pieterse 1998.
8. When spending time in Sri Lanka I certainly thought so (cf. e.g. Nithiyanandam 2000).
9. A full discussion of these ethnicities is Nederveen Pieterse 1997a; this section and the next draw on this while developing the argument further.
10. I don't accept Portes' (2000) distinction between *linear ethnicity* and *reactive ethnicity*; there is no such thing as linear ethnicity: if it were linear it would be dormant ethnicity; ethnicity is always relational (or else it would not be ethnicity) and thus reactive.
11. One might argue further that ethnicity implies ethnicities and therefore also a "multiculturalism" for the coexistence of ethnicities always involves a normative component and collective representations and ideological frameworks of differences-in-relation. Yet this would stretch the term "multiculturalism" beyond its usual meaning of positive valuation of cultural diversity, to *any* valuation of cultural difference (i.e. antisemitism, Jim Crow, and Apartheid would then be forms of multiculturalism too).
12. Furnivall's original term "plural economy" (1939) was later stretched to plural society. This section draws on Nederveen Pieterse 2001a.
13. Ethnicity (multiethnicity, ethnonationalism, secession etc.) remains the common heading in the global South; yet multiculturalism is an emerging discourse in countries such as Mexico, Turkey, and Singapore. Parekh 2000 takes multiculturalism beyond experiences in the North.

14. A related notion is Terence Turner's "difference multiculturalism" (1994).
15. As rejoinder McLaren (2001: 416–17) proposes a materialist multiculturalism.

REFERENCES

Ali, Y. (1992) "Muslim women and the politics of ethnicity and culture in North
England." In G. Saghal, and N. Yuval-Davis (eds.), *Refusing Holy Orders:
Women and Fundamentalism in Britain*. London: Virago, pp. 101–23.
Bayart, J.-F., S. Ellis, and B. Hibou (1999) *The Criminalization of the State in
Africa*. London: James Currey.
Bernasconi, R. (1998) "'Stuck inside of mobile with the Memphis blues again':
interculturalism and the conversation of races." In Cynthia Willett (ed.),
Theorizing Multiculturalism. Oxford: Blackwell, pp. 276–97.
Bulmer, M. and J. Solomos (eds.) (1999) *Ethnic and Racial Studies Today*. London,
Routledge.
Chabal, P. and J.-F. Daloz (1999) *Africa Works: Disorder as Political Instrument*.
London, James Currey.
Chicago Cultural Studies Group (1994) "Critical multiculturalism." In David
Theo Goldberg (ed.), *Multiculturalism: A Critical Reader*. Oxford: Blackwell.
pp. 114–39.
Denitch, Bogdan (1994) *Ethnic Nationalism: The Tragic Death of Yugoslavia*.
Minneapolis: University of Minnesota Press.
Dwyer, D. and S. R. Drakakis (eds.) (1996) *Ethnicity and Development: Geograph-
ical Perspectives*. Chichester: Wiley.
Etzioni, Amitai (1997) "'Other' Americans help break down racial barriers."
International Herald Tribune, May 10.
Fraser, Nancy (1998) "From redistribution to recognition? Dilemmas of justice
in a 'post-socialist' age." In Cynthia Willett (ed.), *Theorizing Multiculturalism*.
Oxford: Blackwell, pp. 19–49.
Furnivall, J. S. (1939) *Netherlands India: A Study of Plural Economy*. Cambridge:
Cambridge University Press.
   (1956) *Colonial Policy and Practice: A Comparative Study of Burma and Nether-
lands India*. New York: New York University Press.
Goldberg, David Theo (1994) "Introduction: multicultural conditions." In Gold-
berg (ed.), *Multiculturalism: A Critical Reader*. Oxford: Blackwell, pp. 1–41.
Goudsblom, J. (1967) *Dutch Society*. New York, Random House.
Hollander, A. N. J. den, O. van den Muijzenberg, J. D. Speckmann, and W. F.
Wertheim (1966) *De plurale samenleving*. Meppel: Boom.
Hollinger, D. (1995) *Postethnic America: Beyond Multiculturalism*. New York, Basic
Books.
Humphrey, M. (1997) "Civil war, identity and globalisation." *New Formations*
31: 67–82.
Jameson, F. (1991) *Postmodernism, or the Cultural Logic of Late Capitalism*. London:
Verso.
Jenkins, R. (1999) "Ethnicity etcetera: social anthropological points of view." In
Bulmer and Solomos (eds.), pp. 85–97.

Kaplan, R. D. (2000) *The Coming Anarchy*. New York, Random House.

Knippenberg, H. and B. de Pater (1988) *De eenwording van Nederland*. Nijmegen, SUN.

Kukathas, C. (1998) "Liberalism and multiculturalism: the politics of indifference." *Political Theory* 26 (5): 686–99.

Kymlicka, Will (1998) "American multiculturalism in the international arena." *Dissent* (Fall): 73–79.

Lake, David A. (1995) "Ethnic conflict and international intervention." La Jolla, University of California, Institute on Global Conflict and Cooperation Policy Brief No. 3.

Lijphart, Arend (1975) *The Politics of Accommodation: Pluralism and Democracy in the Netherlands*. Berkeley: University of California Press.

(1977) *Democracy in Plural Societies: A Comparative Exploration*. New Haven, CT: Yale University Press.

Marable, Manning (1998) "Black fundamentalism: Farrakhan and conservative black nationalism." *Race & Class* 39 (4): 1–22.

Martin, Bill (1998) "Multiculturalism: consumerist or transformational." In Cynthia Willett (ed.), *Theorizing Multiculturalism*. Oxford: Blackwell, pp. 121–50.

Matustík, M. J. B. (1998) "Ludic, corporate and imperial multiculturalism: impostors of democracy and cartographers of the New World Order." In Cynthia Willett (ed.), *Theorizing Multiculturalism*. Oxford: Blackwell, pp. 100–18.

May, Stephen (ed.) (1999) *Critical Multiculturalism: Rethinking Multicultural and Antiracist Education*. London: Routledge Falmer.

McLaren, Peter (1995) *Critical Pedagogy and Predatory Culture*. London, Routledge.

(1997) *Revolutionary Multiculturalism: Pedagogies of Dissent for the New Millennium*. Boulder, CO: Westview Press.

(2001) "Wayward multiculturalists: a reply to Gregor McLennan." *Ethnicities* 1 (3): 408–20.

McLennan, Gregor (2001) "Can there be a "critical" multiculturalism?" *Ethnicities* 1 (3): 389–407.

Moynihan, D. P. (1992) *Pandemonium*. New York: Random House.

Nederveen Pieterse, J. (1997a) "Deconstructing/reconstructing ethnicity." *Nations and Nationalism* 3 (3): 1–31.

(1997b) "Traveling Islam: mosques without minarets." In Ayse Öncü and Petra Weyland (eds.), *Space, Culture and Power*. London: Zed, pp. 177–200.

(1998) "Sociology of humanitarian intervention: Bosnia, Rwanda and Somalia compared." In Nederveen Pieterse (ed.), *Humanitarian Intervention and Beyond: World Orders in the Making*. London and New York: Macmillan and St Martin's Press, pp. 230–65.

(2001a) "The case of multiculturalism: kaleidoscopic and long-term views." *Social Identities* 7 (3): 393–407.

(2001b) *Development Theory: Deconstructions/Reconstructions*. London: Sage.

(2002) "Fault lines of transnationalism: border matters." *Bulletin of the Royal Institute of Inter-Faith Studies (Amman)* 4 (2): 33–48.

(2004) *Globalization and Culture: Global Mélange*. Boulder, CO: Rowman & Littlefield.

Nithiyanandam, V. (2000) "Ethnic politics and Third World development: some lessons from Sri Lanka's experience." *Third World Quarterly* 21 (2): 283–312.

Parekh, Bhikhu (2000) *Rethinking Multiculturalism*. London: Macmillan.

Portes, A. (2000) "Globalization from below: the rise of transnational communities." In D. Kalb, M. van der Land, R. Staring, B. van Steenbergen, and N. Wilterdink (eds.), *The Ends of Globalization: Bringing Society Back In*. Lanham, MD: Rowman & Littlefield, pp. 253–70.

Prazauskas, Algis (1998) "Ethnicity, nationalism and politics." The Hague: Institute of Social Studies Working Paper 280.

Ramet, Sabrina Petra (1996) "Nationalism and the 'idiocy' of the countryside: the case of Serbia." *Ethnic and Racial Studies* 19 (1): 70–87.

Rupesinghe, K. and V. A. Tishkov (eds.) (1996) *Ethnicity and Power in the Contemporary World*. Tokyo: United Nations University Press.

Salih, Mohamed M. A. (1999) "Taking ethnicity seriously: another development and democracy in Africa." The Hague: Institute of Social Studies, unpublished paper.

Shaw, T. (1986) "Ethnicity as the resilient paradigm for Africa: from the 1960s to the 1980s." *Development and Change* 17 (4): 587–606.

Taylor, R. (1999) "Political science encounters 'race' and 'ethnicity'." In Bulmer and Solomos (eds.), pp. 115–23.

Turner, T. (1994) "Anthropology and multiculturalism: what is anthropology that multiculturalists should be mindful of it?" In David Theo Goldberg (ed.), *Multiculturalism: A Critical Reader*. Oxford: Blackwell, pp. 406–25.

Uvin, Peter (1999) "Ethnicity and power in Burundi and Rwanda: different paths to mass violence." *Comparative Politics* 31 (3): 253–72.

Wamba-dia-Wamba, E. (1991) "Philosophy in Africa: challenges of the African philosopher." In T. Serequeberhan (ed.), *African Philosophy: The Essential Readings*. New York: Paragon, pp. 211–46.

Waters, Mary C. (1990) *Ethnic Options: Choosing Identities in America*. Berkeley: University of California Press.

(1996) "Ethnic and racial groups in the USA: conflict and cooperation." In K. Rupesinghe and V. A. Tishkov (eds.), *Ethnicity and Power in the Contemporary World*. Tokyo: United Nations University Press, pp. 236–62.

Wiseman, J. A. (1997) "The rise and fall and rise (and fall?) of democracy in sub-Saharan Africa." In D. Potter, D. Goldblatt, M. Kiloh, and P. Lewis (eds.), *Democratization*. Cambridge: Polity and Open University, pp. 272–93.

Young, Iris (1998) "Unruly categories: a critique of Nancy Fraser's dual systems theory." In Cynthia Willett (ed.), *Theorizing Multiculturalism*. Oxford: Blackwell, pp. 50–67.

Zizek, S. (1997) "Multiculturalism or the cultural logic of multinational capitalism." *New Left Review*, 225.

3   Ethnicity without groups

Rogers Brubaker

Common sense groupism

Few social science concepts would seem as basic, even indispensable, as that of group. In disciplinary terms, "group" would appear to be a core concept for sociology, political science, anthropology, demography, and social psychology. In substantive terms, it would seem to be fundamental to the study of political mobilization, cultural identity, economic interests, social class, status groups, collective action, kinship, gender, religion, ethnicity, race, multiculturalism, and minorities of every kind.[1]

Yet despite this seeming centrality, the concept "group" has remained curiously unscrutinized in recent years. There is, to be sure, a substantial social psychological literature addressing the concept (Hamilton *et al.* 1998; McGrath 1984), but this has had little resonance outside that sub-discipline. Elsewhere in the social sciences, the recent literature addressing the concept "group" is sparse, especially by comparison with the immense literature on such concepts as class, identity, gender, ethnicity, or multiculturalism – topics in which the concept "group" is implicated, yet seldom analyzed its own terms.[2] "Group" functions as a seemingly unproblematic, taken-for-granted concept, apparently in no need of particular scrutiny or explication. As a result, we tend to take for granted not only the concept "group," but also "groups" – the putative things-in-the-world to which the concept refers.

My aim in this chapter is not to enter into conceptual or definitional casuistry about the concept of group. It is rather to address one problematic consequence of this tendency to take groups for granted in the study of ethnicity, race, and nationhood, and in the study of ethnic, racial, and national conflict in particular. This is what I will call groupism: the tendency to take discrete, sharply differentiated, internally homogeneous and externally bounded groups as basic constituents of social life, chief protagonists of social conflicts, and fundamental units of social analysis.[3] In the domain of ethnicity, nationalism, and race, I mean by "groupism" the tendency to treat ethnic groups, nations, and races as substantial entities to which interests and agency can be attributed. I mean the tendency to reify such groups, speaking of Serbs, Croats, Muslims, and Albanians in the former Yugoslavia, of Catholics and Protestants in Northern Ireland, of Jews and Palestinians in Israel and the occupied territories, of Turks and Kurds in Turkey, or of Blacks, Whites, Asians, Hispanics, and Native Americans in the US as if they were internally homogeneous, externally bounded groups, even unitary collective actors with common purposes. I mean the tendency to represent the social and cultural world as a multichrome mosaic of monochrome ethnic, racial, or cultural blocs.

From the perspective of broader developments in social theory, the persisting strength of groupism in this sense is surprising. After all, several distinct traditions of social analysis have challenged the treatment of groups as real, substantial things-in-the-world. These include such sharply differing enterprises as ethnomethodology and conversation analysis, social network theory, cognitive theory, feminist theory, and individualist approaches such as rational choice and game theory. More generally, broadly structuralist approaches have yielded to a variety of more "constructivist" theoretical stances, which tend – at the level of rhetoric, at least – to see groups as constructed, contingent, and fluctuating. And a diffuse postmodernist sensibility emphasizes the fragmentary, the ephemeral, and the erosion of fixed forms and clear boundaries. These developments are disparate, even contradictory in analytical style, methodological orientation, and epistemological commitments. Network theory, with its methodological (and sometimes ontological) relationalism (Emirbayer and Goodwin 1994; Wellman 1988) is opposed to rational choice theory, with its methodological (and sometimes ontological) individualism; both are sharply and similarly opposed, in analytical style and epistemological commitments, to postmodernist approaches. Yet these and other developments have converged in problematizing groupness and undermining axioms of stable group being.

Challenges to "groupism," however, have been uneven. They have been striking – to take just one example – in the study of class, especially in the study of the working class, a term that is hard to use today without quotation marks or some other distancing device. Yet ethnic groups continue to be understood as entities and cast as actors. To be sure, constructivist approaches of one kind or another are now dominant in academic discussions of ethnicity. Yet everyday talk, policy analysis, media reports, and even much ostensibly constructivist academic writing routinely frame accounts of ethnic, racial, and national conflict in groupist terms as the struggles "of" ethnic groups, races, and nations.[4] Somehow, when we talk about ethnicity, and even more when we talk about ethnic conflict, we almost automatically find ourselves talking about ethnic groups.

Now it might be asked: "What's wrong with this?" After all, it seems to be mere common sense to treat ethnic struggles as the struggles of ethnic groups, and ethnic conflict as conflict between such groups. I agree that this is the – or at least *a* – commonsense view of the matter. But we cannot rely on common sense here. Ethnic common sense – the tendency to partition the social world into putatively deeply constituted, quasi-natural intrinsic kinds (Hirschfeld 1996) – is a key part of what we want to explain, not what we want to explain things *with*; it belongs to our empirical data, not to our analytical toolkit.[5] Cognitive anthropologists and social psychologists have accumulated a good deal of evidence about commonsense ways of carving up the social world – about what Lawrence Hirschfeld (1996) has called "folk sociologies." The evidence suggests that some commonsense social categories – and notably commonsense ethnic and racial categories – tend to be essentializing and naturalizing (Rothbart and Taylor 1992; Hirschfeld 1996; Gil-White 1999). They are the vehicles of what has been called a "participants' primordialism" (Smith 1998: 158) or a "psychological essentialism" (Medin 1989). We obviously cannot ignore such commonsense primordialism. But that does not mean we should simply replicate it in our scholarly analyses or policy assessments. As "analysts *of* naturalizers," we need not be "analytic naturalizers" (Gil-White 1999: 803).

Instead, we need to break with vernacular categories and commonsense understandings. We need to break, for example, with the seemingly obvious and uncontroversial point that ethnic conflict involves conflict between ethnic groups. I want to suggest that ethnic conflict – or what might better be called ethnicized or ethnically framed conflict – need not, and should not, be understood as conflict *between ethnic groups*, just as racial or racially framed conflict need not be understood as conflict between *races*, or nationally framed conflict as conflict between *nations*.

Participants, of course, regularly do represent ethnic, racial, and national conflict in such groupist, even primordialist terms. They often cast ethnic groups, races, or nations as the protagonists – the heroes and martyrs – of such struggles. But this is no warrant for analysts to do so. We must, of course, take vernacular categories and participants' understandings seriously, for they are partly constitutive of our objects of study. But we should not uncritically adopt *categories of ethnopolitical practice* as our *categories of social analysis*. Apart from the general unreliability of ethnic common sense as a guide for social analysis, we should remember that participants' accounts – especially those of specialists in ethnicity such as ethnopolitical entrepreneurs, who, unlike nonspecialists, may live "off" as well as "for" ethnicity – often have what Pierre Bourdieu has called a *performative* character. By invoking groups, they seek to evoke them, summon them, call them into being. Their categories are *for doing* – designed to stir, summon, justify, mobilize, kindle, and energize. By reifying groups, by treating them as substantial things-in-the-world, ethnopolitical entrepreneurs may, as Bourdieu notes, "contribute to producing what they apparently describe or designate" (1991a: 220).[6]

Reification is a social process, not simply an intellectual bad habit. As a social process, it is central to the *practice* of politicized ethnicity. And appropriately so. To criticize ethnopolitical entrepreneurs for reifying ethnic groups would be a kind of category mistake. Reifying groups is precisely what ethnopolitical entrepreneurs are in the business of doing. When they are successful, the political fiction of the unified group can be momentarily yet powerfully realized in practice. As analysts, we should certainly try to *account* for the ways in which – and conditions under which – this practice of reification, this powerful crystalization of group feeling, can work. This may be one of the most important tasks of the theory of ethnic conflict. But we should avoid unintentionally *doubling* or *reinforcing* the reification of ethnic groups in ethnopolitical practice with a reification of such groups in social analysis.

Beyond groupism

How, then, are we to understand ethnic conflict, if not in commonsense terms as conflict between ethnic groups? And how can we go beyond groupism? Here I sketch eight basic points and then, in the following section, draw out some of their implications. In the final section, I illustrate the argument by considering one empirical case.

Rethinking ethnicity. We need to rethink not only ethnic conflict, but also what we mean by ethnicity itself. This is not a matter of seeking agreement on a definition. The intricate and everrecommencing definitional casuistry in studies of ethnicity, race, and nationalism has done little to advance the discussion, and indeed can be viewed as a symptom of the non-cumulative nature of research in the field. It is rather a matter of critically scrutinizing our conceptual tools. Ethnicity, race, and nation should be conceptualized not as substances or things or entities or organisms or collective individuals – as the imagery of discrete, concrete, tangible, bounded, and enduring "groups" encourages us to do – but rather in relational, processual, dynamic, eventful, and disaggregated terms. This means thinking of ethnicity, race, and nation not in terms of substantial groups or entities but in terms of *practical categories, cultural idioms, cognitive schemas, discursive frames, organizational routines, institutional forms, political projects,* and *contingent events.* It means thinking of *ethnicization, racialization,* and *nationalization* as political, social, cultural, and psychological *processes.* And it means taking as a basic analytical category not the "group" as an entity but *groupness* as a contextually fluctuating conceptual variable. Stated baldly in this fashion, these are of course mere slogans; I will try to fill them out more fully in what follows.

The reality of ethnicity. To rethink ethnicity, race, and nationhood along these lines is in no way to dispute their reality, minimize their power, or discount their significance; it is to construe their reality, power, and significance in a different way. Understanding the reality of race, for example, does not require us to posit the existence of races. Racial idioms, ideologies, narratives, categories, and systems of classification, and racialized ways of seeing, thinking, talking, and framing claims are real and consequential, especially when they are embedded in powerful organizations. But the reality of race – and even its overwhelming coercive power in some settings – does not depend on the existence of "races." Similarly, the reality of ethnicity and nationhood – and the overriding power of ethnic and national identifications in some settings – does not depend on the existence of ethnic groups or nations as substantial groups or entities.

Groupness as event. Shifting attention from groups to groupness, and treating groupness as variable and contingent rather than fixed and given,[7] allows us to take account of – and, potentially, to account for – phases of extraordinary cohesion, and moments of intensely felt collective solidarity, without implicitly treating high levels of groupness as constant, enduring, or definitionally present. It allows us to treat groupness as an *event,* as something that "happens," as E. P. Thompson famously said about class. At the same time, it keeps us analytically attuned to the possibility that groupness may *not* happen, that high levels of groupness may *fail* to crystalize, despite the group-making efforts of ethnopolitical entrepreneurs, and even in situations of intense elite-level ethnopolitical conflict. Being analytically attuned to "negative" instances in this way enlarges the domain of relevant cases, and helps correct for the bias in the literature toward the study of striking instances of high groupness, successful mobilization, or conspicuous violence – a bias that can engender an "overethnicized" view of the social world, a distorted representation of whole world regions as "seething cauldrons" of ethnic tension (Brubaker 1998), and an overestimation of the incidence of ethnic violence (Fearon and Laitin 1996). Sensitivity to such negative instances can also direct potentially fruitful analytical attention toward the problem of explaining failed efforts at ethnopolitical mobilization.

Groups and categories. Much talk about ethnic, racial, or national groups is obscured by the failure to distinguish between groups and categories.

If by "group" we mean a mutually interacting, mutually recognizing, mutually oriented, effectively communicating, bounded collectivity with a sense of solidarity, corporate identity, and capacity for concerted action, or even if we adopt a less exigent understanding of "group," it should be clear that a category is not a group (Sacks 1995, I: 41, 401; Handelman 1977; McKay and Lewins 1978; Jenkins 1997: 53ff.).[8] It is at best a potential basis for group-formation or "groupness."[9]

By distinguishing consistently between categories and groups, we can problematize – rather than presume – the relation between them. We can ask about the degree of groupness associated with a particular category in a particular setting, and about the political, social, cultural, and psychological processes through which categories get invested with groupness (Petersen 1987). We can ask how people – and organizations – *do things* with categories. This includes limiting access to scarce resources or particular domains of activity by excluding categorically distinguished outsiders (Weber 1968 [1922]: 43ff., 341ff.; Barth 1969; Brubaker 1992; Tilly 1998), but it also includes more mundane actions such as identifying or classifying oneself or others (Levine 1999) or simply "doing being ethnic" in an ethnomethodological sense (Moerman 1968). We can analyze the organizational and discursive careers of categories – the processes through which they become institutionalized and entrenched in administrative routines (Tilly 1998) and embedded in culturally powerful and symbolically resonant myths, memories, and narratives (Armstrong 1982; Smith 1986). We can study the politics of categories, both from above and from below. From above, we can focus on the ways in which categories are proposed, propagated, imposed, institutionalized, discursively articulated, organizationally entrenched, and generally embedded in multifarious forms of "governmentality" (Noiriel 1991; Slezkine 1994; Brubaker 1994; Torpey 2000; Martin 2001). From below, we can study the "micropolitics" of categories, the ways in which the categorized appropriate, internalize, subvert, evade, or transform the categories that are imposed on them (Domínguez 1986). And drawing on advances in cognitive research, ethnomethodology, and conversation analysis,[10] we can study the sociocognitive and interactional processes through which categories are used by individuals to make sense of the social world; linked to stereotypical beliefs and expectations about category members;[11] invested with emotional associations and evaluative judgments; deployed as resources in specific interactional contexts; and activated by situational triggers or cues. A focus on categories, in short, can illuminate the multifarious ways in which ethnicity, race, and nationhood can exist and "work" without the existence of ethnic groups as substantial entities. It can help us envision ethnicity without groups.

Group-making as project. If we treat groupness as a variable and distinguish between groups and categories, we can attend to the dynamics of *group-making* as a social, cultural, and political project, aimed at transforming categories into groups or increasing levels of groupness (Bourdieu 1991a, 1991b). Sometimes this is done in quite a cynical fashion. Ethnic and other insurgencies, for example, often adopt what is called in French a *politique du pire*, a politics of seeking the worst outcome in the short run so as to bolster their legitimacy or improve their prospects in the longer run. When the small, ill-equipped, ragtag Kosovo Liberation Army (KLA) stepped up its attacks on Serb policemen and other targets in early 1998, for example, this was done as a deliberate – and successful – strategy of provoking massive regime reprisals. As in many such situations, the brunt of the reprisals was borne by civilians. The cycle of attacks and counterattacks sharply increased groupness among both Kosovo Albanians and Kosovo Serbs, generated greater support for the KLA among both Kosovo and diaspora Albanians, and bolstered KLA recruitment and funding. This enabled the KLA to mount a more serious challenge to the regime, which in turn generated more brutal regime reprisals, and so on. In this sense, group crystalization and polarization were the result of violence, not the cause (Brubaker 1999).

Of course, this group-making strategy employed in the late 1990s did not start from scratch. It began already with relatively high levels of groupness, a legacy of earlier phases of conflict. The propitious "raw materials" the KLA had to work with no doubt help explain the success of its strategy. Not all group-making projects succeed, and those that do succeed (more or less) do so in part as a result of the cultural and psychological materials they have to work with. These materials include not only, or especially, "deep" *longue-durée* cultural structures such as the *mythomoteurs* highlighted by Armstrong (1982) and Smith (1986), but also the moderately durable ways of thinking and feeling that represent "middle-range" legacies of historical experience and political action. Yet while such raw materials – themselves the product and precipitate of past struggles and predicaments – constrain and condition the possibilities for group-making in the present, there remains considerable scope for deliberate group-making strategies. Certain dramatic events, in particular, can serve to galvanize and crystalize a potential group, or to ratchet up pre-existing levels of groupness. This is why deliberate violence, undertaken as a strategy of provocation, often by a very small number of persons, can sometimes be an exceptionally effective strategy of group-making.

Groups and organizations. Although participants' rhetoric and common-sense accounts treat ethnic groups as the protagonists of ethnic conflict, in fact the chief protagonists of most ethnic conflict – and *a fortiori* of most ethnic violence – are not ethnic groups as such but various kinds of organizations, broadly understood, and their empowered and authorized incumbents. These include states (or, more broadly, autonomous polities) and their organizational components such as particular ministries, offices, law enforcement agencies, and armed forces units; they include terrorist groups, paramilitary organizations, armed bands, and loosely structured gangs; and they include political parties, ethnic associations, social movement organizations, churches, newspapers, radio and television stations, and so on. Some of these organizations may represent themselves, or may be seen by others, as organizations of and for particular ethnic groups.[12] But even when this is the case, organizations cannot be equated with ethnic groups. It is because and insofar as they are organizations, and possess certain material and organizational resources, that they (or, more precisely, their incumbents) are capable of organized action, and thereby of acting as more or less coherent protagonists in ethnic conflict.[13] Although common sense and participants' rhetoric attribute discrete existence, boundedness, coherence, identity, interest, and agency to ethnic groups, these attributes are in fact characteristic of organizations. The IRA, KLA, and PKK claim to speak and act in the name of the (Catholic) Irish, the Kosovo Albanians, and the Kurds; but surely analysts must differentiate between such organizations and the putatively homogeneous and bounded groups in whose name they claim to act. The point applies not only to military, paramilitary, and terrorist organizations, of course, but to all organizations that claim to speak and act in the name of ethnic, racial, or national groups (Heisler 1991).

A fuller and more rounded treatment of this theme, to be sure, would require several qualifications that I can only gesture at here. Conflict and violence vary in the degree to which, as well as the manner in which, organizations are involved. What Donald Horowitz (2001) has called the deadly ethnic riot, for example, differs sharply from organized ethnic insurgencies or terrorist campaigns. Although organizations (sometimes ephemeral ones) may play an important role in preparing, provoking, and permitting such riots, much of the actual violence is committed by broader sets of participants acting in relatively spontaneous fashion, and in starkly polarized situations characterized by high levels of groupness. Moreover, even where organizations are the core protagonists, they may depend on a penumbra of ancillary or supportive action on the part of sympathetic non-members. The "representativeness" of organizations – the degree to which an organization can justifiably claim to represent the will, express the interests, and enjoy the active or passive support of its constituents – is enormously variable, not only between organizations, but also over time and across domains. In addition, while organizations are ordinarily the *protagonists* of conflict and violence, they are not always the *objects* or *targets* of conflict and violence. Entire population categories – or putative groups – can be the objects of organized action, much more easily than they can be the subjects or undertakers of such action. Finally, even apart from situations of violence, ethnic conflict may be at least partly amorphous, carried out not by organizations as such but spontaneously by individuals through such everyday actions as shunning, insults, demands for deference or conformity, or withholdings of routine interactional tokens of acknowledgment or respect (Bailey 1997). Still, despite these qualifications, it is clear that organizations, not ethnic groups as such, are the chief protagonists of ethnic conflict and ethnic violence, and that the relationship between organizations and the groups they claim to represent is often deeply ambiguous.

Framing and coding.[14] If the protagonists of ethnic conflict cannot, in general, be considered ethnic groups, then what makes such conflict count as *ethnic* conflict? And what makes violence count as ethnic violence? Similar questions can be asked about racial and national conflict and violence. The answer cannot be found in the intrinsic properties of behavior. The "ethnic" quality of "ethnic violence," for example, is not intrinsic to violent conduct itself; it is attributed to instances of violent behavior by perpetrators, victims, politicians, officials, journalists, researchers, relief workers, or others. Such acts of framing and narrative encoding do not simply *interpret* the violence; they *constitute* it *as ethnic*.

Framing may be a key mechanism through which groupness is constructed. The metaphor of framing was popularized by Goffman (1974), drawing on Bateson 1985 [1955]. The notion has been elaborated chiefly in the social movement literature (Snow *et al.* 1986; Snow and Benford 1988; Gamson and Modigliani 1989; Gamson 1992; uniting rational choice and framing approaches, Esser 1999). When ethnic framing is successful, we may "see" conflict and violence not only in ethnic, but in groupist terms. Although such imputed groupness is the product of prevailing interpretive frames, not necessarily a measure of the groupness felt and experienced by the participants in an event, a compelling *ex post* interpretive framing or encoding may exercise a powerful feedback effect, shaping subsequent experience and increasing levels of groupness. A great deal is at stake, then, in struggles over the interpretive framing and narrative encoding of conflict and violence.

Interpretive framing, of course, is often contested. Violence – and more generally, conflict – is regularly accompanied by social struggles to label, interpret, and explain it. Such "metaconflicts" or "conflict[s] over the nature of the conflict," as Donald Horowitz has called them (1991: 2), do not simply shadow conflicts from the outside, but are integral and consequential parts of the conflicts. To impose a label or prevailing interpretive frame – to cause an event to be seen as a "pogrom" or a "riot" or a "rebellion" – is no mere matter of external interpretation, but a constitutive act of social definition that can have important consequences (Brass 1996a). Social struggles over the proper coding and interpretation of conflict and violence are therefore important subjects of study in their own right (Brass 1996b, 1997; Abelmann and Lie 1995).

Coding and framing practices are heavily influenced by prevailing interpretive frames. Today, ethnic and national frames are accessible and legitimate, suggesting themselves to actors and analysts alike. This generates a "coding bias" in the ethnic direction. And this, in turn, may lead us to overestimate the incidence of ethnic conflict and violence by unjustifiably seeing ethnicity everywhere at work (Bowen 1996). Actors may take advantage of this coding bias, and of the generalized legitimacy of ethnic and national frames, by strategically using ethnic framing to mask the pursuit of clan, clique, or class interests. The point here is not to suggest that clans, cliques, or classes are somehow more real then ethnic groups, but simply to note the existence of structural and cultural incentives for strategic framing.

Ethnicity as cognition.[15] These observations about the constitutive significance of coding and framing suggest a final point about the cognitive dimension of ethnicity. Ethnicity, race, and nationhood exist only in and through our perceptions, interpretations, representations, categorizations, and identifications. They are not things *in* the world, but perspectives *on* the world.[16] These include ethnicized ways of seeing (and ignoring), of construing (and misconstruing), of inferring (and misinferring), of remembering (and forgetting). They include ethnically oriented frames, schemas, and narratives, and the situational cues that activate them, such as the ubiquitous televised images that have played such an important role in the latest intifada. They include systems of classification, categorization, and identification, formal and informal. And they include the tacit, taken-for-granted background knowledge, embodied in persons and embedded in institutionalized routines and practices, through which people recognize and experience objects, places, persons, actions, or situations as ethnically, racially, or nationally marked or meaningful.

Cognitive perspectives, broadly understood,[17] can help advance constructivist research on ethnicity, race, and nationhood, which has stalled in recent years as it has grown complacent with success. Instead of simply asserting *that* ethnicity, race, and nationhood are constructed, they can help specify *how* they are constructed. They can help specify how – and when – people identify themselves, perceive others, experience the world, and interpret their predicaments in racial, ethnic, or national rather than other terms. They can help specify how "groupness" can "crystalize" in some situations while remaining latent and merely potential in others. And they can help link macrolevel outcomes with microlevel processes.

Implications

At this point a critic might interject: "What is the point of all this? Even if we *can* study 'ethnicity without groups,' why should we? Concepts invariably simplify the world; that the concept of discrete and bounded ethnic groups does so, suggesting something more substantial and clear-cut than really exists, cannot be held against it. The concept of ethnic group may be a blunt instrument, but it's good enough as a first approximation. This talk about groupness and framing and practical categories and cognitive schemas is all well and good, but meanwhile the killing goes on. Does the critique matter in the real world, or – if at all – only in the ivory tower? What practical difference does it make?"

I believe the critique of groupism does have implications, albeit rather general ones, for the ways in which researchers, journalists, policymakers, NGOs, and others come to terms, analytically and practically, with what we ordinarily – though perhaps too readily – call ethnic conflict and ethnic violence. Here I would like to enumerate five of these, before proceeding in the final section to discuss an empirical case.

First, sensitivity to framing dynamics, to the generalized coding bias in favor of ethnicity, and to the sometimes strategic or even cynical use of ethnic framing to mask the pursuit of clan, clique, or class interests can alert us to the risk of overethnicized or overly groupist interpretations of (and interventions in) situations of conflict and violence (Bowen 1996). One need not subscribe to a reductionist "elite manipulation" view of politicized ethnicity (Brubaker 1998) to acknowledge that the "spin" put on conflicts by participants may conceal as much as it reveals, and that the representation of conflicts as conflicts between ethnic or national groups may obscure the interests at stake and the dynamics involved. What is represented as ethnic conflict or ethnic war – such as the violence in the former Yugoslavia, may have as much or more to do with thuggery, warlordship, opportunistic looting, and black-market profiteering than with ethnicity (Mueller 2000; cf. Collier 1999).

Second, recognition of the centrality of organizations in ethnic conflict and ethnic violence, of the often equivocal character of their leaders' claims to speak and act in the name of ethnic groups, and of the performative nature of ethnopolitical rhetoric, enlisted in the service of group-making projects, can remind us not to mistake groupist rhetoric for real groupness, the putative groups of ethnopolitical rhetoric for substantial things-in-the-world.

Third, awareness of the interest that ethnic and nationalist leaders may have in living *off* politics, as well as *for* politics, to borrow the classic distinction of Max Weber (1946: 84), and awareness of the possible divergence between the interests of leaders and those of their putative constituents, can keep us from accepting at face value leaders' claims about the beliefs, desires, and interests of their constituents.

Fourth, sensitivity to the variable and contingent, waxing and waning nature of groupness, and to the fact that high levels of groupness may be more the result of conflict (especially violent conflict) than its underlying cause, can focus our analytical attention and policy interventions on the processes through which groupness tends to develop and crystalize, and those through which it may subside. Some attention has been given recently to the former, including tipping and cascade mechanisms (Laitin 1995; Kuran 1998) and mechanisms governing the activation and diffusion of schemas and the "epidemiology of representations" (Sperber 1985). But declining curves of groupness have not been studied systematically, although they are just as important, theoretically and practically. Once ratcheted up to a high level, groupness does not remain there out of inertia. If not sustained at high levels through specific social and cognitive mechanisms, it will tend to decline, as everyday interests reassert themselves, through a process of what Weber (in a different but apposite context [1968 (1922): 246–54]) called "routinization" (*Veralltaeglichung*, literally, "towards everydayness").

Lastly, a disaggregating, nongroupist approach can bring into analytical and policy focus the critical importance of intraethnic mechanisms in generating and sustaining putatively interethnic conflict (Brubaker and Laitin 1998: 433). These include in-group "policing," monitoring, or sanctioning processes (Laitin 1995); the "ethnic outbidding" through which electoral competition can foster extreme ethnicization (Rothschild 1981; Horowitz 1985); the calculated instigation or provocation of conflict with outsiders by vulnerable incumbents seeking to deflect in-group challenges to their positions; and in-group processes bearing on the dynamics of recruitment into gangs, militias, terrorist groups, or guerrilla armies, including honoring, shaming, and shunning practices, rituals of manhood, intergenerational tensions, and the promising and provision of material and symbolic rewards for martyrs.

Ethnicity at work in a Transylvanian town

At this point, I would like to add some flesh to the bare-bones analytical argument sketched above. It is tempting to comment on the United States. It would be easy to score rhetorical points by emphasizing that the "groups" taken to constitute the canonical "ethnoracial pentagon" (Hollinger 1995) – African Americans, Asian Americans, Whites, Native Americans, and Latinos – are (with the partial exception of African Americans) not groups at all but categories, backed by political entrepreneurs and entrenched in governmental and other organizational routines of social counting and accounting (Office of Management and Budget 1994). It would be easy to highlight the enormous cultural heterogeneity within these and other putative "groups," and the minimal degree of groupness associated with many ethnic categories in the US (Gans 1979; Heisler 1991).

But, rather than take this tack, I will try to address a harder case, drawn from a region historically characterized by much higher degrees of ethnic and national groupness. I want to consider briefly how ethnicity works in an East Central European context characterized by continuous and often intense elite-level ethnonational conflict since the fall of communism (and, of course, by a much longer history of ethnonational tension). Here too, I want to suggest, we can fruitfully analyze ethnicity without groups.

The setting, familiar to me from field research conducted in the second half of the 1990s, is the city of Cluj, the main administrative, economic, and cultural center of the Transylvanian region of Romania. Of the approximately 330,000 residents, a substantial minority – somewhere between 14 and 23 percent – identify themselves as Hungarian by ethnocultural nationality.[18] The city, as I indicated, has been the site of protracted and seemingly intractable ethnonational conflict since the collapse of the Ceauşescu regime in December 1989. But this is not, I will argue, best understood as a conflict between ethnic or national groups. To think of it as a conflict between groups is to conflate categories ("Hungarian" and "Romanian") with groups ("the Hungarians," "the Romanians"); to obscure the generally low, though fluctuating, degree of groupness in this setting; to mistake the putative groups invoked by ethnonational rhetoric for substantial things-in-the-world; to accept, at least tacitly, the claims of nationalist organizations to speak for the "groups" they claim to represent; and to neglect the everyday contexts in which ethnic and national categories take on meaning and the processes through which ethnicity actually "works" in everyday life.

Here, as elsewhere, the protagonists of the conflict have been organizations, not groups. The conflict has pitted the town's three-term mayor – the flamboyant Romanian nationalist Gheorghe Funar – and the statewide Romanian nationalist parties against the Cluj-based Democratic Association of Hungarians of Romania (DAHR), at once a statewide political party with its electoral base in Transylvania and an organization claiming to represent and further the interests of the Hungarian minority in Romania. Rhetoric has been heated on both sides. Mayor Funar has accused Hungary of harboring irredentist designs on Transylvania;[19] he has called the DAHR a "terrorist organization"; and he has accused Transylvanian Hungarians of secretly collecting weapons, forming paramilitary detachments, and planning an attack on Romanians. Funar has ordered bilingual signs removed from the few buildings that had them; banned proposed celebrations of the Hungarian national holiday; called for the suspending of Hungarian language broadcasts on Romanian state television; called for punishment of citizens for displaying the Hungarian flag or singing the Hungarian anthem; and proposed to rename after Romanian personages the few Cluj streets that bear the names of Hungarians.

The DAHR, for its part, is committed to a number of goals that outrage Romanian nationalists.[20] It characterizes Hungarians in Romania as an "indigenous community" entitled to an equal partnership with the Romanian nation as a constituent element of the Romanian state – thereby directly challenging the prevailing (and constitutionally enshrined) Romanian understanding of the state as a unitary nation-state like France. At the same time, it characterizes Transylvanian Hungarians as an "organic part of the Hungarian nation," and as such claims the right to cultivate relations with the "mother country" across the border, which leads Romanian nationalists to call into question their loyalty to the Romanian state. It demands collective rights for Hungarians as a national minority, and it demands autonomy, including territorial autonomy, for areas in which Hungarians live as a local majority, thereby raising the specter of separatism in the minds of Romanian nationalists. It demands that Hungarians have their own institutional system in the domain of education and culture – yet that this institutional system should be financed by the Romanian state. It demands the right to public, state-funded education in Hungarian at every level and in every branch of the educational system, including vocational education. It demands the right to take entrance exams to every school and university in Hungarian, even if the school or department to which the student is applying carries out instruction in Romanian. And it demands the reestablishment of an independent Hungarian university in Cluj, and the establishment of publicly funded but independent Hungarian language radio and TV studios.

Like ethnic and nationalist organizations everywhere, the DAHR claims to speak for the Hungarian minority in Romania, often characterizing it as a singular entity, "the Hungariandom of Romania" (*a romániai magyarság*). But no such entity exists.[21] The many Cluj residents who self-identify as Hungarian are often sharply critical of the DAHR, and there is no evidence that the demands of the DAHR are the demands of "the Hungarians." On the question of a Hungarian university – the most contentious political issue of the last few years – a survey conducted by a Hungarian sociologist found that a plurality of Hungarian university students in Cluj preferred an autonomous system of Hungarian-language education within the existing university to the DAHR goal of reestablishment of a separate Hungarian university (Magyari-Nándor and Péter 1997). Most Hungarians, like most Romanians, are largely indifferent to politics, and preoccupied with problems of everyday life – problems that are not interpreted in ethnic terms. Although survey data and election results suggest that they appear to vote *en bloc* for the DAHR, most Hungarians are familiar only in a vague way with the DAHR program. Similarly, there is no evidence that Mayor Funar's anti-Hungarian views are widely shared by the town's Romanian residents. When Funar is praised, it is typically as a "good housekeeper" (*bun gospodar*); he is given credit for sprucing up the town's appearance and for providing comparatively good municipal services. Almost everyone – Romanian and Hungarian alike – talks about ethnic conflict as something that "comes from above" and is stirred up by politicians pursuing their own interests. The near-universal refrain is that ethnicity is "not a problem." To be sure, a similar idiom – or perhaps ideology – of everyday interethnic harmony can be found in many other settings, including some deeply divided, violence-plagued ones. So the idiom cannot be taken as evidence of the irrelevance of ethnicity. The point here is simply to underscore the gap between nationalist organizations and the putative "groups" in whose names they claim to speak.

Despite the continuous elite-level ethnopolitical conflict in Cluj since the fall of Ceauşescu, "groupness" has generally remained low. At no time did Hungarians and Romanians crystalize as distinct, solidary, bounded groups; in this sense groupness failed to "happen." The contrast with Târgu Mureş, another Transylvanian city where groups did crystalize in 1990, is instructive. In Târgu Mureş, ethnically framed conflict over the control of a high school and over the control of local government in the immediate aftermath of the fall of Ceauşescu intensified and broadened into a generalized conflict over the "ownership" and control of the ethnodemographically evenly divided city. The conflict culminated in mass assemblies and two days of street fighting that left at least 6 dead and 200 injured. In the days leading up to the violent denouement, categories had become palpable, sharply bounded groups, united by intensely felt collective solidarity and animated by a single overriding distinction between "us" and "them." The violence itself reinforced this sense of

groupness, which then subsided gradually as life returned to normal, and
no further Hungarian–Romanian violence occurred, here or elsewhere in
Transylvania.

No such crystalization occurred in Cluj. There were, to be sure, a
few moments of moderately heightened groupness. One such moment –
among Hungarians – occurred when Mayor Funar ordered a new plaque
installed on the base of a monumental equestrian statue of Matthias
Corvinus, celebrated king of Hungary during the late fifteenth century, in
the town's main square. The statue, erected at the turn of the last century
at a moment of, and as a monument to, triumphant Hungarian nationalism, is perceived by many Hungarians as "their own," and the new plaque
deliberately affronted Hungarian national sensibilities by emphasizing the
(partly) Romanian origin of Matthias Corvinus and representing him –
contrary to the triumphalist image projected by the statue – as having
been defeated in battle by "his own nation," Moldavia (Feischmidt 2001).
Another moment occurred when archeological excavations were begun
in front of the statue, again in a manner calculated to affront Hungarian
national sensibilities by highlighting the earlier Roman – and by extension,
Romanian – presence on the site. A third moment occurred in March
1998, when Mayor Funar tried to bar Hungarians from carrying out their
annual March 15 celebration commemorating the revolution of 1848,
this year's celebration, in the sesquicentennial year, having special significance (Brubaker and Feischmidt 2002).[22] A final moment occurred
in June 1999 at the time of a much-hyped soccer match in Bucharest
between the national teams of Romania and Hungary. In Cluj, the match
was televised on a huge outdoor screen in the main square, and some fans
chanted *Afara, afara, cu Ungurii din ţara!* (Out, out, Hungarians out of the
country!) and vandalized cars with Hungarian license plates (Adevărul
de Cluj 1999).

In each of these cases, groupness – especially among Hungarians,
though in the final case among Romanians as well – was heightened,
but only to a modest degree, and only for a passing moment. The first
event occasioned a substantial but isolated Hungarian protest, the second a smaller protest, the third some concern that the commemoration
might be broken up (in the event it proceeded without serious incident),
and the last some moments of concern for those who happened to be in
the town center during and immediately after the soccer match. But even
at these maximally group-like moments, there was no overriding sense
of bounded and solidary groupness for those not immediately involved
in the events.[23] In short, when one shifts one's focus from presupposed
groups to variable groupness, and treats high levels of groupness as a
contingent event, a crystalization, something that happens, then what

is striking about Cluj in the 1990s is that groupness remained low and groups failed to happen, to crystalize.

To note the relatively low degree of groupness in Cluj, and the gap between organizations and the putative groups they claim to represent, is not to suggest that ethnicity is somehow not "real" in this setting, or that it is purely an elite phenomenon. Yet to understand how ethnicity works, it may help to begin not with "the Romanians" and "the Hungarians" as groups, but with "Romanian" and "Hungarian" as categories. Doing so suggests a different set of questions than those that come to mind when we begin with "groups." Starting with groups, one is led to ask what groups want, demand, or aspire toward; how they think of themselves and others; and how they act in relation to other groups. One is led almost automatically by the substantialist language to attribute identity, agency, interests, and will to groups. Starting with categories, by contrast, invites us to focus on processes and relations rather than substances. It invites us to specify how people and organizations do things with, and to, ethnic and national categories; how such categories are used to channel and organize processes and relations; and how categories get institutionalized, and with what consequences. It invites us to ask how, why, and in what contexts ethnic categories are used – or not used – to make sense of problems and predicaments, to articulate affinities and affiliations, to identify commonalities and connections, to frame stories and self-understandings.

Consider here just two of the many ways of pursuing a category-centered rather than a group-centered approach to ethnicity in Cluj. First, a good deal of commonsense cultural knowledge about the social world and one's place in it, here as in other settings, is organized around ethnonational categories.[24] This includes knowledge of one's own and others' ethnocultural nationality, and the ability to assign unknown others to ethnonational categories on the basis of cues such as language, accent, name, sometimes dress, hair style, even phenotype. It includes knowledge of what incumbents of such categories are like,[25] how they typically behave, and how ethnonational category membership matters in various spheres of life. Such commonsense category-based knowledge shapes everyday interaction, figures in stories people tell about themselves and others, and provides ready-made explanations for certain events or states of affairs. For Hungarians, for example, categorizing an unknown person as Hungarian or Romanian may govern how one interacts with him or her, determining not only the language but also the manner in which one will speak, a more personal and confidential (*bizalmas*) style often being employed with fellow Hungarians. Or for Romanians, categorizing two persons speaking Hungarian in a mixed-language setting as

Hungarian (rather than, for example, as friends who happen to be speaking Hungarian) provides a ready-made explanation for their conduct, it being commonsense knowledge about Hungarians that they will form a *bisericuţa* (clique; literally: small church) with others of their kind, excluding copresent Romanians, whenever they have the chance. Or again for Hungarians, categorically organized commonsense knowledge provides a ready-made framework for perceiving differential educational and economic opportunities as structured along ethnic lines, explaining such differentials in terms of what they know about the bearing of ethnic nationality on grading, admissions, hiring, promotion, and firing decisions, and justifying the commonly voiced opinion that "we [Hungarians] have to work twice as hard" to get ahead (Feischmidt 2001; Fox 2001). These and many other examples suggest that ethnicity is, in important part, a cognitive phenomenon, a way of seeing and interpreting the world, and that, as such, it works in and through categories and category-based commonsense knowledge.

Ethnic categories shape institutional as well as informal cognition and recognition. They not only structure perception and interpretation in the ebb and flow of everyday interaction but channel conduct through official classifications and organizational routines. Thus ethnic (and other) categories may be used to allocate rights, regulate actions, distribute benefits and burdens, construct category-specific institutions, identify particular persons as bearers of categorical attributes, "cultivate" populations, or, at the extreme, "eradicate" unwanted "elements."[26]

In Cluj – as in Romania generally – ethnic categories are not institutionalized in dramatic ways. Yet there is one important set of institutions built, in part, around ethnic categories. This is the school system.[27] In Cluj, as in other Transylvanian cities, there is a separate Hungarian-language school system paralleling the mainstream system, and running from preschool through high school. These are not private schools, but part of the state school system. Not all persons identifying themselves as Hungarian attend Hungarian schools, but most do (85–90 percent in grades 1–4, smaller proportions, though still substantial majorities, in later grades).[28] In Cluj, moreover, there are also parallel tracks at the university level in many fields of study.

Categories need ecological niches in which to survive and flourish; the parallel school system provides such a niche for "Hungarian" as an ethnonational category. It is a strategically positioned niche. Hungarian schools not only provide a legitimate institutional home and a protected public space for the category. They also generate the social structural foundations for a small Hungarian world within the larger Romanian one (Feischmidt 2001). Since the schools shape opportunity structures and contact probabilities, and thereby influence friendship patterns (and, at the high school and university level, marriage patterns as well), this world is to a certain extent a self-reproducing one. Note that the (partial) reproduction of this social world – this interlocking set of social relationships linking school, friendship circles, and family – does not require strong nationalist commitments or group loyalties. Ethnic networks can be reproduced without high degrees of groupness, largely through the logic of contact probabilities and opportunity structures and the resulting moderately high degrees of ethnic endogamy.[29]

This brief case study has sought to suggest that even in a setting of intense elite-level ethnic conflict and (by comparison to the United States) deeply rooted and stable ethnic identifications, one can analyze the workings of ethnicity without employing the language of bounded groups.

Conclusion

What are we studying when we study ethnicity and ethnic conflict? This chapter has suggested that we need not frame our analyses in terms of ethnic groups, and that it may be more productive to focus on practical categories, cultural idioms, cognitive schemas, commonsense knowledge, organizational routines and resources, discursive frames, institutionalized forms, political projects, contingent events, and variable groupness. It should be noted in closing, however, that by framing our inquiry in this way, and by bringing to bear a set of analytical perspectives not ordinarily associated with the study of ethnicity – cognitive theory, ethnomethodology, conversation analysis, network analysis, organizational analysis, and institutional theory, for example – we may end up not studying ethnicity at all. It may be that "ethnicity" is simply a convenient – though in certain respects misleading – rubric under which to group phenomena that, on the one hand, are highly disparate, and, on the other, have a great deal in common with phenomena that are not ordinarily subsumed under the rubric of ethnicity.[30] In other words, by raising questions about the *unit* of analysis – the ethnic group – we may end up questioning the *domain* of analysis – ethnicity itself. But that is an argument for another occasion.

NOTES

1. This chapter was first published in *Archives européennes de sociologie* 43 (2) (2002): 163–89.
2. Foundational discussions include Cooley 1962 [1909], ch. 3 and Homans 1950 in sociology; Nadel 1957, ch. 7 in anthropology; Bentley 1908, ch. 7 and Truman 1951 in political science. More recent discussions include Olson 1965, Tilly 1978, and Hechter 1987.

3. In this very general sense, groupism extends well beyond the domain of ethnicity, race, and nationalism to include accounts of putative groups based on gender, sexuality, age, class, abledness, religion, minority status, and any kind of "culture," as well as putative groups based on combinations of these categorical attributes. Yet while recognizing that it is a wider tendency in social analysis, I limit my discussion here to groupism in the study of ethnicity, race, and nationalism.

4. For useful critical analyses of media representations of ethnic violence, see the collection of essays in Allen and Seaton 1999, as well as Seaton 1999.

5. This is perhaps too sharply put. To the extent that such intrinsic-kind categories are indeed constitutive of commonsense understandings of the social world, to the extent that such categories are used as a resource for participants, and are demonstrably deployed or oriented to by participants in interaction, they can also serve as a resource for analysts. But as Emanuel Schegloff notes in another context, with respect to the category "interruption," the fact that this is a vernacular, commonsense category for participants "does not make it a first-order category usable for professional analysis. Rather than being employed *in* professional analysis, it is better treated as a target category *for* professional analysis" (2000: 27). The same might well be said of commonsense ethnic categories.

6. Such performative, group-making practices, of course, are not specific to ethnic entrepreneurs, but generic to political mobilization and representation (Bourdieu 1991b: 248–51).

7. For accounts (not focused specifically on ethnicity) that treat groupness as variable, see Tilly 1978: 62ff.; Hechter 1987: 8; Hamilton *et al.* 1998. These accounts, very different from one another, focus on variability in groupness across cases; my concern is primarily with variability in groupness over time.

8. Fredrik Barth's introductory essay to the collection *Ethnic Groups and Boundaries* (1969) was extraordinarily influential in directing attention to the workings of categories of self- and other-ascription. But Barth does not distinguish sharply or consistently between categories and groups, and his central metaphor of "boundary" carries with it connotations of boundedness, entitativity, and groupness.

9. This point was already made by Max Weber, albeit in somewhat different terms. As Weber argued – in a passage obscured in the English translation – ethnic commonality, based on belief in common descent, is "in itself mere (putative) commonality [(geglaubte) Gemeinsamkeit], not community [Gemeinschaft] . . . but only a factor facilitating communal action [Vergemeinschaftung]" (1964: 307; cf. 1968: 389). Ethnic commonality means more than mere category membership for Weber. It is – or rather involves – a category that is employed by members themselves. But this shows that even self-categorization does not create a "group."

10. Ethnomethodology and conversation analysis have not focused on the use of ethnic categories as such, but Sacks, Schegloff, and others have addressed the problem of situated categorization in general, notably the question of the procedures through which participants in interaction, in deploying categories, choose among alternative sets of categories (since there is always

more than one set of categories in terms of which any person can be correctly described). The import of this problem has been formulated as follows by Schegloff (2000: 30–31): "And given the centrality of . . . categories in organizing vernacular cultural 'knowledge,' this equivocality can be profoundly consequential, for *which* category is employed will carry with it the invocation of commonsense knowledge about *that* category of person and bring it to bear on the person referred to on some occasion, rather than bringing to bear the knowledge implicated with *another* category, of which the person being referred to is equally a member." For Sacks on categories, see 1995 (I, 40–48, 333–40, 396–403, 578–96; II, 184–87).

11. The language of "stereotypes" is, of course, that of cognitive social psychology (for a review of work in this tradition, see Hamilton and Sherman 1994). But the general ethnomethodological emphasis on the crucial importance of the rich though tacit background knowledge that participants bring to interaction, and – more specifically – Harvey Sacks' discussion of the "inference-rich" categories in terms of which much everyday social knowledge is stored (1995: I, 40ff. *et passim*; cf. Schegloff 2000: 29ff.) and of the way in which the knowledge thus organized is "protected against induction" (ibid., 336ff.), suggest a domain of potentially converging concern between cognitive work on the one hand and ethnomethodological and conversation-analytic work on the other – however different their analytic stances and methodologies.

12. One should remember, though, that organizations often compete with one another for the monopolization of the right to represent the same (putative) group.

13. In this respect, the resource mobilization perspective on social movements, eclipsed in recent years by identity-oriented new social movement theory, has much to offer students of ethnicity. For an integrated statement, see McCarthy and Zald 1977.

14. These paragraphs draw on Brubaker and Laitin 1998.

15. These paragraphs draw on Brubaker *et al.* 2004.

16. As Emanuel Schegloff reminded me in a different context, this formulation is potentially misleading, since perspectives *on* the world – as every Sociology 1 student is taught – are themselves *in* the world, and every bit as "real" and consequential as other sorts of things.

17. Cognitive perspectives, in this broad sense, include not only those developed in cognitive psychology and cognitive anthropology but also those developed in the post- (and anti-)Parsonian "cognitive turn" (DiMaggio and Powell 1991) in sociological and (more broadly) social theory, especially in response to the influence of phenomenological and ethnomethodological work (Schutz 1962; Garfinkel 1967; Heritage 1984). Cognitive perspectives are central to the influential syntheses of Bourdieu and Giddens and – in a very different form – to the enterprise of conversation analysis.

18. In the US and much of northern and western Europe, "nationality" ordinarily means "citizenship," that is, membership of the state; and "nation" and "state" are often used interchangeably. In central and eastern Europe, by contrast, "nation" and "nationality" do not refer in the first instance to the state, but ordinarily invoke an ethnocultural frame of reference independent

of – and often cutting across the boundaries of – statehood and citizenship. To identify oneself as Hungarian by nationality in Transylvania is to a invoke a state-transcending Hungarian ethnocultural "nation." In the text, following the usage in this setting, I use "ethnic" and "national" interchangeably.

At the last census, conducted in 1992, 23 percent of the population of Cluj identified as Hungarian. More recent statistics, however, suggest a smaller population identifying as Hungarian, at least among younger age cohorts. Of persons getting married in 1999, 14.4 percent identified their nationality as Hungarian. Of primary, middle school, and secondary school students in 1999–2000, 15.1 percent, 14.3 percent, and 14.8 percent, respectively, identified as Hungarian. Contextual differences in identification may account for part of the difference, as might different age structures of Romanian and Hungarian populations and differential emigration rates during the 1990s.

19. Transylvania had belonged to Hungary for half a century before the First World War, and again for four years during the Second World War.

20. The DAHR program can be found in English at http://www.rmdsz.ro/angol/aboutus/prog.htm

21. Of course this point holds not only, or especially, of the Hungarian minority, or of minorities generally. In Romania as elsewhere, those who claim to speak for dominant nations – nations that are closely identified with the states that bear their names, referred to in German as *Staatsvölker* or "state peoples" – also routinely reify those "nations" and characterize them as singular entities with a common will and common interests, where in fact no such entity exists.

22. To Romanian nationalists, Hungarians' commemoration of 1848 is illegitimate, for it celebrates a regime that was as much nationalist as revolutionary, aspiring to – and briefly securing – unitary control over Transylvania. Romanian nationalist mythology commemorates not the revolution, but the guerrilla struggle against the Hungarian revolutionary regime, led by Avram Iancu, to whom a colossal monument was erected under Funar's sponsorship in 1993.

23. Even for those who were involved in the events, one should be cautious about inferring an overriding sense of groupness. I was in Cluj in the summer of 1994, when excavations in the main "Hungarian" square were about to begin. I was staying with the family of a leading figure of the DAHR, albeit one of the more liberal figures. At one point, he proposed: "Menjünk ásni? [Shall we go dig?]." At a moment of overriding groupness, such a joke would be unthinkable; here, the nationalist projects of Mayor Funar were – at least for some – a joking matter. One further incident is worth mentioning in this connection. In 1997, a long-closed Hungarian Consulate reopened in Cluj, reflecting a warming of relations between Budapest and the newly elected pro-Western government in Bucharest. Funar protested – in vain – against its opening, and when it opened, tried to fine it for flying the Hungarian flag. A few weeks after its opening, five men pulled up in a pickup truck, placed an extendable ladder against the side of the building, and removed the flag from the building, in broad daylight, as a small crowed looked on. The next day, they were apprehended by the police; Funar characterized them as "Romanian heroes." Elsewhere, this sort of incident – which could easily be

construed as involving the desecration of a sacred national symbol – has been enough to trigger a riot. Here, nobody paid much attention; the incident was coded as farce, not as sacred drama.

24. On categories as "repositor[ies] for commonsense knowledge" generally (Schegloff 2000:29), see Sacks (1995: I, 40–48, 333–40). For cognitive perspectives on social categories as structures of knowledge, with special regard to ethnic, racial, and other "natural kind"-like categories, see Rothbart and Taylor 1992; Hamilton and Sherman 1994; Hirschfeld 1996.

25. Even when such commonsense, category-based stereotypical knowledge is overridden, the very manner of overriding may testify to the existence (and the content) of the category-based knowledge that is being overridden. On the general phenomenon of "modifiers" that work by asserting that what is generally known about members of a category is not applicable to some particular member, see Sacks (1995: I, 44–45). Among Hungarians – even liberal, cosmopolitan Hungarians – I have on several occasions heard someone referred to as "Román, de rendes" (Romanian, but quite all right) or something to that effect.

26. On "population politics" and the metaphor of the gardening state, see Holquist 1997: 131; Bauman 2000; Weiner 2001. Genocide, as Bauman observes, "differs from other murders in having a *category* for its object" (2000: 227, italics in original).

27. Traditional churches, too, are built around ethnic categories, with two "Hungarian" churches (Roman Catholic and Calvinist) and two "Romanian" churches (Orthodox and Greek-Catholic or Uniate). With aging congregations, dwindling influence, and increased competition from less ethnically marked neo-Protestant denominations, the traditional churches are less significant than schools as institutional loci of ethnic categories.

28. Data are drawn from figures provided by the School Inspectorate of Cluj County.

29. Of the Hungarians who married in Cluj in 1999, nearly 75 percent married other Hungarians, while about 25 percent married Romanians. This suggests a moderately high degree of ethnic endogamy, but only moderately high, for about 40 percent of all marriages involving Hungarians were mixed marriages. Data were compiled from forms filled out by couples, consulted at the Cluj branch of the National Commission for Statistics.

30. As Weber put it nearly a century ago (1964 [1922]: 313; cf. 1968 [1922]: 394–95), a precise and differentiated analysis would "surely throw out the umbrella term 'ethnic' altogether," for it is "entirely unusable" for any "truly rigorous investigation."

REFERENCES

Abelmann, Nancy and John Lie (1995) *Blue Dreams: Korean Americans and the Los Angeles Riots*. Cambridge, MA: Harvard University Press.

Adevărul de Cluj. (1999) "Confruntarea dintre România şi Ungaria a continuat şi după meci [The confrontation between Romania and Hungarian continued also after the match]." June 7, 1999.

Allen, Tim and Jean Seaton (eds.) (1999) *The Media of Conflict: War Reporting and Representations of Ethnic Violence.* London: Zed Books.

Armstrong, John A. (1982) *Nations Before Nationalism.* Chapel Hill: University of North Carolina Press.

Bailey, Benjamin (1997) "Communication of respect in interethnic service encounters." *Language in Society* 26: 327–56.

Barth, Fredrik (1969) "Introduction." In Fredrik Barth (ed.), *Ethnic Groups and Boundaries: The Social Organization of Culture Difference.* London: George Allen & Unwin, pp. 9–38.

Bateson, Gregory (1985 [1955]) "A theory of play and fantasy." In Robert E. Innis (ed.), *Semiotics: An Introductory Anthology*, pp. 131–44.

Bauman, Zygmunt (2000 [1989]) *Modernity and the Holocaust.* Ithaca: Cornell University Press.

Bentley, Arthur F. (1908) *The Process of Government: A Study of Social Pressures.* Chicago: University of Chicago Press.

Bourdieu, Pierre (1991a) "Identity and representation: elements for a critical reflection on the idea of region." In Pierre Bourdieu, *Language and Symbolic Power.* Cambridge, MA: Harvard University Press, pp. 220–28.

(1991b) "Social space and the genesis of 'classes'." In Pierre Bourdieu, *Language and Symbolic Power.* Cambridge, MA: Harvard University Press, pp. 229–51.

Bowen, John R. (1996) "The myth of global ethnic conflict." *Journal of Democracy* 7(4): 3–14.

Brass, Paul R. (1996a) "Introduction: discourse of ethnicity, communalism, and violence." In Paul R. Brass (ed.), *Riots and Pogroms.* New York: New York University Press, pp. 1–55.

Brass, Paul R. (ed.) (1996b) *Riots and Pogroms.* New York: New York University Press.

(1997) *Theft of an Idol: Text and Context in the Representation of Collective Violence.* Princeton: Princeton University Press.

Brubaker, Rogers (1992) *Citizenship and Nationhood in France and Germany.* Cambridge, MA: Harvard University Press.

(1994) "Nationhood and the national question in the Soviet Union and post-Soviet Eurasia." *Theory and Society* 23 (1): 47–78.

(1998) "Myths and misconceptions in the study of nationalism." In John Hall (ed.), *The State of the Nation: Ernest Gellner and the Theory of Nationalism.* New York: Cambridge University Press, pp. 272–306.

(1999) "A shameful debacle." *UCLA Magazine* (summer): 15–16.

Brubaker, Rogers and Margit Feischmidt (2002) "1848 in 1998: the politics of commemoration in Hungary, Romania, and Slovakia." *Comparative Studies in Society and History* 44 (4) (October): 700–44.

Brubaker, Rogers and David D. Laitin (1998) "Ethnic and nationalist violence." *Annual Review of Sociology* 24: 423–52.

Brubaker, Rogers, Mara Loveman, and Peter Stamatov (2004) "Ethnicity as cognition." *Theory and Society* 33 (1): 31–64.

Collier, Paul (1999) "Doing well out of war." http://www.worldbank.org/research/conflict/papers/econagenda.htm

Cooley, Charles H. (1962 [1909]) *Social Organization*. New York: Schocken Books.

DiMaggio, Paul J. and Walter W. Powell (1991) "Introduction." In Walter W. Powell and Paul J. DiMaggio (eds.), *The New Institutionalism in Organizational Analysis*. Chicago: University of Chicago Press, pp. 1–38.

Domínguez, Virginia R. (1986) *White by Definition: Social Classification in Creole Louisiana*. New Brunswick: Rutgers University Press.

Emirbayer, Mustafa and Jeff Goodwin (1994) "Network analysis, culture, and the problem of agency." *American Journal of Sociology* 99 (6): 1411–54.

Esser, Hartmut (1999) "Die Situationslogik ethnischer Konflikte: Auch eine Anmerkung zum Beitrag 'Ethnische Mobilisierung und die Logik von Identitätskämpfen' von Klaus Eder und Oliver Schmidtke." *Zeitschrift für Soziologie* 28 (4): 245–62.

Fearon, James and David D. Laitin (1996) "Explaining interethnic cooperation." *American Political Science Review* 90 (4): 715–35.

Feischmidt, Margit (2001) "Zwischen Abgrenzung und Vermischung: Ethnizität in der siebenbürgischen Stadt Cluj (Kolozsvár, Klausenburg)." Ph.D. dissertation, Humboldt University, Berlin.

Fox, Jon E. (2001) "Nationness and everyday life: Romanian and Hungarian university students in Transylvania." Paper presented to the Center for Comparative Social Analysis Workshop, Department of Sociology, UCLA.

Gamson, William A. (1992) *Talking Politics*. New York: Cambridge University Press.

Gamson, William A. and Andre Modigliani (1989) "Media discourse and public opinion on nuclear power: a constructionist approach." *American Journal of Sociology* 95: 1–37.

Gans, Herbert J. (1979) "Symbolic ethnicity: the future of ethnic groups and cultures in America." *Ethnic and Racial Studies* 2: 1–20.

Garfinkel, Harold (1967) *Studies in Ethnomethodology*. Englewood Cliffs, NJ: Prentice-Hall.

Gil-White, Francisco (1999) "How thick is blood? The plot thickens . . . : If ethnic actors are primordialists, what remains of the circumstantialist/primordialist controversy?" *Ethnic and Racial Studies* 22 (5): 789–820.

Goffman, Erving (1974) *Frame Analysis*. San Francisco: Harper Colophon Books.

Hamilton, David L. and Jeffrey W. Sherman (1994) "Stereotypes." In Robert S. Wyer and Thomas K. Srull (eds.), *Handbook of Social Cognition*, 2nd ed. Hillsdale, NJ: L. Erlbaum Associates, pp. 1–68.

Hamilton, David L., Steven J. Sherman, and Brian Lickel (1998) "Perceiving social groups: the importance of the entitativity continuum." In Constantine Sedikides, John Schopler, and Chester A. Insko (eds.), *Intergroup Cognition and Intergroup Behavior*. Mahwah, NJ: Lawrence Erlbaum Associates, pp. 47–74.

Handelman, Don (1977) "The organization of ethnicity." *Ethnic Groups* 1: 187–200.

Hechter, Michael (1987) *Principles of Group Solidarity*. Berkeley: University of California Press.

Heisler, Martin (1991) "Ethnicity and ethnic relations in the modern West." In Joseph Montville (ed.), *Conflict and Peacemaking in Multiethnic Societies.* Joseph Montville. Lexington: Lexington Books, pp. 21–52.

Heritage, John (1984) *Garfinkel and Ethnomethodology.* Cambridge: Polity Press.

Hirschfeld, Lawrence A. (1996) *Race in the Making: Cognition, Culture and the Child's Construction of Human Kinds.* Cambridge, MA: MIT Press.

Hollinger, David A. (1995) *Postethnic America: Beyond Multiculturalism.* New York: Basic Books.

Holquist, Peter (1997) "'Conduct merciless mass terror': decossackization on the Don, 1919." *Cahiers du monde russe* 38 (1–2): 127–62.

Homans, George C. (1950) *The Human Group.* New York: Harcourt, Brace & World.

Horowitz, Donald L. (1985) *Ethnic Groups in Conflict.* Berkeley, CA: University of California Press.

(1991) *A Democratic South Africa?: Constitutional Engineering in a Divided Society.* Berkeley: University of California Press.

(2001) *The Deadly Ethnic Riot.* Berkeley: University of California Press.

Jenkins, Richard (1997) *Rethinking Ethnicity.* London: Sage.

Kuran, Timur (1998) "Ethnic norms and their transformation through reputational cascades." *Journal of Legal Studies* 27: 623–59.

Laitin, David D. (1995) "National revivals and violence." *Archives Européennes de sociologie* 36 (1): 3–43.

Levine, Hal B. (1999) "Reconstructing ethnicity." *Journal of the Royal Anthropological Institute (New Series)* 5: 165–80.

Magyari-Nándor, László and László Péter (1997) "Az egyetemről magyar diákszemmel [Hungarian students' views on the university]." *Korunk* 4: 112–19.

Martin, Terry (2001) *The Affirmative Action Empire.* Ithaca: Cornell University press.

McCarthy, John D. and Mayer N. Zald (1977) "Resource mobilization and social movements: a partial theory." *American Journal of Sociology* 82 (6): 1212–41.

McGrath, Joseph E. (1984) *Groups: Interaction and Performance.* New York: Prentice-Hall.

McKay, James and Frank Lewins (1978) "Ethnicity and the ethnic group: a conceptual analysis and reformulation." *Ethnic and Racial Studies* 1 (4): 412–27.

Medin, Douglas L. (1989) "Concepts and conceptual structure." *The American Psychologist* 44: 1469–81.

Moerman, Michael (1968) "Being Lue: uses and abuses of ethnic identification." In June Helm (ed.), *Essays on the Problem of Tribe.* Washington: University of Washington Press.

Mueller, John (2000) "The banality of 'ethnic war'." *International Security* 25: 42–70.

Nadel, S. F. (1957) *A Theory of Social Structure.* London: Cohen & West.

Noiriel, Gérard (1991) *La Tyrannie du national: le droit d'asile en Europe 1793–1993.* Paris: Calmann-Lévy.

Office of Management and Budget (1994) "Standards for the classification of federal data on race and ethnicity". http://www.whitehouse.gov/omb/fedreg/notice_15.html

Olson, Mancur (1965) *The Logic of Collective Action: Public Goods and the Theory of Groups*. Cambridge, MA: Harvard University Press.

Petersen, William (1987) "Politics and the measurement of ethnicity." In William Alonso and Paul Starr (eds.), *The Politics of Numbers*. New York: Russell Sage Foundation, pp. 187–233.

Rothbart, Myron and Marjorie Taylor (1992) "Category labels and social reality: do we view social categories as natural kinds?" In Gün R. Semin and Klaus Fiedler (eds.), *Language, Interaction and Social Cognition*. London: SAGE Publications.

Rothschild, Joseph (1981) *Ethnopolitics: A Conceptual Framework*. New York: Columbia University Press.

Sacks, Harvey (1995) *Lectures on Conversation*. Oxford: Blackwell.

Schegloff, Emanuel A. (2000) "Accounts of conduct in interaction: interruption, overlap and turn-taking." Forthcoming in J. H. Turner (ed.), *Handbook of Sociological Theory*. New York: Plenum.

Schutz, Alfred (1962) *Collected Papers I: The Problem of Social Reality*. Maurice Natanson (ed.). The Hague: Marinus Nijhoff.

Seaton, Jean (1999) "Why do we think the Serbs do it? The new 'ethnic' wars and the media." *Political Quarterly* 70 (3): 254–70.

Slezkine, Yuri (1994) "The USSR as a communal apartment, or how a socialist state promoted ethnic particularlism." *Slavic Review* 53 (4): 414–52.

Smith, Anthony D. (1986) *The Ethnic Origins of Nations*. Oxford: Basil Blackwell.
   (1998) *Nationalism and Modernism: A Critical Survey of Recent Theories of Nations and Nationalism*. London: Routledge.

Snow, David A. and Robert D. Benford (1988) "Ideology, frame resonance, and participant mobilization." *International Social Movement Research* 1: 197–217.

Snow, David A., E. B. Rochford Jr., Steven K. Worden, and Robert D. Benford (1986) "Frame alignment processes, micromobilization, and movement participation." *American Sociological Review* 51: 464–81.

Sperber, Dan (1985) "Anthropology and psychology: towards an epidemiology of representations." *Man* 20: 73–89.

Thompson, E. P. (1963) *The Making of the English Working Class*. New York: Vintage, p. 9.

Tilly, Charles (1978) *From Mobilization to Revolution*. Reading, MA: Addison-Wesley Publishing Company.
   (1998) *Durable Inequality*. Berkeley: University of California Press.

Torpey, John (2000) *The Invention of the Passport: Surveillance, Citizenship and the State*. Cambridge: Cambridge University Press.

Truman, David B. (1951) *The Governmental Process: Political Interests and Public Opinion*. 2nd edn. New York: Alfred A. Knopf.

Weber, Max (1946) *From Max Weber: Essays in Sociology*. Gerth and Wright Mills (eds.). New York: Oxford University Press.
   (1964) *Wirtschaft und Gesellschaf*. 4th edn. Cologne: Kiepenheurer & Witsch.

(1968 [1922]) *Economy and Society*. Guenther Roth and Claus Wittich (eds.). Berkeley: University of California Press.

Weiner, Amir (2001) *Making Sense of War: The Second World War and the Fate of the Bolshevik Revolution*. Princeton: Princeton University Press.

Wellman, Barry (1988) "Structural analysis: from method and metaphor to theory and substance." In Barry Wellman and S. D. Berkowitz (eds.), *Social Structures: A Network Approach*. Cambridge: Cambridge University Press, pp. 19–61.

4 Ethnicity, class, and the 1999 Mauritian riots

Thomas Hylland Eriksen

Introduction

A few recurring issues regarding ethnic pluralism have been raised regularly during the last couple of decades.

1. *Issues concerning discrimination and racism, or group hegemony.* Many sociological and anthropological studies of urban or immigrant minorities, indigenous peoples or territorial minorities, postcolonial plural societies and stable nation-states, raise these problems in various ways. Are equal rights enjoyed by all citizens in a given state, and what do "equal rights" entail in practice? Under what circumstances do conflicts emerge? The extant social science literature covers judicial systems, language policies, labor markets, educational systems, and so on.

2. *Questions concerning discursive hegemonies.* Particularly in the related fields of literary and cultural studies, symbolic power has been a key variable in work on pluralism and minorities. The key issues, which can be traced back to the work of Frantz Fanon (1971 [1952]), concern whether or not members of traditionally oppressed groups can express their identity on their own terms, that is to say, to what extent they are forced into reproducing the hegemonic discourse.

3. *Cultural rights versus individual rights.* These problems have been raised particularly among social philosophers, and have been dealt with in very sophisticated, if occasionally US-centric, ways in the communitarianism–liberalism debate (see Taylor 1992), where communitarians argue that cultural communities are more fundamental than individuals and defend notions of collective group rights, while liberals argue the need for universal, individual human rights that do not make concessions to cultural variation.

4. *Assimilation, integration, and segregation.* Studies of historical change involving majority–minority relations inevitably deal with these options: whether the minority eventually melts into the majority (or, more rarely, vice versa), whether the minority achieves equality

without having to sacrifice certain cultural diacritica, or whether the groups are kept strictly apart in a form of enforced or voluntary apartheid.

5. *Pluralism versus hybridity.* A related, but more recent perspective, especially developed among anthropologists (Appadurai 1996; Hannerz 1996), discusses the cultural dynamics of multiethnic societies, investigating to what extent the constituent groups influence each other, and to what extent they remain culturally discrete.

6. *Constructivist studies of history and ideology.* Drawing inspiration both from Foucault and from the justly famous *The Invention of Tradition* (Hobsbawm and Ranger 1983), these studies show how strong group identities, where enemy images of others frequently figure prominently, are constructed through selective, ideological, and sometimes fraudulent narratives about the past or dramatic rituals involving powerful symbols of community.

7. *Globalization and localization.* The founding paradox of contemporary ethnicity studies is the fact that the seeming economic, social, and cultural homogenization engendered by globalization has led to strong ethnic revitalization, nationalism, and other essentialistic assertions of rooted cultural identities (Friedman 1994).

A few more areas could have been mentioned, but these frequently intersecting topics are arguably some of the most central ones in the field.[1] However, this chapter will not take on any of these central debates, all of which I consider important, and all of which I have spent many years engaging with (see e.g. Eriksen 2002). What I propose to do instead is to present a case of apparent ethnic conflict which none of these currently dominant perspectives seems able to account for properly.

Seen as a whole, the contemporary literature on ethnically plural societies depicts a conflict-ridden world of volatile minority situations, precarious equilibriums, racial oppression, and ethnic discrimination, predicaments of culture and tricky political situations where cultural rights and individual human rights are confronted. The truly successful polyethnic societies are few and far between in this literature; that is, societies where individual rights are balanced with tolerance and cultural diversity, where religious differences go together with economic growth, patriotism and functioning political democracy; where interethnic marriages are grudgingly or even enthusiastically accepted, where the relationship between class and ethnicity is sufficiently complex that the one could not be reduced to the other, and where no single ethnic group could be said to have monopolised the state apparatus or the imagery of nationbuilding. A strong candidate for a place in this apparently rare category until recently was – or still is, this is as yet uncertain – Mauritius. Below, I shall trace the itinerary of interethnic relations in that society since the late 1960s, while drawing some parallels to other societies, particularly in Europe. I then move to an analysis of the recent ethnic riots that shocked Mauritians and shook the very foundation of their society in 1999.[2] In the course of this analysis, I shall argue that an important dimension seems to be missing from the current academic discourse on identity politics, namely that of class in a wide sense, which incorporates symbolic dominance as well as economic power.

The ethnic dimension in Mauritian politics and everyday life

Mauritius is an oceanic island 800 kilometres east of Madagascar, with a population of slightly over a million. With no indigenous population, all the inhabitants are the descendants of immigrants, largely brought there in the successive waves of slavery and indentureship during the eighteenth and nineteenth centuries. The main ethnic groups are Hindus of North Indian descent, Creoles (Catholics of African, Malagasy and mixed descent), Muslims of North Indian descent, Tamils and Telegus of South Indian descent, Sino-Mauritians of Chinese descent and Franco-Mauritians of French and British descent. The wealthiest groups are the Franco and Sino-Mauritians, while the largest and politically dominant group are the Hindus. Ethnic classification in Mauritius is an intricate and fascinating matter, but there is no need to go deeper into it in the present context (cf. Eriksen 1988, 1998).

After having been colonized first by France (1715–1810) and then by Britain (1810–1968), Mauritius became a constitutional monarchy within the Commonwealth in 1968, changing its status to that of a republic in 1992. Politics in independent Mauritius is deeply ethnic in character. By contrast with many other multiethnic countries, such as Tito's Yugoslavia, ethnicity is not officially regarded as politically irrelevant, and the main political parties have always more or less openly catered to particular ethnic groups. With a number of important exceptions, Mauritian politics is identity politics in the sense that the ethnic identity of voters is crucial for their voting patterns. The Labor Party and the Mouvement Socialiste Mauricien (MSM) compete for the Hindu vote, the Mouvement Militant Mauricien (MMM) and the Parti Mauricien Social Démocrate (PMSD) compete for the Creole vote, while the majority of the Muslims have tended to vote either for the MMM or, in the 1960s, for a Muslim party. Politicians representing smaller ethnic groups unable to win simple majorities in any constituency tend to enter into strategic alliances with one of the large parties. As documented almost weekly in the Mauritian press, patronage and ethnic favoritism are widespread, and, since independence, the public sector has become gradually more dominated by Hindus, that is the politically dominant group.

At the same time, Mauritian politics has followed democratic principles and practices for over three decades of independence. Moreover, it cannot easily be argued that the Hindus are simply the hegemonic group. A large proportion of Mauritian Hindus are rural and poor, while there are many rich Muslims and influential Creoles. The media sphere is dominated by Catholics, the sugar industry by Franco-Mauritians, and small trade by Sino-Mauritians. It could be argued therefore that Mauritius has to a great extent achieved a viable, if precarious, model of power-sharing, ensuring members of all ethnic groups the possibility of social mobility along different lines. That is to say, this holds true with one notable exception, pointed out by many commentators over the years: other things being equal, working-class Creoles are generally faced with poorer opportunities than other Mauritians. Although Mauritian economic statistics do not reveal correlations between class and mobility, it is easy to see that the very considerable economic growth which has transformed Mauritian society since the mid-1980s has affected Creole-dominated areas to a much lesser extent than the rest of the island. This is evident in the housing standard, the availability of employment and the general infrastructure.

The emphasis on ethnic membership in the political sphere echoes a similar preoccupation with ethnicity in other domains. Since Mauritius is a fairly small island (1800 sq kms) and the ethnic groups are not physically isolated in monoethnic enclaves, the inhabitants encounter members of other ethnic groups many times every day. As a result, cultural differences diminish while group consciousness remains strong. Endogamy is the rule and not the exception, and since kinship is an important principle of local organization in virtually all the ethnic groups (with the partial exception of the Creoles), ethnic networks tend to be important in a person's everyday life. Now, it could be argued, and has indeed been argued (in Eriksen 1986, 1988), that differences in kinship structure can be a factor when accounting for differential access to certain resources. Creole kinship is based on the nuclear family, with shallow, bilateral genealogies and loose connections with remote kin. By contrast, the patrilineal Hindu, Muslim and Sino-Mauritian families form the backbone of strong corporate lineage-based groups with deep moral obligations towards relatives. In other words, a Hindu in a powerful position is obliged to help his or her relatives in a way that a Creole would not be. The *social capital* of

Creoles gives more limited possibilities for investment than that of other groups.

Mauritian multiculturalism is not without its detractors. As early as the 1950s, the Mauritian author Malcolm de Chazal (1951) wrote contemptuously of his country of origin as a "tropical inferno" where nobody meets anybody outside of the "freemasonries of blood." Since Independence, cultural and political radicals have tried to undermine ethnic boundaries, frequently either by promoting creolization at the individual level (mixing various influences according to personal whim), or by arguing, along Marxist lines, the primacy of class over ethnicity. Others have pointed out that ethnic identity seems to become gradually weaker in some segments of the population, particularly in the towns, and that it may eventually lose its practical significance for a growing minority of the population, provided that the division of labor continues to move away from ethnic segmentation, and that kinship and religion are weakened as dimensions of identification. Be this as it may, it is beyond dispute that for a majority of Mauritians, ethnic identity remains important both at a symbolic or existential level and at a practical, social level. The "fruit salad" metaphor is frequently invoked in domestic discourse (borrowing, presumably, from the US metaphor of the "salad bowl"), suggesting that the various pieces of different fruits – banana, papaya, pineapple etc. – must be kept discrete lest Mauritians lose their sense of roots and identity. Critics argue, against this description, that the fruit salad metaphor is a euphemism for "apartheid with a human face," but it cannot be denied that for a majority of Mauritians, their ethnic identity provides them with personal networks as well as a sense of ontological security.

The recent ethnic unrest in Mauritius began with a public manifestation of Creole resentment, and it is therefore necessary to take a look at the situation of the Creoles, seen as a community, before proceeding further.

The *malaise créole*

In the years before Mauritius achieved independence, many authoritative warnings were issued to the effect that social and economic disaster might be imminent. Burton Benedict, the island's only major ethnographer before independence, concluded an analysis of Mauritian by stating that: "The ethnic divisions of Mauritius are changing. They are no longer mere categories but are becoming corporate groups. The danger of communal conflict increases" (Benedict 1965: 67). Also in the 1960s, the Report of the Meade Commission, published and endorsed by the

Colonial Office, argued that the combination of rapid population growth (about 3.5 percent in the 1960s), ethnic diversity and extreme economic dependence on a single crop, sugar, was a recipe for disaster (Meade *et al.* 1961). Independent Mauritius would prove these grim predictions to be wrong; population growth was reduced to less than 1.5 percent, economic diversification ensured that the economy eventually rested on three pillars rather than one (sugar, manufacturing and tourism), and by the 1980s, it was evident that Mauritius had evolved into a functioning parliamentary democracy where governments had been peacefully replaced through multiparty general elections. While the unemployment rate was 20 percent as late as 1985, the country was importing labor only a couple of years later.

Although the vast majority of scholars and commentators – foreign and Mauritian alike – had been impressed mainly by the unexpected economic and political success of independent Mauritius during the 1980s and 1990s (see Simmons 1982; Bowman 1991), worries began to be voiced, particularly in the second half of the 1990s, to the effect that social unrest might be brewing – especially among the Catholics of mainly African descent, the Creoles. This population segment had, on the whole, experienced a slower upward mobility than other groups, and it was visibly underrepresented in a number of vital professions. As the Mauritian government has been dominated by Hindus since Independence, due to their strength in numbers, tendencies towards favoritism and nepotism, which have been well documented in a number of cases, did not usually benefit the Creoles. The most impoverished sections of the population were – and are, with a few exceptions – Creoles. Lacking a strong kinship-based corporate organization, they did not profit collectively from individual mobility either. Besides, the Creole elite, many of whom belong to the category formerly known as *gens de couleur*, and who are of mixed European-African or Asian-African origin, is concentrated in the liberal professions, where it is neither customary nor easy to help distant relatives with job opportunities, and where ethnic identification tends to be weak.

By the early 1990s, it was well established in Mauritian public discourse that Creoles had generally enjoyed weaker social mobility than the rest of the population during the otherwise booming 1980s, and that they were affected by social problems much less common in the other groups: teenage pregnancies, long-term unemployment, low educational levels and petty crime. The term *le malaise créole* (the Creole ailment) was coined by a Creole priest, Père Roger Cervaux, in this period, and it immediately caught on among Creoles and non-Creoles alike, as an apt description of an acute social problem.

Complaints against what was and is perceived as unjust Hindu dominance in politics and the state apparatus have been common since independence, but Creoles are traditionally weakly politically organized. Either their political organizations were ill-fated and short-lived, or they voted for parties that would either never achieve power (PMSD) or that had formed coalitions where non-Creoles were the leaders (MMM). During the latter half of the 1990s, a new social movement and later political party, saw the light of day, namely the *Mouvement Républicain*. Led by a lawyer formerly close to the late PMSD leader Gaëtan Duval, this essentially populist movement had a strong libertarian and antigovernment rhetoric, sprinkled with elements of Afrocentric resentment and anarchist visions of social justice. Support for the movement grew quickly, particularly in poor urban neighborhoods and especially among the young, as it seemed to promise the Creoles their just share of the Mauritian miracle without going into ultimately self-defeating and humiliating compromises with Hindus and Muslims.[3]

It can be argued that some elements of the *Mouvement Républicain* may be seen as a result of globalization, the belated arrival of Black Power to Mauritius. (Its ethnic orientation, however, is not definitive; the leader, Rama Valayden, has an ambiguous ethnic identity.) Since Mauritius is located far away from the USA and the Caribbean, and its main literary language is French, not English, Black Power and militant Rastafarianism did not catch on there in the 1960s and 1970s. Only in the late 1980s did local musicians adopt the rhythms and sounds of the reggae (amalgamating it with the traditional *séga* into a hybrid form called *seggae*), and efforts to improve the conditions for the Creoles were largely associated with certain trade unions, French-educated intellectuals, and the Catholic Church, none of which favored postcolonial resentment and aggressive antiwhite, anti-Hindu or antistate rhetoric as political tools.

There is nevertheless one major exception to this picture, which reveals that the recent riot had its precursor not just in form, but also in content. The most important Creole politician for thirty years, Gaëtan Duval (who died in 1996), regularly used ethnic resentment as a tool in his political work, although he frequently went into strategic coalitions with non-Creoles. During the lengthy negotiations for independence in the mid-1960s, he infamously coined the slogan *Malbar nou pa oulé* (We don't want Hindus), *malbar* being a pejorative term comparable to "nigger" in English. His party, the PMSD, has been connected – if obliquely – to the ethnic riots of 1965 and 1968, a series of violent incidents that were for three decades considered the final ethnic riots in Mauritius.

Before proceeding to an analysis of the 1999 riots, a couple of preliminary points must be made. First, quite unlike contemporary ethnic movements in many other countries, the right to be different has not been a major issue in independent Mauritius. The country's citizens have always enjoyed complete freedom of religion and a language policy which has sought compromise between the many languages used in various contexts. Although Duval warned his supporters in the mid-1960s that Mauritius was about to become a "little India," there is little to indicate that this happened, although the MBC (Mauritius Broadcasting Corporation) increased the proportion of Indian feature films in its programming in the late 1990s. Mauritius is complex and creolized at the level of culture; fashionable revitalizations of ethnic traditions thrive side by side with modernization and individualism. Typical expressions of Creole identity, such as the *séga* music and dance, are regarded as symbols of national culture, not as expressions of a minority identity. To the extent that culture has been politicized, as I shall show later, it has been as a symbol for particular rights, not as an end in itself.

Second, the Westminster system of political representation in Mauritius – a legacy from colonialism – creates stable majorities, but it does not entail proportionate representation. However, all major ethnic groups are represented in Parliament, partly because the geographical distribution of Hindus, Creoles, Muslims, and Chinese ensures that all groups get their MLAs (Members of the Legislative Assembly), partly because an ingenious "Best Loser" system guarantees seats in Parliament for eight runners-up (of a total of 70 MLAs). In other words, unlike say, Sami in Norway, North Africans in France or indigenous peoples in Canada, Creoles are reasonably well represented in Parliament – in spite of being loosely politically organized. In the present Legislative Assembly (elected in September 2000), 21 percent of the members belong to the general population, and most of them could be considered Creoles – which is an obvious, but not catastrophic underrepresentation of a population segment which comprises about 30 percent of the total population. In the government, the representation is poorer (currently three of twenty-four cabinet ministers), and there has been an obvious downward mobility of Creoles in Mauritian politics since the Second World War.

In sum, the plight of the Mauritian Creoles does not fit into the current scholarly debate over minority situations. To reiterate the claims made in the Introduction: theirs is not a clear-cut case of discrimination or racism; no single group is hegemonic in Mauritius; non-Creoles do not have a discursive hegemony (indeed, Catholics dominate in the media); debates over cultural rights versus individual rights do not affect Creoles particularly; assimilation into the dominant group is not an option; the pluralism–hybridity issue and social constructions of the past are largely irrelevant; and the issue is not one of global influences versus local identities. Politically and culturally, Mauritius seems to have found a viable and stable compromise between universalist values and ethnic particularism (cf. Eriksen 1997). Yet, interethnic tensions have grown steadily since the early 1990s.

The 1999 riots

Two of the core symbols of the new Creole movement are cannabis and *seggae* music, incidentally the most popular domestic music in the island. In February 1999, a mass meeting in favor of legalization was held, and among the participants was the island's most popular singer, who performed and recorded under the sobriquet Kaya in deference to Bob Marley. Kaya openly smoked cannabis at the meeting, and was detained by the police. Four days later, on Sunday February 21, it was announced that he had died in custody. According the the police, he had died from a violent epileptic fit, but his supporters were convinced that he had been murdered. On the evening of February 21, violence against the police broke out in three Mauritian towns, and police stations were set on fire. The next day, the riot spread to other locations in Mauritius, and a man was shot dead when the police opened fire against the rioters. Looting, arson, widespread material destruction and violence between demonstrators and police, as well as violence between Hindus and Creoles, continued for several days, until peace was restored on Friday, February 26, following appeals from religious leaders (notably Mgr. Jean Margéot of the Catholic Church) and the President, Sir Cassam Uteem. The riots left six people dead and over a hundred injured, and the material damage was very considerable. Although the initial target of the rioters was the police and by extension the state, the violence eventually took a communal turn.

The February riots left the Mauritian public sphere in a state of shock. Although peace was restored and life went back to normal in a matter of days, the damage caused to the fragile social fabric of Mauritius was – if difficult to assess – considerable. Comments in the Mauritian press ranged from indignation and rage directed against the "criminal elements" responsible for the chaotic situation, to more far-sighted calls for greater social justice for the Creoles, and several – including Paul Bérenger, the leader of the Opposition – asked Navin Ramgoolam's government to resign.

Soon after the riots, an initiative was taken to organize a peace march in order to demonstrate that the majority of Mauritians were committed to interethnic harmony. The result was the impressive *Chaînes d'amitié* a month after the riots, where many thousands of Mauritians formed a human chain across the island. Many now came to see the February riot as a timely warning to the government and the public sector, telling them that the struggle to combat ethnic favoritism and systematic discrimination on ethnic grounds, to which virtually every postindependence politician had paid lip service, had to be taken seriously.

More unrest was nevertheless still to come. In mid-May, a minor riot erupted unexpectedly following a road accident near the village of Palma, and a week later, disaster struck in the capital. In the final and decisive match in the first division of the Mauritian football league, the Creole team Fire Brigade met the Muslim team Scouts on May 23. Following an 89th minute goal, the Fire Brigade won the game and, as a result, became Mauritian champions, but the Scouts had two goals annulled by the referee, including an equalizer on overtime. Furious Scouts supporters tore up their seats, players ransacked the dressing room, a Scouts official attacked the referee, while others set fire to surrounding cane fields; by evening, the violence had spread to Port-Louis. Among other things, a police station had its windows smashed. As a climax of sorts, a famous old gambling club run by a Sino-Mauritian family was set on fire, and seven people died.

Football riots are far from unknown in other parts of the world, and if this incident did not have an ethnic dimension, it could have been seen merely as an isolated tragedy – the first of its kind in Mauritius. The Muslim/Creole dimension in the football match itself is evident, if undercommunicated; in the 1980s, the formerly ethnic teams (Muslim Scouts, Hindu Cadets, Tamil Sunrise etc.) were forced to change their names, but they remained associated with ethnic "communities" nonetheless. Still, it would be misleading to see the football riot as an expression of deep Creole/Muslim hatred; it was a spontaneous outburst of rage and anger, and most of the casualties happened to be Sino-Mauritians, members of a community that has little to do with politics or sports, and which is no more associated with Creoles than with Muslims. One of the dead was actually a Muslim employee at the club, while others were Sino-Mauritians. The February riots had much deeper causes and a greater political significance; what the football riot signals, is that the threshold for mob violence has been lowered during the spring of 1999, and that – Mauritius being what it is – such violence is more likely than not to be framed in ethnic terms.

In the end, the government did not resign, but on the contrary promised to make law and order a top priority. Newspaper reports later in 1999 indicated that violent crimes were on the rise, and in early August, five prisoners escaped, apparently with the complicity of a prison guard, from the local *Bastille*. Public confidence in the police is generally low. The political opposition further called for the establishment of independent commissions of inquiry to look into corruption, nepotism, and ethnic favoritism, and accused the government, with its law-and-order talk, of merely confronting the symptoms, not the causes, of the social unrest.

The situation gradually calmed down. However, at the September 2000 General Elections, the voters showed their dissatisfaction with the government by giving the opposition a landslide victory, returning former Prime Minister Anerood Jugnauth to power. Few dramatic changes have seen the light of day following the elections, and the current government contains twenty-four cabinet ministers, two of them relatives of the Prime Minister and only three members of the general population.

Class, ethnicity, and kinship

There are several causes for the collective failure of the Creoles to benefit from Mauritius' recent economic growth – internal, external, cultural, and structural. First, Creole kinship and local organization tend to place comparatively weak moral obligations on individuals; marriage is entirely an individual, voluntary contract, and Creoles are not expected to help relatives or other Creoles with employment or places in institutions of higher education. Their social capital is, in a word, very limited in a situation of group competition.

Second, the Creole ethos and collective stereotype of self depicts them as individualists, in contrast to the Hindus, who have a strong ethic of kin solidarity. While it is common among non-Creole Mauritians to see Creole values as an African "survival," it is more correct to trace them and the accompanying social organization back to the social conditions of slavery (Eriksen 1986). In the context of the present argument, it is nonetheless sufficient to note that there are systematic differences regarding values and local organization between Creoles and Hindus.

Third, the systematic use of kinship and ethnic networks by the other Mauritian "communities" for collective economic and political ends has placed the Creoles at a relative disadvantage. The civil service and the police are, partly due to the logic of kinship obligations, dominated by Hindus, and among working-class Creoles, there is a widespread feeling that their best opportunity for social mobility lies in migration. They are in a minority situation *and* lack the cultural resources necessary to profit from an employment culture of kinship obligations. Furthermore, the state is not just the largest employer in Mauritius, but it also consists of a number of institutions that Mauritians have to relate to in order to get on with their lives, such as the State Bank, the national educational board, the tax office, the postal services and, naturally, the police. When any of these common institutions loses its legitimacy for a certain segment of the population, a likely outcome is social unrest.

It should be kept in mind that the small *Mouvement Républicain*[4] is not a revolutionary one aiming at systemic change. The target of the recent Creole resentment, culminating in the Kaya riots, is neither cultural discrimination nor even the inequalities resulting from libertarian capitalism, but public-sector clientilism working to their disadvantage, and as a result, a lack of confidence in the state apparatus. None of the men in top positions in Mauritian state organizations are Creoles: the Prime Minister is a Hindu, as is the Governor of the Bank of Mauritius. The President is a Muslim, and the Vice-President is a Hindu. The Commissioner of Police is also a Hindu. The Secretary-General of the powerful Mauritius Chamber of Commerce is also a Hindu.

The death of Kaya, incidentally, was not the first Creole casualty in police custody; similar deaths were recorded both in 1994 and 1995. His death gained a particular symbolic significance for obvious reasons: he had participated at a peaceful public meeting promoting Creole causes, doing something the majority of male Mauritians have done at least a few times, that is, smoking marijuana; and he was a successful Creole artist who both embodied the aspirations of his fellow Creoles as an exemplar and gave voice to their hopes and fears. Killing Kaya, if that is what the policemen did,[5] was possibly the worst single action that could have been envisioned for communal relations in the island. This was further aggravated in the killing, by the police, of another Creole singer during the February riots.

Be this as it may, the main source of the recent riots in Mauritius does not lie in cultural differences, religious intolerance, the suppression of cultural identities, or unequal civil rights. On the contrary, one may ask virtually any Mauritian, and he or she will express pride in the "cultural mosaic" and diversity of the small "rainbow society," its variety being promoted as the very essence of Mauritius by politicians and tourist agencies alike. Unlike in many other multiethnic societies, religious and cultural pluralism are positively encouraged by the state, and nobody openly aspires to turn the country into an ethnically hegemonic state of the European kind.

The ultimate cause of the Mauritian state's current crisis of legitimacy, I will argue, is a particular kind of kinship solidarity and the obligations associated with it, frequently extended to metaphoric kinship, that is ethnic identity and ethnic social organization. In a liberal state, kinship solidarity may be encouraged in family businesses, accepted in larger enterprises, and condemned in the public sector. Yet this ethos of reciprocity and caring for the family, values that have incidentally often been highly praised by politicians in nonspecific ways during rural campaigning, has led to a feeling of exclusion among Creoles. The low number of Creoles in high bureaucratic positions lends credibility to this feeling, which is further strengthened by the sense of relative downward mobility which is so widespread among Creoles as to have become virtually an emblem of their ethnic identity.

The riots and models of ethnicity

The Mauritian example, I have argued, does not fit nicely into any of the current academic debates over minority rights, nationalism, and identity politics, and I shall therefore take this opportunity to use it for a brief critique of some dominant perspectives.

We should first keep in mind that a short generation ago, Marxist analyses of social life were offered wholesale as alternatives to "bourgeois" or "liberal" social science. Regarding Mauritian ethnicity, the most complete Marxist analysis was that of two French sociologists who published a book more than two decades ago (Durand and Durand 1978). They saw ethnic revitalization chiefly as a middle-class affectation intended to preserve privileges associated with caste and class, and argued that while class consciousness could provide the disenfranchised with equal rights, ethnic consciousness was a form of false consciousness that led nowhere for the masses. Whatever its merits, by concentrating on ostentatious symbolic displays of ethnic identity (one of their examples is the revitalization of the sari, a garment that had become obsolete among rural and working-class Hindu women), the Durands neglected the foundation of ethnic identity in everyday life; the fact that not only social classification of self and other, but also the flow of material and nonmaterial resources is largely directed by ethnic connections, networks, and associations. Although some factors, such as education, individualism, and the emergence of an increasingly nonethnic private-sector labor market, reduce the importance of ethnicity, the monoethnic networks of trust and mutual commitment continue to confirm and reinforce ethnicity in most Mauritian settings. This has nothing to do with the cultural differences spoken about by ethnic ideologists in Europe and North America. As every Mauritian knows, their country might well be organized along ethnic lines even if the cultural differences between the groups were negligible. At present, as noted earlier, the cultural differences between ethnic groups in Mauritius nonetheless remain considerable and socially relevant. Their relative lack of social capital (a cultural factor) partly explains the difficult situation of the Creoles, but such differences are not necessary for ethnicity to be socially important.

Since Marxism went out of fashion, a main controversy regarding these matters has been the ongoing debate in social philosophy between communitarians and liberals. While communitarians like Michael Walzer and Alasdair Macintyre have argued the primacy of the group over the individual, and have thereby defended ethnic movements and nonoffensive nationalist collectivism, liberals like John Rawls, Ronald Dworkin, and Jürgen Habermas have argued in favor of individual rights, pointing out the predicaments inherent in a collectivism that treats people differently on the basis of presumed cultural differences. Some theorists, like Will Kymlicka, have tried to transcend this opposition, suggesting ways in which a concern for cultural rootedness among minorities or even majorities can be reconciled with liberal individualism (Kymlicka 1995). While this ongoing debate in social philosophy can be useful as a starting point for analyses of Mauritian discourses and policies relating to religion, language, education, and the electoral system, it is less helpful when we try to unravel the causes of the Kaya riots. The issue at the core here is not the question of cultural rights versus individual rights, but the extension of kinship solidarity to the metaphoric realm of ethnicity, applied to the public service of the multiethnic nation. One distinction highlighted in the communitarianism/liberalism debate nevertheless seems highly relevant, namely, that obtaining between the private and the public sphere. In the scholarly discourse about urban minorities in Western Europe as well as ethnic nationalism in Eastern Europe, it is common to argue that expressions of ethnic or cultural distinctiveness are acceptable in the private sphere but not in the public sphere; one may be different at home but not at school or at work. While this argument can also be found in Mauritian discourse, it is notoriously difficult to apply in practice, since rights and obligations anchored in the domestic sphere inevitably have ramifications in public spheres. Nowhere is this more evident than in cases of nepotism and ethnic favoritism.

Whether liberal or communitarian in normative orientation, this literature generally has surprisingly little to tell us about the current Mauritian crisis, as does the kind of Marxist analysis referred to above. The country is a well-functioning democracy with an excellent human rights record, and it has achieved a clever reconciliation between cultural rights and individual rights – yet a sizeable ethnic minority is excluded from a variety of career opportunities for structural and cultural reasons. This kind of exclusion requires no formal organization and no ideology; kinship and, by extension, ethnicity as classificatory kinship, are sufficient. Unless one looks at this dimension of ethnic identity, which is reproduced through socialization, largely in the private sphere, there is little to suggest that Mauritius is anything but a country where liberals and communitarians can live comfortably together.

Another large body of literature, dominated by political scientists, deals with ethnic conflict, its causes and its solutions (see Horowitz 1985; Lijphart 1977 for two different, important contributions). Although few would today go as far as to claim that cultural incompatibilities explain ethnic hostilities, many of the writers dealing with these issues take the ethnic identity for granted; what needs to be accounted for seems to be not the strength of ethnic loyalty, but the outbreak of conflict. In my view, given a society with strongly incorporated ethnic groups, it is fairly easy to explain why conflict is likely to erupt under specific circumstances involving competition over scarce resources. The present challenge is not so much to explain discrimination and conflict, but why they emerge as *ethnic* phenomena. It is a straightforward task to demonstrate that, say, Pakistani immigrants are discriminated against in the labor and housing markets in Oslo, or that African Americans systematically receive an inferior education, or that the Yugoslav wars were fought on the basis of ethnicity. It is even relatively easy to offer a persuasive argument about the causes of these outcomes, provided one takes the ethnic structure of society for granted.

Like the social philosophers and social scientists writing about majorities, minorities, cultures, and individuals, alluded to above and in the introduction to this chapter, the ethnic conflict analysts have rarely shown how ethnic identity is being reproduced – it is not chiefly through overt ideologies of roots and supremacy, nor through large-scale rituals of community, but through the more low-key and less easily observable institutions of primary socialization and kinship. This is where the ultimate causes of the Kaya riots must be sought. The appropriate comparison, therefore, should not be made between the ethnic unrest in Mauritius and violent ethnic conflict in, say, Sri Lanka, Kosovo, or Rwanda; but between the Mauritian class structure and the class structure of other perfectly democratic countries where kinship, interpersonal networks and social distinctions ensure the reproduction of systematically differential access to coveted resources. In other words, the British class structure is a more relevant comparative horizon here than Scottish separatism or Cornish revivalism, or even identity politics among Muslims in West Yorkshire.

In the Mauritian case as elsewhere, it may – and will doubtless – be argued that the official multiculturalism of the country is a foil concealing systematic discrimination against particular ethnic groups: they are granted equal symbolic significance, cultural rights, and formal equality, but are discriminated against in informal, nearly invisible, but no less efficient ways. This description fits the Mauritian situation well, but if it is invoked as an argument against cultural rights or a moderate version of multiculturalism, it must be pointed out that it conflates two separate issues: the current unrest involving part of the Creole population is not fought out over cultural rights relating to, for example, religion, language or "way of life." The right to pursue a culturally specific way of life has never been threatened in independent Mauritius, and indeed, when cultural radicals in the 1970s tried to make Kreol – the ancestral language of the Creoles, an official language in the media and the state, many of the latter were against the proposition, since they saw French as a more sophisticated and useful language. As I have shown, the conflict can be traced to certain practices in the public sphere related to socialization patterns, not to culture. It can therefore be argued that the moderate multiculturalism institutionalized in the Mauritian public sphere – equal rights, but cultural variation – is part of the solution, not part of the problem. Since the existence of discrete "ethnic communities" is recognized both in the Mauritian constitution and in Mauritian society as a whole, it follows that ethnic particularism and favoritism are deemed possible – unlike what would have been the case in a more dogmatic liberal state, where only individuals and their families are acknowledged, or in a socialist state like Tito's Yugoslavia, where ethnicity was officially seen as a phenomenon belonging to an earlier social formation. Similarly, in societies where the existence of social classes is denied by the dominant ideology, accusations of systemic reproductions of a particular class structure are likely to be met with limited understanding.

Concluding remarks

I hope to have shown two things in this analysis of the February 1999 riots in Mauritius. First, ethnicity is, when all is said and done, chiefly a property of social relations, not of ideology. As long as ethnic identity has a firm foundation in kinship and social networks, it can manage quite well and even be socially dominant, without an overarching ideology or ostentatious symbolic display; in Mauritius, if anything, French-language discourse conducted by nonwhite Catholics is dominant in the public sphere, while the wider ethnic category associated with them is subordinated.

Second, this particular conflict is properly seen not as an ethnic conflict in the usual sense, despite its appearance as one. Neither of the groups wishes to annihilate, enslave, or dominate the other, achieve political independence or strengthen its collective sense of identity. Rather, the Creoles revolted against particularist practices in the public service curtailing their individual social mobility and depriving them of equal treatment. The Creole quest for equality, taken at face value for the sake of the present argument, therefore deserves to be seen in the context of the emancipatory liberal tradition rather than as yet another expression of sectarian identity politics. In other words, not every conflict that involves two ethnic groups is an ethnic conflict. In general, conflicts involving territorial minorities and indigenous peoples confronting a more or less belligerent state are ethnic in character, while the antiracist movement and other social movements involving immigrant groups in Western Europe tend to belong to the liberal tradition in that they argue in favor of equality, *against* the ethnic logic of society. These two kinds of social movements have little in common, and deserve not to be lumped together as "ethnic" ones. One is similar to class struggle (in the wide sense including cultural aspects of class), the other to nationalism; one favors equality, the other difference. This distinction, often obscured by the blanket term "ethnic conflict," is not a trivial one, whether one's concern is intellectual or political.

NOTES

A previous version of this chapter was delivered at the conference "Nationalism, Identity and Minority Rights," Department of Sociology, University of Bristol, September 16–19, 1999. Thanks are due to the organizers for creating a stimulating setting, and, in their subsequent role as editors of this volume, for useful comments on an earlier version of the chapter.

1. The philosophical debate between communitarians and liberals is also an important one; it will be dealt with separately below.
2. Thanks are due to Malenn Oodiah, Vinesh Hookoomsing, and Elisabeth Boullé for keeping me posted on the crisis before I could come myself (I went in October 1999).
3. It then all but collapsed, like many former movements of the same structure.
4. The actual importance of this movement is negligible. It is interesting as a symptom, not as a force in itself.
5. An independent autopsy on Kaya, carried out by a foreign physician, concluded that he died from head injuries which could not have been self-inflicted, noting that the injuries could have been caused by violent shaking of the body or it being thrown to the ground. He also noted slight injuries on the singer's face and body. The government has nonetheless called on other specialists, and nearly a year after Kaya's death, there was officially not sufficient evidence to suggest he was murdered.

REFERENCES

Appadurai, Arjun (1996) *Modernity at Large: Cultural Dimensions of Globalization.* Minneapolis: University of Minnesota Press.

Benedict, Burton (1961) *Mauritius: Problems of a Plural Society.* London: Pall Mall.

(1965) *Mauritius: Problems of a Plural Society.* London: Pall Mall.

Bowman, Larry (1991) *Mauritius: Democracy and Development in the Indian Ocean.* Boulder: Westview.

Chazal, Malcolm de (1979 [1951]) *Petrusmok.* Port-Louis: Editions de la Table Ovale.

Durand, J.-P. and J. Durand (1978) *L'Ile Maurice et ses populations.* Paris: P.U.F.

Eriksen, Thomas Hylland (1986) "Creole culture and social change." *Journal of Mauritian Studies* 1 (2): 59–72.

(1988) *Communicating Cultural Difference and Identity. Ethnicity and Nationalism in Mauritius.* Oslo: Department of Social Anthropology, Occasional Papers in Social Anthropology, 16.

(1997) "Multiculturalism, individualism and human rights." In Richard Wilson (ed.), *Human Rights, Culture and Context.* London: Pluto, pp. 49–69.

(1998) *Common Denominators: Ethnicity, Nation-Building and Compromise in Mauritius.* Oxford: Berg.

(2002) *Ethnicity and Nationalism: Anthropological Perspectives.* 2nd edn. London: Pluto.

Fanon, Frantz (1971 [1952]) *Peau noire, masques blancs.* Paris: Seuil.

Friedman, Jonathan (1994) *Cultural Identity and Global Process.* London: Sage.

Hannerz, Ulf (1996) *Transnational Connections: Culture, People, Places.* London: Routledge.

Hobsbawm, Eric and Terence Ranger (eds.) (1983) *The Invention of Tradition.* Cambridge: Cambridge University Press.

Horowitz, Donald L. (1985) *Ethnic Groups in Conflict.* Berkeley: University of California Press.

Kymlicka, Will (1995) *Multicultural Citizenship: A Liberal Theory of Minority Rights.* Oxford: Clarendon.

Lijphart, Arend (1977) *Democracy in Plural Societies: A Comparative Exploration.* New Haven: Yale University Press.

Meade, J. E. *et al.* (1961) *The Social and Economic Structure of Mauritius.* London: Her Majesty's Stationery Office.

Simmons, Adele Smith (1982) *Modern Mauritius: The Politics of Decolonialization.* Bloomington: Indiana University Press.

Taylor, Charles (1992) "The politics of recognition." In A. Gutman (ed.), *Multiculturalism: examining the politics of recognition.* Princeton: Princeton University Press.

5 Black nationalism and African American ethnicity: the case of Afrocentrism as civil religion

Patricia Hill Collins

The changes generated by postcoloniality, global capitalism, and new technologies have sparked a lively debate about the contours and meaning of the "new" racism in the United States. Some scrutinize the transformation of contemporary US society as a racialized social system composed of structural and ideological dimensions (Bonilla-Silva 1996). When it comes to African Americans, structurally, American society has not made the gains in desegregating its housing, schools, and employment promised by the civil rights movement (Massey and Denton 1993). One study of Atlanta, Georgia revealed that neighborhood-level racial resegregation is emerging as a new spatial pattern within major American cities, even those with a politically enfranchised and highly visible Black middle class (Orfield and Ashkinaze 1991). Emerging research points to the growth of a prison-industrial complex as an important new site for institutionalized racism confronting working-class and poor African Americans and Latinos (Miller 1996). Ideologically, a belief in upholding "colorblindness" masks the continued inequalities of contemporary racism. By proclaiming that equal treatment of *individuals* under the law is sufficient for addressing racism, this ideology redefines *group*-based, antiracist remedies such as affirmative action as being "racist" (Crenshaw 1997).

How should African Americans respond to the promise and the disappointments of this "new" racism that operates through the curious combination of a structurally incomplete desegregation cloaked by an ideology of "color-blind" inclusiveness? In this chapter, I sketch out how some African Americans refashioned the core ideas of Black Nationalism in attempts to negotiate the dilemmas of the "new" racism. Despite considerable variability in how African Americans understand and articulate Black Nationalist ideology, I suggest that Black Nationalism's main ideas of self-definition, self-determination, and self-reliance resonate with the experiences of large numbers of African Americans and with important cultural norms of American society. In this context, the core ideas of

Black Nationalism can be used to craft an African American racial/ethnic identity that in turn articulates with historical models of ethnic political mobilization used by other racial/ethnic groups.[1]

My argument constitutes a major departure from standard approaches to Black Nationalism. Most scholarship defines Black Nationalism as a political ideology, one of many (e.g. socialism or integrationism) that historically have framed African American politics (Robinson 2001). Such approaches further categorize the philosophical distinctions among Black Nationalisms. Cultural nationalism, revolutionary nationalism, religious nationalism, Black feminist nationalism, and the like have all been classified as diverse strands of an overarching Black Nationalist philosophy (Van DeBurg 1997; Moses 1978; Pinkney 1976). This approach, while valuable, remains limited, because it ignores how African Americans may use Black Nationalist ideology in forming political organizations and for influencing voting patterns. For example, despite class differences among African Americans that should result in differential voting patterns, unlike White Americans, African Americans continue to vote along racial lines (Dawson 1994). Moreover, focusing on ideological strands of Black Nationalism also obscures how African Americans may use its core ideas as a system of meaning. Black Nationalism can be used to organize social institutions and social relations within African American communities as well as African American group behavior within American society.

Part of Black Nationalism's appeal may lie in its usefulness to individual African Americans searching for meaning within their everyday lives; in its utility in mobilizing African Americans as a collectivity for quite diverse activities that are not overtly political; and in its versatility to have diverse meanings for segments of African American civil society distinguished by social class, color, gender, immigrant status, and religion. This malleability constitutes Black Nationalism's promise and its danger. Political ideologies and religions both claim this ability to construct group identities that move people to action. Individuals who believe in Christianity, capitalism, Islam, Marxism, and similar systems of thought use the main ideas of these systems of belief to guide everyday decisionmaking and group mobilization. At the same time, despite sharing a common set of ideas, how individuals interpret these core ideas as well as the actual practices undertaken under their guidance can vary widely.

Honed at the intersection of political ideology and religion, Black Nationalism may have a similar utility for African Americans. Historically, Black Nationalism's flexibility allowed African Americans to reshape it in response to the specific political challenges raised by slavery, Jim Crow segregation, industrialization, and urbanization. Given this resiliency and potential functionality for our times, either presenting Black Nationalism as an overly homogeneous political ideology in order to claim or reject it (nationalism versus integrationism), or restricting analysis to the specific content of strands of Black Nationalism (cultural nationalism versus religious nationalism) seems shortsighted. Instead, a more intriguing and potentially useful approach lies in exploring the diverse ways in which African Americans deploy Black Nationalism as a system of meaning, especially in constructing responses to the "new" racism.

Racism: the erasure of African American ethnicity

Racism and religion were both foundational to the very essence of American national identity as well as the nation-state policies of the United States. The external racism directed against indigenous peoples who occupied the land desired by European settlers and the internal racism directed against enslaved African workers both were integral to the *founding* moments of the United States as a nation-state (Collins 2001). During the US colonial period, Whiteness, whether claimed by propertied Whites or White indentured servants, became defined in opposition to, and elevated above, the nonwhite status assigned to indigenous peoples and enslaved Africans. This core racial triangle among White settlers, indigenous peoples, and enslaved Africans lay at the heart of the new US nation-state. In forming a settler society that privileged Whiteness, European American settlers saw their search for land and resources as their right as a new people or nation. Because national identity itself was so compromised by such deeply embedded racial processes, it has been virtually impossible to conceive of American national identity in terms other than racial. Moreover, accomplishing this racialized American national identity required reducing the myriad of ethnicities that characterized European, American Indian, and African populations into these three core racial categories.

Christian religion mattered greatly during this foundational period and served as a template for the creation of an American Civil Religion that also articulated with American national identity. On the one hand, a fundamental principle of American national identity – the identity of the American "nation" or "people" – protects religious freedom through the separation of church and state. On the other hand, European colonists were deeply Christian and valued religion, yet this same protection of religious freedom forbade making Christianity the formal state religion of the new nation-state. Crafting an American Civil Religion that worshipped American national identity yet did so in a legally secular fashion addressed this seeming contradiction. By definition, civil religion constitutes the worship of a form of government and the political principles associated with it. The claim that the United States has a civil religion suggests that Americans are not only a religious people in the sense of widespread adherence to religious belief, but that Americans understand American national identity *as* a people in religious terms. In the US context, the substance of civil religion includes the worship of democracy and republican government rooted in principles such as liberty, equality, justice, and law. In short, the American Civil Religion is patriotism infused with and constructed in tandem with "Christian values." Because the United States explicitly does not have a state religion where adherence to and protection of a true faith operates as a qualification for holding government authority, the reliance on civil religion emerged as one mechanism for resolving the contradiction between America as a republic and America as a liberal, constitutional state (Bellah 1992: 169–73). From its inception, religion and nationalism have been deeply intertwined within American politics, and in ways that place people of African descent in the curious position of being inside the body politic as workers, yet outside it as either members of the republican community or as full citizens of the liberal, constitutional state.[2]

Arriving with ethnic identities organized around shared language, culture, religion, and customs, new immigrant groups in the early twentieth century established ethnic enclaves that protected their members and established a beachhead in US society. Many groups quickly realized that politicizing these enclosure ethnicities and using them to compete with other ethnic groups yielded tangible political and economic benefits. Deploying a form of "competition ethnicity" where groups compete with one another in relation to state power, resources, and development, ethnic groups jockeyed for position within the US racial hierarchy (see also Nederveen Pieterse this volume). European immigrant groups were able to use their appearance to become optimally "white," whereas others, Eastern European Jews, for example, settled for becoming "not quite white" (Brodkin 2000: 103–37). The political and economic leverage created via ethnic *group* mobilization generated sufficient opportunities for their children to become "white" *individuals* unencumbered by the limits of enclosure ethnicity (Robinson 2001: 104–17). Caribbean immigrants of African descent encountered a different reality. Their challenge lay in trying to be "not-black." Deploying competitive ethnic identities of Jamaican, Trinidadian, Cuban, and the like served for a time as a shield against falling into the stark racial classification that erased their individuality and made them simply "black." Rigid racial segregation politicized many, and those who believed that the benefits of first-class citizenship were likely to elude them because they were too "black" often threw in their lot with African Americans and became "black." Together, in the 1920s, Afro-Caribbeans and African Americans flocked to the Black Nationalist Garvey Movement, to date, the largest US mass movement of people of African descent.

Whereas the racial category of "white" constructed from European ethnicities remained highly salient within US hierarchical power relations, Whiteness ironically became largely un-raced, primarily because it held the power to erase its own operation. Race was certainly real, but because White Americans enjoyed the state protections of being the dominant racial group, they could claim a curious ignorance concerning the privileges that they accrued in their everyday lives because they were White. All White Americans could self-define as individuals, not as members of a White ethnic group. At the same time, because White Americans were far from homogeneous, some Whites claimed an array of "optional ethnicities" that, depending on historical time and place of arrival in the United States, gained access to the privileges of first-class citizenship. Structures of racial segregation articulated well with these stark racial categories. For African Americans, ethnicity was denied and race became paramount. For White Americans, ethnicity operated as a malleable category that could be deployed in defense of the ethnic group, or could be shed altogether if the price were right. More importantly, for White Americans, race disappeared.

Unlike other immigrant groups that typically arrived in the United States with their ethnic cultures intact, African Americans faced the challenge of constructing a new group identity or African American ethnicity that resisted the derogatory meanings attached to the racial category "black." This new ethnicity both had to draw upon the new syncretic cultural heritage created by diverse African ethnic groups and do so within the distinctly American religious milieu of an overarching American Civil Religion. In this context, religion culled from Christian theology assumed great importance within African American culture and ethnicity (Cone 1972; Paris 1995; Hood 1994). As C. Eric Lincoln points out, "For African Americans, a people whose total experience has been a sustained condition of multiform stress, religion is never far from the threshold of consciousness, for whether it is embraced with fervor or rejected with disdain, it is the focal element of the black experience" (Lincoln 1999: xxiv). Because the racialized social system itself changed shape over time, African American ethnicity also was continually constructed anew, in the context of a persistent core racial triangle as well as the centrality of religiosity to African American ethnicity.

Because African Americans have experienced this unique racial/ethnic history in the United States, negotiating the "new" racism constitutes a special challenge. Historically, African Americans crafted antiracist initiatives in response to deeply entrenched patterns of racial segregation that blocked opportunities in jobs, housing, education, and voting (Berry 1994). In the context of legally sanctioned racial apartheid, designing antiracist strategies seemed to be straightforward – dismantle the legal edifice of racial segregation and racism should wither away. Currently, despite dramatic changes in the legal infrastructure that occurred in the 1950s and 1960s, racial segregation is far from disappearing. As a result, the United States remains characterized by an uneven racial desegregation, especially in housing and schools, with African Americans more heavily segregated in housing, schooling, and marital patterns than any other racial/ethnic group (Massey and Denton 1993). Moreover, because a sizeable portion of the general population believes that American society is more racially integrated than is actually the case, many fail to see new patterns of racial resegregation. Because the victories of the civil rights movement dismantled legal segregation and gave African Americans equal rights, many White Americans feel that to talk of race is tantamount to creating racism. Racially coded language proliferates within this new ideology of colorblindness, with the use of terms such as "street crime," "welfare cheats," "unwed mothers," and "family values" standing in proxy for the racially explicit language of prior eras (Collins 1998: 82–83).

Because the "new" racism operates in the organizational context of desegregation and with the illusion of equality provided by the logic of colorblindness (Crenshaw 1997), it provides new challenges for African Americans. For one, the "new" racism seems to be replicating the foundational racial triangle, yet does so by working differently from ethnicity. Changes in immigration legislation dating from the mid-1960s fostered a huge growth of immigration, this time not from European nations, but primarily from Latin America, Asia, and to a lesser extent, the Caribbean and continental Africa. These new immigrants could not fit the biological criteria of Whiteness and thus physically could not be classified as biologically White.

The use of ethnicity by these new immigrant groups provides a fascinating glimpse of how the ethnic identifications claimed by these heterogeneous immigrant groups articulate with the longstanding racial order. Like the Jewish population before them in the 1950s (Brodkin 2000: 144–53), Asians are also offered the status of "model minorities" as a way of claiming the benefits of Whiteness (Tuan 1998). They remain "not-white" but can aspire to be the best of the "not-blacks." The diverse skin colors, hair textures, and physical features of Latino populations, as well as the vastly different histories that distinguish Cuban Americans from Puerto Ricans, Dominican from Mexican immigrants, for example, stimulate interesting challenges for this bureaucratically created "ethnic" group. In particular, Latino populations typically bring a different sensibility about race and racism. However, the absence of a stark black/white racial divide in Latin countries does not mean that Afro-Latin populations have not experienced a distinctive form of racism organized around concepts of "whitening." Resembling the situation that confronted Caribbean immigrants during the Garvey era, immigrants of African descent from the Caribbean and from continental Africa encounter similar pressures to flatten their ethnic identities and to become simply "black." Nigerians, Cameroonians, Somalians, Haitians, and Jamaicans remain "not-white," but they also must work to remain "not-black," i.e., not African American. In this case, holding fast to ethnic customs as "foreign Blacks" seemingly provides a shield for the first generation against the assaults of racism where the goal is to be anything but "domestic Black."

Racial/ethnic mobilization, religion, and Black Nationalism

African Americans confront this dynamic racial/ethnic context, where virtually any ethnic identity is deemed to be better than being African American or "domestic black." For many, claiming African American ethnic identification potentially can serve as a shield against a negative racial classification as well as form a basis for group-based political mobilization. In this political and social environment, the core ideas of Black Nationalism may take on an importance beyond their logical and empirical merits. Such ideas can guide constructions of an African American ethnicity that can be brokered for political and social power within the context of American pluralism. Moreover, Black Nationalist ideas can be reconfigured in ways that draw upon the religiosity of African Americans so central within African American culture as well as the climate of American Civil Religion that frames American society overall.

Despite the fact that the majority of African Americans most likely can define neither Black Nationalism nor its major ideological strands, the ideas themselves may circulate in everyday life as a template for African American ethnicity. The ideas need not be associated with formal Black Nationalist politics to serve this function for everyday African Americans. C. Eric Lincoln unpacks these interrelationships among ethnicity, religion, and Black Nationalism:

> Because black ethnicity and black identity are often expressed through black religion, black religion is often mistaken for black nationalism. They may, and often do, travel together, but the goals and interests of these two aspects of the

black experience are not the same . . . For the black masses, black religion and black nationalism are often one and the same, *in effect*. Both address the sources of their distress, and these require no labels. Those whose suffering seems most arbitrary are likely to be most impatient with fine distinctions, when in the fervor of black togetherness they finally confront the specter which stalks them all. As a result, black nationalism sometimes assumes the *character* of religion because it promises to the disinherited the swift and certain reversal of the circumstances of their oppression and suffering. (Lincoln 1999: 91–92)

Black Nationalism, religion, and African American ethnicity seemingly construct one another in ways that seem remarkably similar to the connections of American patriotism and American Civil Religion. Religion, nationalism, and ethnicity certainly are prominent in the Black Nationalist projects from the Black Power movement of the 1960s that somehow survived to the present. Dean Robinson identifies the Nation of Islam under the leadership of Louis Farrakhan and Afrocentricity as principally defined by Molefi Kete Asante as being the two most prominent manifestations of contemporary Black Nationalism since the mid-1970s (Robinson 2001: 118). Both forms of Black Nationalism work with the paradigm of ethnic mobilization so prominent in American history. Both Black Nationalist projects simultaneously draw upon the historical religiosity of African Americans yet do so with an eye toward developing ethnic identification among American Americans. At the same time, neither project pushes for the political mobilization used by Irish, Italians, Jews, and other European ethnic groups. Robinson contends, "both make some demands on the state: but, thus far, neither tendency firmly links its political trajectory to the efforts of labor, feminist, or other typically progressive political forces. Both offer, instead, highly idealistic proposals – one explicitly religious, the other quasireligious – for group empowerment" (Robinson 2001: 118).

Both of these Black Nationalist projects came to full fruition during the 1980s and early 1990s, a time when the Christian Right made new demands on the US nation-state via the Republican presidencies of Ronald Reagan and George Bush (1980–92), and a time that was a clear transitional period for the reworking of religion, ethnicity, and race within American politics. However much its theology deviated from traditional Islamic teachings, by organizing its own mosques and other social organizations, the Nation of Islam (NOI) became recognized as a formal religion. Despite the small number of actual NOI members, much has been written about the intersection of religion and politics of this organization (Lee 1996), and I will not summarize this literature here. It seems adequate to point out that ordinary African Americans have either ignored or remain unaware of the often-contentious debates among African American intellectuals in the 1990s that castigated the NOI's patriarchal and heterosexist programs. Voting with their feet by attending the 1995 Million Man March on Washington organized by NOI and Louis Farakkhan in record numbers, everyday African Americans apparently found the core ideas of this conservative version of Black Nationalism more appealing than arguments advanced by well-known Black public intellectuals who opposed the march.

Afrocentrism raises a different set of issues that pivot on one core question: how does Black Nationalism "assume the *character* of religion" in order to address the "oppression and suffering" caused by the "new" racism? The emergence of Afrocentrism in the 1980s among African American academics and its dissemination in the 1990s outside the academy into popular culture illustrate how Black Nationalist ideology can be recast as a civil religion.[3] Within American higher education, Molefi Asante and other African American academics refashioned the main ideas of Black Cultural Nationalism as social theory designed to guide fledgling Black Studies research and teaching (Collins 1998: 155–83). Despite Afrocentrism's expressed function as a social theory within American higher education, its actual use more closely resembled that of a civil religion. As a civil religion, Afrocentrism reinterpreted African American ethnicity by developing African-influenced cultural referents that prescribed the overall values of African diasporic communities, provided social cohesion based on those values, and facilitated the emotional healing of African Americans. In essence, Afrocentric scholars took the framework of American Civil Religion, stripped it of the "American" symbols and rituals that were designed to foster patriotic commitment to the US nation-state, and substituted a Black value system designed to achieve similar ends.

One reason that religious expressions of Black Nationalism have garnered support is that African Americans have long relied upon religion as a source of resistance to racial oppression (Sobel 1979). African Americans have long used faith-based sources of resistance to racism. Unlike the use of religion by immigrant ethnic groups where practicing the traditional religion becomes an important site of a group's success in maintaining its ethnic heritage, for African Americans, religion in general and Christianity in particular evolved in response to African American encounters with racism. Initially, the Black public sphere or African American civil society was virtually synonymous with the Black church. Over time, however, especially with migration from the rural South to urban industrial areas of the South and North, this Black public sphere developed a split between the sacred and the secular as interconnected dimensions of Black community life. Both spheres shared a common belief in spirituality. In this sense, the split between the overwhelmingly Christian and largely Baptist formal religious traditions in Black church culture, and the secular spirituality that has formed the creative foundation of music, dance, and other aspects of African American creative cultural production constitute two sides of the same coin. When combined, a spirituality that can take sacred or secular form constitutes an important dimension of African American ethnicity (Richards 1990).

Sociologist Mary Patillo-McCoy's study of church culture as a strategy of action in one African American community provides ethnographic evidence for the recursive nature of the sacred and the secular within Black civil society and how such a society is infused with an African American religiosity (Patillo-McCoy 1998). Existing research indicates that African Americans are, by many measures, highly religious people, as evidenced by the importance of God and religion in African Americans' lives, the high frequency of church attendance and church membership, and the prevalence of prayer in daily life. Defining church culture as ranging from "the ardent use of formal prayer to the subtle murmurs of encouragement that punctuate public gatherings" (Patillo-McCoy 1998: 767), Patillo-McCoy contends that the Black church provides a cultural blueprint for community activities and thus influences the script and staging of African American community organizations. As Patillo-McCoy points out, "the power of prayer, Christian imagery, and call-and-response interaction lies . . . in the *cultural* familiarity of these tools among African Americans as media for interacting, conducting a meeting, holding a rally, or getting out the vote. Black church culture constitutes a common language that motivates social action" (Patillo-McCoy 1998: 768).

This fluidity between sacred and secular provides the historical backdrop for Afrocentric scholars and others to use the tenets of Black Nationalism to craft new ethnic identifications that, because they share some core features with organized religions, link regular churchgoers to African Americans who rarely set foot in a church, mosque, or synagogue. Moreover, Black ethnic identifications that take religious and/or spiritual forms may be more readily recognizable to far greater numbers of African Americans because they invoke preexisting religious, spiritual, and cultural traditions. By drawing upon this common Black church culture, Afrocentrism attaches the specific content of Black Nationalism to the processes of how social action is constructed within African American communities. Afrocentrism aims to provide a template for African American ethnicity grounded in a shared sense of "blackness" that can be simultaneously theorized (Afrocentricity) and performed (Black church culture).

Black Nationalism as civil religion: the case of Afrocentrism

Examining how Afrocentric scholars have recast the *functions* typically performed by formal religions reveals how Afrocentrism operates as a civil religion. Organized religions have several distinguishing features, some of which Afrocentrism as a civil religion aims to reproduce, others of which remain less attainable. Here I discuss four overlapping features, namely (1) shared belief systems that form the core values of the religion; (2) articles of faith that separate the true believers from everyone else and that provide guidance for everyday life; (3) explanations for suffering, death, and other mysteries of life that affect the religion's membership; and (4) organizational structures, especially shared rituals, meetings and/or other mechanisms that affirm group membership.

First, organized religions have a shared system of beliefs or values that constitute the core, enduring values of faith. Without these core ideas, the religion could not exist. Within Afrocentrism, an unconditional love of Black people lies at the heart of this civil religion. Philosopher Cornel West suggests that nihilism, or the feeling that life has no meaning, constitutes a new, fundamental threat to African Americans: "Nihilism is not overcome by arguments or analysis; it is tamed by love and care. Any disease of the soul must be conquered by a turning of one's soul. This turning is done by one's own affirmation of one's worth – an affirmation fueled by the concern of others. This is why a love ethic must be at the center of a politics of conversion" (West 1993: 19). Within Afrocentrism as a civil religion, the quest to develop Black consciousness or a love of Blackness stems from efforts to develop unconditional love for one's people or "nation."

Identifying and valuing *negritude* is foundational to Afrocentric efforts to develop this core article of faith. In his 1966 essay "Negritude: a humanism of the twentieth century," Leopold Sedar Senghor offers two definitions of negritude, each of which serves as a pillar for the shared values that constitute Afrocentrism as a civil religion. Senghor suggests that "negritude . . . is rooting oneself in oneself, and self-confirmation; confirmations of one's *being*. Negritude is nothing more or less than what some English-speaking Africans have called the *African personality*" (Senghor 1995: 45, italics in original). This use of negritude foreshadows Molefi Asante's approach to Afrocentricity as being centered in a world of Black beliefs. As Asante observes, "Afrocentricity is the active centering of the African in subject place in our historical landscape. This has always been my search; it has been a quest for sanity" (Asante 1993: 43). In essence, Afrocentricity enables African Americans to recognize the irrationality of racism and claim "sanity" within it. Elsewhere Asante defines

Afrocentricity as "*a perspective which allows Africans to be subjects of histor-ical experiences rather than objects* on the fringes of Europe" (Asante 1990: 2, italics in original). Senghor's emphasis on the "African personality" focuses attention on the values and psychological make-up of individ-ual Blacks and encourages efforts to analyze how centered, conscious, African, or Black an individual actually is.

Senghor also suggests another meaning of negritude that has influ-enced another component of the shared system of values that distin-guishes believers in Afrocentrism as a civil religion from nonmembers. Here Senghor defines negritude as "*the sum of the cultural values of the world*" (Senghor 1995: 46, italics in original). Whereas Asante proposes elements of Black values that form the cultural center of Blackness, Maulana Karenga's creation and dissemination of a Black value system has dwarfed all other efforts. The seven principles of Karenga's Nguzo Saba or "Black value system" provide organizing principles for Afrocen-trism as a civil religion.[4] In describing why he created the Nguzo Saba, Karenga notes that the Nguzo Saba is designed to "organize and enrich our [African American] relations with each other on the personal and community level . . . establish standards, commitments and priorities that would tend to enhance our human possibilities as persons and a people . . . and serve as a contribution to a core system of communitarian ethical values for the moral guidance and instruction of the community, especially for children' (Karenga 1995: 276). These functions routinely are carried out by organized religions and simultaneously articulate with notions of Black solidarity advanced within Black Nationalism.

Afrocentrism as civil religion draws from a second feature of orga-nized religions, namely, the importance of articles of faith needed to guide the behavior of the true believers. The tenets and beliefs of formal religions are typically preserved in some sort of authoritative scripture, for example, bibles, griots, and other sources of legitimated knowledge. Afrocentrism's tenets seem designed to function as articles of faith. In particular, the significance of evaluating all thoughts, deeds, and actions in terms of the perceived interests not of God, but of Black people, sug-gests that centering on Blackness serves as the main vehicle for achieving this state of grace (a respite from white racism). This use of Afrocen-tricity not only bears striking resemblance to articles of faith that claim that God be considered in every waking action and thought, it dovetails with a preexisting orientation within African American religious culture whereby spirituality and religiosity infuse African American civil society (Paris 1995; Patillo-McCoy 1998).

As a civil religion, certain elements of nonacademic Afrocentrism are taken as articles of faith – they are not to be questioned. In this context, just as formal scriptures provide interpretive frameworks for formal religions, Karenga's Nguzo Saba can be deployed as articles of faith that are part of a larger authoritative scripture. But if the Nguzo Saba operates as central articles of *faith*, how can it be analyzed or worse yet criticized? Who dares argue against creativity, or purpose, or unity? In this faith-based context, what *is* available for interpretation is the question of *how* these articles of faith are being implemented. For example, while the principle of cooperative economics (*Ujamaa*) is endorsed, as was the case during the Black Power era, widely different strategies can constitute cooperative economic effort. These debates within the rubric of the Nguzo Saba are certainly theoretically possible, but are not common among Afrocentrist thinkers. Rather, just as within formal religions a distinction can be made between articles of faith and religious doctrine, using Afrocentrism as a civil religion can foster an unfortunate slippage between these two uses. Articles of faith are meant to be the principles that pull people together. In contrast, religious doctrines constitute rules to follow that separate the true believers from all others. On the one hand, efforts to hammer out articles of faith in historically specific social contexts, for example, the ways in which African Americans might generate new ways of practicing cooperative economics in the context of the "new" racism, may breath fresh life into seemingly threadbare African American political agendas. On the other hand, as many Black intellectuals quite rightly point out, deploying Afrocentrism as a religious doctrine where some are more authentically Black than others serves to fragment African Americans (Dyson 1993; Lubiano 1997).

Third, just as organized religions typically provide explanations for suffering, death, and other mysteries of life, Afrocentrism as a civil religion strives to account for the origins and purpose of Black suffering and death under racial oppression. Because organized religions must provide some sort of shared history for their members, narratives explaining the origins of the religion as well as its core principles typically are well known by members of the congregation. For African Americans grappling with the aftermath of the slave experience, this need to establish a point of origin takes on special meaning. The origins of Black suffering are clear – the slave trade constituted the original sin that disrupted what is depicted as harmonious African societies and introduced 400 years of Black suffering. Afrocentric origin myths identify Africa as the "motherland" or homeland of all people of African descent. Children of the African diaspora have a homeland that they must revere, reclaim, and protect. By seeing their connections with Africa and defining as African people, the lost children of Africa who were enslaved in America can reclaim a Black consciousness and once again become centered in a true African personality.

This attention to explaining Black suffering often accompanies a corresponding emphasis on Black redemption via adhering to articles of Afrocentric faith. Within models that place blame for all Black suffering at the feet of White supremacy, the suffering of African American individuals occurs because they remain mesmerized by White culture. If Whites and the culture they create are in fact "evil," then salvation occurs via rejecting anything labeled "white." Instead, individuals recentering on Blackness will reverse this lack of consciousness concerning their own importance. "One becomes Afrocentric by exploring the connections, visiting the quiet places, and remaining connected," counsels Molefi Asante (Asante 1993: 143). By destroying both an authentic African-centered identity and an affirming African-centered culture, institutionalized racism fostered a "psychology of oppression" among African Americans (Baldwin 1980). Within this worldview, Black people suffer when they deviate from their true sense of Blackness and become overly influenced by White supremacist institutions. As a step toward recovering their identity and subjectivity, Black people needed to undergo a conversion experience from "Negro" to "Black" (Cross 1971). "Negroes" mesmerized by Whiteness could be distinguished from authentic Black people prepared to participate in liberation struggles by completing a conversion experience. Completing a four-stage transformation – moving through stages of preencounter, encounter with Whites, immersion in Black culture, and internalization of a new Black identity – constituted the path toward a new Black identity. Just as members of many organized religions view themselves as the chosen ones because they are true believers, individuals who follow this particular strand of Afrocentrism may see themselves as being more consciously, authentically, and correctly "Black" than others. Moreover, the certainty that accompanies Afrocentrism as a source of faith and the inherent goodness attributed to Black people within this system of thought can be a valuable collective weapon in confronting the daily assaults of White supremacist institutions and thus can relieve suffering.

A fourth feature of organized religions concerns the need to maintain organizational practices and structures for religious activities. Holding regularly scheduled services in agreed-upon places of worship allows communities of faith to reenact their stories, teachings, and rituals. These repetitive practices are designed to build solidarity among the community of true believers across space and time. In this effort to develop lasting organizational structures for Afrocentrism as a civil religion, being located either inside or outside the academy makes all the difference. Just as organized religions have institutional locations where the faith is ritualized, celebrated, and reproduced, Afrocentrism as a civil religion aspired for similar organizational stability. In the 1980s, Black Studies programs and departments created institutional bases within seemingly hostile White institutions. From these sites, they aimed to install Afrocentrism as the social theory guiding Black Studies scholarship and teaching (Collins 1998: 90–91, 155–57). Regardless of their intellectual products, the very existence of Black Studies initiatives garnered animosity. This very hostility could be used as evidence of the rightness of Black Studies and of the martyrdom of its practitioners/disciples. It should come as no surprise that Molefi Asante and Maulana Ron Karenga chaired two prominent Black Studies programs known for Afrocentrism, namely, those at Temple University in Philadelphia, and at California State University at Long Beach, respectively.

Herein lies the problem – because Black Studies units reside in secular higher education and thus rely on public tax dollars and private fundraising by their institutions to fund their programs, they must be responsive to issues that their host institutions decide are important. Because the seeming separation of church and state leaves religion with no place in the academy except as a subject of study, Afrocentrism has great difficulty functioning in this context precisely because it has organized itself as a civil religion, both in content and in practice. This social positioning accounts for academic Afrocentrism's peculiar hybrid identity. On the one hand, positioning Afrocentrism as a civil religion within US colleges and universities exposed it to the epistemological criteria of science that are valued within the academy. The very standards of judgment within the academy eschew faith-based approaches to understanding the world and instead value scientific epistemologies as the currency of acceptability (Collins 1998: 97–105). All knowledge, including Afrocentric scholarship that is infused with the sensibilities of a civil religion, typically garners censure. On the other hand, the antidote to this censure, namely, trying to attract academic credibility for Afrocentrism as a legitimate field of inquiry by establishing itself as a science of Blackness, was equally doomed. Within academia, a visible and virulent backlash against Afrocentrism in the 1990s challenged the flawed knowledge-claims of Afrocentrism (Lefkowitz 1996). Once it became safe to castigate Molefi Asante as spokesperson for a narrow version of Afrocentrism, its credibility within the academy, one that had never been high, virtually disappeared.

One important criticism of academic Afrocentrism that fostered its demise as a social theory concerned its exclusionary practices, in particular, its creation of narrow, essentialist definitions of Blackness. Because rituals determine the very categories of belonging, some versions of academic Afrocentrism degenerated into policing the evershrinking boundaries of authentic Blackness (Lubiano 1997). Being of African descent makes every African American a potential convert to Afrocentrism, yet being racially categorized as "black" is not enough. One is both *born* Black and *becomes* Black. Afrocentrism installed rituals to identify the authentically "black" from their less conscious counterparts. Just as Christians undergo baptism to demonstrate their membership of their faith-based community, Afrocentric true believers were expected to undergo similar conversion rituals (Cross 1971). For example, changing one's name from a slave name to an African one, changing one's style of dress to that deemed more closely aligned with traditional African styles, and wearing one's hair in braids, cornrows, dreadlocks or some other "natural" style all operated as elements of an individual's conversion experience. All of these indicators were used as ways of signaling to the larger community that the individual had undergone the conversion experience from one kind of Blackness to another. The problem with both the narrow definitions of Blackness and with the conversion experience needed to accomplish it is that some segments of the African American community could *never* become "black enough." Within exclusionary versions of Afrocentrism, women, gays, lesbians, and other sexual minorities, and biracial and multiracial individuals were expected to "prove" their right to belong and their rights of entitlement to the unconditional love for Black people. Increasing numbers of people of African descent, especially those in the hip hop generation, simply refused to do it. Claiming Black Nationalism, African American youth took it in a different direction within Black cultural production (Lusane 1993; Zook 1992). In essence, sexism and homophobia within academic Afrocentrism compromised its own claims for a comprehensive love ethic and fostered its demise (Collins 1998: 174–79).

Afrocentrism's organization as a civil religion outside the academy followed a different and more complex path. Currently, a more diffuse Afrocentric sensibility characterizes African American culture where the meaning of Blackness is increasingly the subject of debate. Interestingly, the holidays, social events, and other practices initially developed by Asante and Karenga within higher education migrated outside the academy and began to fulfill some of the functions of Afrocentrism as a civil religion for church, community groups, and some urban public school systems. For example, within African American popular culture, rites of passage programs provide an important example of how the rituals of Afrocentrism as a civil religion have been crafted for nonacademic settings. Such programs aim to give African American youth new identities through a conversion experience of putting them in touch with their true selves and marking their passage to adulthood. Whereas rites of passage programs are small scale, the ritual of Kwanzaa has moved beyond the academy and African American communities and is part of American popular culture. Organized around the seven principles of the Nguzo Saba and occurring over a seven-day period between Christmas and New Year, Kwanzaa celebrations range from family gatherings to church-based and other large community events. The success of this holiday is evident in the industry that it has spawned – commercial greeting cards and other Kwanzaa paraphernalia can be found in local stores. Kwanzaa remains viable in part because it articulates with capitalist marketplace relations. African American consumers have long been targeted with niche advertising for alcohol projects and gym shoes. Adding Afrocentric greeting cards and other paraphernalia associated with African American ethnic rituals constitutes a logical extension of these practices.

Other rituals inspired by Afrocentrism have taken on a more democratic, inclusive aura. For example, the annual Black family reunions organized by the National Council of Negro Women (NCNW) that are attended by thousands of people represent the most visible expression of this organizational "Afrocentric" enterprise. Many extended African American families use these larger events to organize their own family-specific gatherings. Concerned about the erosion of extended family life, NCNW conceived of the annual reunions as a way to foster family solidarity and thus community and "national" solidarity. On the one hand, these gatherings do articulate with the family values and faith-based ideology of American national identity and thus also dovetail with American Civil Religion. At the same time, whereas people of African descent constitute the bulk of reunion attendees, the actual families who attend include members from many racial and ethnic groups. This is not an exclusionary, patriarchal racial identification advanced under some narrow versions of Afrocentrism. Instead, the Black family reunions more closely resemble rituals that are designed to reinforce the core Afrocentric principle of an unconditional love of Black people by recruiting diverse people to that task.

African American ethnicity and the "new" racism

The troubled history of Afrocentrism in the academy does not erase the significance of its approach to ethnic identification. Linking Black Nationalist ideas to a preexisting spirituality has influenced the sacred and secular contours of contemporary African American civil society. Rites of passage programs, Kwanzaa celebrations, and Black family reunions constitute tangible actions that African Americans now take to address suffering associated with the "new" racism. If Cornel West is right about the dangers of nihilism for African Americans, then cultural responses such as those of Afrocentrism that place a love ethic at the heart of Black political mobilization become vitally important. Beyond the specific case of Afrocentrism, Black Nationalist inspired efforts to construct African American ethnicity raise one crucial question: can this or other strategies of ethnic identification deliver the same economic and political benefits for African Americans grappling with the "new" racism as ethnic mobilization strategies of the past did for Irish, Italians, Jews, and other ethnic groups?

On the one hand, the increasingly segregated racial landscape obscured by a "color-blind" ideology eschews group-based politics of all sorts. Groups should not make claims on the state, that right is reserved for individuals. Thus, the "color-blind" ideology speaks to equal treatment of *individuals* by the state and before the law as the penultimate expression of the nation-state. The attacks on affirmative action and other group-based remedies for past racial practices flow directly from this belief that any group-based discrimination can violate individual rights and thus is unsatisfactory. This ideology enables group-based politics to be redefined as "special interests," and thus violating the fundamental tenets of American Civil Religion that protect individual freedom, especially from the incursions of the state. Faith-based remedies take on added importance within this context, because they aim to minister not to the group but to individuals.

On the other hand, group-based politics remain an important reality within all aspects of American society. Despite expressed commitments to American individualism, the arrival of new immigrant groups of color has revived longstanding understandings of ethnic mobilization as a route to political power within the US nation-state. Racial/ethnic immigrant groups are advised to prove their worthiness for Americanization by not making demands on the nation-state. Selected Asian groups are depicted as "model minorities" not just because they engage in family businesses and encourage their children to study hard in school – these groups make limited demands on state services. In contrast, other groups who are deemed to be less worthy are derogated. For example, Mexican American immigrant women are stigmatized as getting unearned entitlements from the nation-state, primarily because their American-born children consume educational and social services to which they are entitled as American citizens. The message seems clear – groups are fine, just as long as they make few demands on the state and do not organize around Blackness.

This political context of a painfully slow case-by-case remedy of individual claims where the nation-state has virtually turned its back on reforms to address contemporary group-based racial disparities such as residential racial segregation with appropriate group-based remedies leaves African Americans adrift. Traditional civil rights groups have produced few tangible victories in confronting this nonresponsive nation-state. Their efforts quite rightly have been consumed with trying to defend the civil rights gains that ushered in the period of the "new" racism. In this situation, the persistence of Black Nationalist initiatives cannot be explained away simply as a wrong-headed ideology foisted upon falsely conscious African American masses. Despite African American rejection of the politics advanced by both the Nation of Islam and a conservative Afrocentrism, the fact that so many African Americans are familiar with and/or respect these versions of Black Nationalism speaks more to the vacuum in African American politics and intellectual thought than to the strength of the programs offered by either version of Black Nationalism. As Robinson observes, "despite its strange cosmology, the NOI stands as the sole national Black political organization that has a strategy explicitly aimed at improving the lot of the most disadvantaged" (Robinson 2001: 119). As long as this remains the case, Black Nationalism is unlikely to disappear anytime soon.

NOTES

1. I rely on sociologist Eduardo Bonilla-Silva's (1996) distinction between race and ethnicity as different bases for group association. Unlike ethnicity, racialized social systems contain power hierarchies that distinguish between superiors and subordinates. I use the term "racial/ethnic" groups to reference the interaction between racial/ethnic group assignment by the nation-state and racial/ethnic identification as constructed by individuals and groups within it. Using a similar language of "ethnoracial assignment" and "ethnoracial identity," Karen Brodkin points out the conceptual distinction between the two. Tracing the history of US census classifications of citizens into racial categories and into categories of native-born versus immigrant, Brodkin examines the changing categories of racial/ethnic assignment within US society. In contrast to this classification process, individuals and groups construct racial/ethnic identities, but do so within the context of their racial/ethnic assignments (Brodkin 2000). I capitalize the terms "Black" and "White" because both refer to specific racial/ethnic groups in American society. African Americans use the terms "African American" and "Black" interchangeably to self-describe this racial/ethnic identification. If national identities such as "French," "Italian," or "British" can be substituted for "Black," then I capitalize the term. Capitalizing "White" is more troublesome, precisely because Whites reject an ethnic identification as "Whites."

2. Via a set of cultural ideas, symbols, and practices, American Civil Religion encourages members of American society to worship the "American way of life." Two of the sacred texts of American Civil Religion, the Declaration of Independence and the Constitution, are in conflict. The Declaration

encompasses the ideas of a republican form of government with clear attention to a Deity, whereas the Constitution represents the liberal democratic state of the Enlightenment (Bellah 1992). Within American Civil Religion, the "Founding Fathers" can be seen as demigods, American presidents serve as high priests, and citizens who die in the service of democracy (warfare) become the martyrs.

3. In this section, I distinguish between the narrow concept of Afrocentrism advanced by selected academics within US higher education (Asante 1990), and a broader definition of Afrocentrism that speaks to the use of actual or imagined African-influenced customs among African Americans. It is important to note that African Americans may deploy the ideas of Black consciousness or Afrocentrism without using this terminology to describe their beliefs and/or activities.

4. The seven principles of the Nguzo Saba seem designed to provide guidance for African American behavior in everyday lived experience. They are *Umoja* or unity; *Kujichagulia* or self-determination; *Ujima* or collective work and responsibility; *Ujamaa* or cooperative economics; *Nia* or purpose; *Kuumba* or creativity; and *Imani* or faith (Karenga 1995). In the same way that formal religions identify articles of faith used to guide their everyday behavior, the Nguzo Saba fulfills a similar function. Together, the seven principles outline a way of life for true believers and specify a framework within which African Americans can express Black solidarity via Black consciousness.

REFERENCES

Asante, Molefi K. (1990) *Kemet, Afrocentricity and Knowledge*. Philadelphia: Temple University Press.

(1993) "Racism, consciousness, and Afrocentricity." In Gerald Early (ed.), *Lure and Loathing: Essays on Race, Identity, and the Ambivalence of Assimilation*. New York: Penguin Books, pp. 127–43.

Baldwin, Joseph (1980) "The psychology of oppression." In Molefi K. Asante (ed.), *Contemporary Black Thought: Alternative Analyses in Social and Behavioral Sciences*. Beverly Hills, CA: Sage Publications, pp. 95–110.

Bellah, Robert N. (1992) *The Broken Covenant: American Civil Religion in a Time of Trial*. Chicago: University of Chicago.

Berry, Mary F. (1994) *Black Resistance, White Law: A History of Constitutional Racism in America*. New York: Penguin.

Bonilla-Silva, Eduardo (1996) "Rethinking racism: toward a structural interpretation." *American Sociological Review* 62 (June): 465–80.

Brodkin, Karen (2000) *How Jews Became White Folks & What that Says about Race in America*. New Brunswick, NJ: Rutgers University Press.

Collins, Patricia H. (1998) *Fighting Words: Black Women and the Search for Justice*. Minneapolis: University of Minnesota.

(2001) "Like one of the family: race, ethnicity, and the paradox of US national identity." *Ethnic and Racial Studies* 24 (1): 3–28.

Cone, James H. (1972) *The Spirituals and the Blues: An Interpretation*. New York: Seabury Press.

Crenshaw, Kimberle W. (1997) "Color blindness, history, and the law." In Wahneema Lubiano (ed.), *The House That Race Built*. New York: Pantheon, pp. 280–88.

Cross, William (1971) "The Negro to Black conversion experience: toward a psychology of Black Liberation." *Black World* 20 (9): 13–27.

Dawson, Michael C. (1994) *Behind the Mule: Race and Class in African-American Politics*. Princeton: Princeton University Press.

Dyson, Michael R. (1993) *Reflecting Black: African-American Cultural Criticism*. Minneapolis: University of Minnesota Press.

Hood, Robert E. (1994) *Begrimed and Black: Christian Traditions on Blacks and Blackness*. Minneapolis: Fortress Press.

Karenga, Maulana R. (1995) "The Nguzo Saga (The Seven Principles): their meaning and message." In William L. Van Deburg (ed.), *Modern Black Nationalism: From Marcus Garvey to Louis Farrakhan*. New York: New York University Press, pp. 276–87.

Lee, Martha F. (1996) *The Nation of Islam: An American Millenarian Movement*. Syracuse: Syracuse University Press.

Lefkowitz, Mary (1996) *Not Out of Africa: How Afrocentrism Became an Excuse to Teach Myth as History*. New York: Basic Books.

Lincoln, C. Eric (1999) *Race, Religion, and the Continuing American Dilemma*. New York: Hill and Wang.

Lubiano, Wahneema (1997) "Black Nationalism and Black common sense: policing ourselves." In Wahneema Lubiano (ed.), *The House That Race Built: Black Americans, US Terrain*. New York: Pantheon, pp. 232–352.

Lusane, Clarence (1993) "Rap, race and politics." *Race and Class* 35 (1): 41–55.

Massey, Douglas S. and Nancy A. Denton (1993) *American Apartheid: Segregation and the Making of the Underclass*. Cambridge, MA: Harvard University Press.

Miller, Jerome G. (1996) *Search and Destroy: African-American Males in the Criminal Justice System*. New York: Cambridge University Press.

Moses, Wilson J. (1978) *The Golden Age of Black Nationalism, 1850–1925*. New York: Oxford.

Orfield, Gary and Carole Ashkinaze (1991) *The Closing Door: Conservative Policy and Black Opportunity*. Chicago: University of Chicago.

Paris, Peter J. (1995) *The Spirituality of African Peoples: The Search for a Common Moral Discourse*. Minneapolis: Fortress Press.

Patillo-McCoy, Mary (1998) "Church culture as a strategy of action in the Black community." *American Sociological Review* 63 (Dec.): 767–84.

Pinkney, Alphonso (1976) *Red, Black, and Green: Black Nationalism in the United States*. London: Cambridge University Press.

Richards, Dona (1990) "The implications of African-American spirituality." In Molefi K. Asante and K. W. A. Asante (eds.), *African Culture: The Rhythms of Unity*. Trenton, NJ: Africa World Press, pp. 207–31.

Robinson, Dean E. (2001) *Black Nationalism in American Politics and Thought*. New York: Oxford University Press.

Senghor, Leopold (1995) "Negritude: a humanism of the twentieth century." In Fred L. Hord and J. S. Lee (eds.), *I Am Because We Are: Readings in Black Philosophy*. Amherst: University of Massachusetts Press, pp. 45–54.

Sobel, Mechal (1979) *Trabelin' On: The Slave Journey to an Afro-Baptist Faith.* Princeton: Princeton University Press.

Tuan, Mia (1998) *Forever Foreigners or Honorary Whites? The Asian Ethnic Experience Today.* New Brunswick, NJ: Rutgers University Press.

Van DeBurg, William L. (1997) *Modern Black Nationalism: From Marcus Garvey to Louis Farrakhan.* New York: New York University Press.

West, Cornel (1993) *Race Matters.* Boston: Beacon Press.

Zook, Kristal B. (1992) "Reconstructions of nationalist thought in Black music and culture." In Reebee Garofalo (ed.), *Rockin' the Boat: Mass Music and Mass Movements.* Boston: South End Press, pp. 255–66.

Part II

The state and minority claims

6 New nationalisms and collective rights: the case of South Asia

T. K. Oommen

Two historical moments, and conceptualizations anchored to them, gave birth to much of the current confusion around the issue of nationalism and collective rights. The Treaty of Westphalia, concluded in 1648, initiated the notion of the nation-state which ineluctably linked nation and state. But the state is inherently uncomfortable with the idea of cultural diversity and it is prone to count and label citizens; the lesser the number of social categories the more comfortable the state is. In order to be comprehended by the state the sociocultural world had to be standardized and simplified; the idea of "uniform, homogeneous citizenship" had to be created (Scott 1998: 32). Consequently, the single most important project of nation-state was, and continues to be, homogenization.

In this respect, the state's tendency to homogenize minorities is particularly evident. Native Americans, an aggregation of over 250 First Nations, and "Asian Americans," a wide variety of peoples drawn from the two civilizations of China and India present in the United States of America, are but two examples. Similarly, the Scheduled Tribes is a common label for over 400 First Nations of India, and Scheduled Castes is an aggregation of numerous caste groups drawn from over a dozen "nations" of India. In contrast, the distinctiveness of the collectivity is not eroded in the case of dominant groups, as exemplified in the case of White Anglo-Saxon Protestants or Brahmins. Thus viewed, project homogenization was mainly an effort to liquidate the identity of minority groups so that their claim for collective rights can be put in jeopardy and delegitimized.

Nation, in contrast to state, is basically diversifying; it is incessantly in search of roots. Roots, to be meaningful, will have to be specific and to be specified. This tendency to differentiate "our community" from the rest is the sustaining élan of nation. This is utterly against the homogenizing orientation of the state. Therefore, the yoking together of nation and state was and continues to be tension-generating as they pull in two different directions. Yet for 300 years after the Treaty of Westphalia the trends and tides favored the state against nation. Many nations were

121

liquidated and assimilated, several others accepted a subordinate position within a federal framework and a few others persisted and fought for their identity. The coterminality between state and nation is absent even in Europe. That is why Smith (1983 [1971]) reported that there were seventy-three nations but only twenty-four states in Europe when he was writing and Nielsson identified twenty-eight states fourteen years later but the "nation-groups" were many more (Nielsson 1985: 27–56). With the break up of several multinational socialist states in East Europe in 1989 the number of states increased still further, although of course the number of nations remained constant.

The second historical moment that I am referring to occurred nearly one and a half centuries after the Treaty of Westphalia was concluded. The Enlightenment project celebrated its triumph of inventing the universal man (man-as-such) over "particular human beings set in specific traditions, each with its own integrity" (Sacks 1997: 100). The French National Assembly in its Declaration of Rights in 1789 asserted: "All men are born, and remain, free and equal in rights." Against the background of anti-Jewish riots that had broken out in Alsace, the Count of Claremont-Tonnerre said in December of that year : "The Jews should be denied everything as a nation, but granted everything as individuals. . . . Every one of them must individually become a citizen; if they do not want this, they must inform us and we shall then be compelled to expel them" (quoted in Sacks 1997: 98–99). Why should the Jews be denied their nationhood in France? Not simply because they are immigrants but also because: "They had allegiances to one another as well as to the state . . ." (Sacks 1997: 101). Jews were good citizens and were appreciated for their patriotism but they were not entirely trustworthy because "they had allegiances to one another"; their loyalty to France was not terminal. If the Jews were recognized as a minority, a group or a nation, logically it follows that the possibility of their demanding collective rights was perennially present. The Enlightenment project overemphasized the universality of human beings and completely ignored the specificities of human groups.

If one were to follow the spirit of the Enlightenment project to its logical end humanity would become an aggregate of atomized individuals floating around without any anchorage. But the fact is that individuals are at once citizens, consumers, and communitarians. Which is to say that they are simultaneously attached to state, market, and civil society. They have multiple identities and multiple loyalties. The fact that most polities remain multinational and/or multicultural attests to the need to recognize the possibility of several horizontal loyalties coexisting, not necessarily always competing fiercely. It is time to recognize that there is no hierarchy of loyalties but only contexts of identity. This is an important rationale behind examining the linkage between nationalism and collective rights.

With the above considerations in mind, the discussion in this chapter is organized into three parts. Part 1 provides the required historical background and conceptual clarifications. Part 2 describes the specificity of the South Asian situation, and Part 3 brings together the salient points as concluding remarks.

Part 1

It is necessary to make three conceptual clarifications to start with. First, the difference between multinational and multicultural situations. Four multinational and two multicultural polities evolved gradually and yet most writers do not clearly identify them. The multinational situations that I am referring to are: premodern empires, colonial plural societies, postcolonial polities, and socialist states. The multicultural situations comprise the New World settlements and contemporary multicultural polities. In the case of multinational polities, peoples with distinct homelands and cultures, particularly language and religion, coexist in one polity. In contrast, multicultural polities are products of the deterritorialization of national groups who migrated to new homelands. However, the social texture of each of the six situations referred to above was varied, the discussion of which follows.

Premodern empires were formed through conquests or dynastic marriages and/or inheritance. There was no collective self-determination or democratic process in their formation; they had no citizens but only subjects. However, considerable religious, linguistic, and legal diversity were permitted among the subjects. While the imperial powers did not indulge in cultural homogenization, they insisted on submission of the subjects to the authority of the supreme power. Some, like the Ottoman Empire, had even conceded political representation to cultural communities through the millet system (Lijphart 1980). This is neither to deny the existence of monarchies with considerable cultural uniformity, such as those of Japan and Korea, nor to ignore attempts made by emperors like Akbar for creative fusion of cultures. The point to be noted here is that "multinational" empires did exist during premodern times. But these were nations without national consciousness.

The colonial situation gave birth to "plural societies" wherein different segments, usually of racial collectivities, one national (the colonized) and the other ethnic (that of the colonizer), coexisted uneasily. As Furnivall describes:

Each group holds its own religion, its own culture, its own ideas and ways. As individuals they meet but only in the market place, in buying and selling . . . There is a plural society, with different sections of the community living side by side, but separately within the same political unit. Even in the economic sphere there is a division of labor on racial lines. (1948: 304)

Later writers (e.g. Smith 1965; Van den Berghe 1983: 238–52) refined the notion of plural societies and extended it to postcolonial empirical contexts. But all of them conceded that plural societies were multinational and multicultural. This is the second multinational situation that I am referring to.

The postcolonial states emerged when the colonizers retreated. In most of these states the political and cultural boundaries did not coincide, as exemplified by the South Asian and African states. Often the same nation was vivisected between two or more states. However, these new states accepted the crucial political, economic, and sociocultural institutions and values of colonizers, leading to the coexistence of alien and native cultural elements. Finally, the multinational socialist states were consciously constructed political entities wherein the distinction between citizenship and nationality was clearly recognized, as in the cases of the former Soviet Union, Yugoslavia, and Czechoslovakia. But great nation chauvinism had led to their breakup into unicultural nations by the 1980s, although most of them do contain nonnational elements constituted by migrants from erstwhile dominant nations.

The above four multinational situations were/are qualitatively different from the two multicultural settlements in that, while the former were predominantly populated by nationals, the latter drew their population mainly from territorially dislocated people, the ethnies (cf. Smith 1998). The "New World" produced the first multicultural situation. There were three main raciocultural streams in those settlements. First, those of European descent, the voluntary migrants who established their hegemony in their new homeland. Second, those of African extraction who were imported as slaves. Third, the marginalized "natives" who have been largely dislocated from their ancestral habitats. That is, if multinational polities are predominantly populated by nationals, multicultural settlements are mainly populated by ethnies (see Oommen 1997, 2002).

The contemporary multicultural polities are products of a cultural dynamic which is neither prenational as in empires, proethnic as in the New World settlements, nor a mixture of national and ethnic groups, as in postcolonial and socialist states. It is a post-nation-state situation in that both citizens and noncitizens drawn from a multiplicity of cultural backgrounds coexist in these polities. Contemporary multiculturality recognizes the fact that cultural homogenization launched by the project of the nation-state has failed and that cultural hegemonization is not plausible any more.

If multiculturality was merely a social fact in the New World settlements in the beginning, it is also a favored social value in contemporary multicultural polities. It incorporates the emerging new voices of African Americans, British Asians, Australian Aboriginal Peoples, and the like, in addition to the voices of women, homosexuals and the physically challenged. It is reinforced by the new waves of interstate and intercontinental immigration. It recognizes the social fact that in a globalizing world not only capital but labor too migrate, which renders even Western Europe, traditionally a continent of out-migration and homogeneous nation-states, a continent of net immigration and a conglomerate of culturally heterogeneous polities. Thus the cradle of nation-states now has not only nationals but a substantial number of ethnies in them, a significant proportion of the latter being citizens too. This is the context in which the notion of multicultural citizenship assumes authenticity, although its initial formulation was based on the Canadian experience (see Kymlicka 1995).

If multiculturalism is understood as a value orientation which promotes the coexistence and preservation of a multiplicity of cultural communities within the territory of a state, the issue of national self-determination is not germane to multicultural polities (cf. Murphy 2001). At any rate, linking multiculturalism with national self-determination arises out of the confusion wrought by two conflations: (a) between state and nation (see Connor 1994; Fenton and May 2002) and (b) between nation and ethnie (see Oommen 1997, 2002), both of which are unsustainable. Territory is a shared feature between state and nation but its meanings for them vary vastly; for the nation, territory is a moral entity, for the state, it is a legal entity (cf. Brubaker 1996; Smith 1998; May 2001). Similarly, culture is a shared feature between nation and ethnie, but while territory and culture in unison create nation, dissociation between the two leads to the formation of ethnie (cf. Smith 1998; Eriksen 1993; Fenton 1999). To put it pithily, ethnies are cultural groups living outside their ancestral homelands, usually in multicultural societies, interspersed with other cultural groups. However, if they are exclusive or major occupants of the territory to which they migrate, they may gradually become nations through the process of national self-determination. That is, just as national groups can be subjected to a process of ethnification, ethnies can be transformed into nations. This processual dynamic needs to be clearly recognized (for an elaboration, see Oommen 1997). This brings me to the second conceptual clarification which needs to be attempted.

Tilly's (1993) distinction between state-seeking and state-led nationalisms covers most cases in Europe but leaves out some. Neither Scotland nor Wales, which were "joined" to England, fits into these categorizations. Catalonians, although they insisted upon a certain level of economic, political, and cultural autonomy, did happily form part of the Spanish state (Pi-Sunyer 1985: 254–76). Most nations in the Indian subcontinent did not insist on a separate sovereign state of their own. Which is to say that one can also legitimately speak of state-renouncing nationalisms; these nations only insist on maintaining their cultural identity within a federal polity. Such a situation gives birth to the necessity of accepting certain collective national rights because citizenship rights or even human rights anchored to individuals will not help sustain their collective identity. While individuals of these nations insist on citizenship rights and the equality they enjoy in the federal polity, they are not willing to assimilate into the state-contrived cultural mainstream. The bartering of collective identity for individual equality, the motif of the nation-state, is not acceptable to them, hence the need to examine the linkage between nationalism and collective rights.

The state-seeking nationalism of Western Europe was based on the principle of national self-determination and yet there are more nations than states there. Therefore, there are several empirical situations that call for the recognition of collective rights, even in Western Europe. The first arises out of the fact that the principle of self-determination was denied to some of the "nations". Leading examples are the Basques, the Irish, the people of Brittany, Occitanians and others. Second, there are "nation-states" in which two or more "nations" and/or collectivities are equally important, as exemplified in the cases of Belgium and Holland. In such cases, political pluralism, which implies the recognition of the collective rights of the constituent groups, is designated as consociational democracy (see Lijphart 1980). Third, there are deterritorialized groups or ethnies (see Oommen 1997) which came to inhabit European countries. Both Jews and Roma belong to this category. Although such communities are often willing to adopt the country of their residence as their homeland they are not accepted as conationals and hence remain as ethnies. Fourth, there are immigrants, refugees and exiles who are dislocated for totally different reasons. While the first usually come as guest workers, the second flee their homeland to escape political and/or religious persecution, and the third are expelled for political treason. But these groups end up as residents, if not citizens, at their point of destination and their collective rights are often at risk.

The state-led nationalism of Eastern Europe abandoned in principle the maxim of one nation one state, although state–nation congruence largely did exist in some cases. Examples were/are Albania, German Democratic Republic, Hungary, and Poland. However, in three cases – Czechoslovakia, USSR, and Yugoslavia – there was substantial cultural heterogeneity. In all these cases, Great Nation Chauvinism led to their breakdown and resulted in the formation of relatively homogeneous "nation-states" of West European vintage. However, even now in all the East European states, national minorities, ethnies as well as immigrants and refugees exist whose collective rights need to be recognized.

Anti-colonial "nationalism" was also state-seeking. However, viewed in terms of collective rights, the Old World anticolonial nationalism of Africa and Asia and the New World anticolonial nationalism of the Americas, Australia, and New Zealand varied drastically. The principle of national self-determination was not found to be admissible to the colonial masters, albeit for different reasons, in Africa and Asia. The African "primitives" were deemed to be peoples without history and hence were not nations according to the colonizers. The principle of self-determination is mean-ingless in their cases "because the people cannot decide until somebody decides who are the people," to recall the pregnant statement of Ivor Jennings (1956: 56). The African paradox is aptly articulated by King Mutesa II of Baganda, who wrote:

I have never been able to pin down precisely the difference between a tribe and a nation and [to] see why one is thought to be despicable and the other is so admired . . . the Baganda have a common language, tradition, history and cast of mind . . . Does this justify our being totally dominated by our neighbours, unnaturally yoked to us as they were by Britain? (1967: 78–79)

Most of the modern African states are the products of such unnatural yoking, which reduced and mutilated nation-groups into minorities and even deterritorialized ethnies (cf. Fenton and May 2002). Admittedly, their collective personality cannot be nurtured through individual rights.

It could not be argued that the "Orientals" of Asia were peoples with-out history and hence their supposed incapacity for self-rule had to be located elsewhere. Assuming that democracy is possible only in those societies where individual autonomy exists, the Asians were adjudged to be incapable of self-rule. Further, slavery, the caste system, oppression of women, were all features which obstructed the potentiality of a possible democratic regime. Admittedly, to "civilize" is a prerequisite to "democ-ratize" and hence the need for and justification of colonialism. In this process of "civilizing," the British colonial regime completely ignored the existence of numerous nations in the Indian subcontinent, some of which are much larger than most of the European nations. To complicate mat-ters, the colonizer found it expedient to acknowledge the sociopolitical strength of the "two-nation theory," invoking religion as the sole basis of nation, ignoring history, language, lifestyle, and several other aspects of culture. The artificial vivisection of British India created two states – India and Pakistan – with several nations and parts thereof, as well as ethnies within them. Individual rights in and by themselves are incapable of preserving the integrity of these nations and ethnies.

If the colonizers retreated from the Old World of Asia and Africa, they settled into the New World of the Americas, Australia and New Zealand, treating these, with varying degrees (less so in New Zealand), as empty spaces. There was a cognitive blackout regarding the First Nations of the New World in the mental horizon of the colonizer. Admittedly, the principle of national self-determination was not applied to them. However, once the settlers far exceeded the number of nationals the former's right had to be recognized. But they could not be reckoned as nationals by any stretch of the imagination and, hence, to apply the doctrine of national self-determination to them was a contradiction in terms. The way out of this dilemma was to concede individual-based human rights to settler-Europeans of the New Nations. In this process, the indigenous "First Nations" of the New World have been subjected to a process of ethnification which marginalized and mutilated their collective identity (Oommen 1997; 1989: 279–305). To rehabilitate them, in the deepest sense of the word, one has to treat them as communities and concede them collective rights.

From what I have said so far, it is evident that collective rights in Europe after the Treaty of Westphalia have been endorsed as the right to national self-determination. However, this doctrine has been withheld by Europeans from the rest of the peoples of the world, through a series of rationalizations. But the creation of the United Nations in 1945, in the aftermath of the First World War, dramatically changed the situation; more than 70 percent of the "nation-states" of the world today emerged after that, and barely 10 percent of them are culturally homogeneous. Several processes have contributed to the emergence of multicultural and multiracial states which necessitated the recognition of collective rights within polities.

The first is the deterritorialization of race, religion, and language, which started with geographical explorations and the colonialism that followed it. If during the colonial times the flow was mainly from Europe to the rest of the world, after the Second World War the flow to Europe and the New World from Asia and Africa increased. Even the Africans and Asians who were taken to new destinations as slaves and/or indentured labor became free citizens whose voices started becoming audible. One of the manifestations of this new audibility is the demand for collective/minority rights.

The second process is the tendency to recognize separate spaces for state and nation leading to a delinking of the two. In turn, this led to the bifurcation of citizenship and nationality, patriotism and nationalism, and "instrumental nationalism" attached to the state and "symbolic nationalism" linked to the nation. If instrumental nationalism fends for equality, symbolic nationalism plumbs for identity. In turn, individual-centered citizenship rights and human rights came to be differentiated from national and ethnic rights linked to nations and ethnies.

A third process, which is gradually crystalizing, is the abandoning of the notion of terminal loyalty to the state. With the unbundling of the nation-state, differentiation of the loyalty system too is taking place. Loyalties are no longer vertically ordered with loyalty to the state at the apex. There is a shift from the verticality of loyalties to their horizontality. In turn, this facilitates the latching of qualitatively different layers of loyalty to specific contexts. As the content of loyalty varies, its context also differs. The loyalty of a Catholic or a Muslim on matters religious is not confined to her "nation-state." The loyalty of a French or Chinese speaker in matters cultural is not confined to his state but to his cultural community irrespective of its geographical locus. The "racity" (loyalty to the race) of the Black American transcends the boundaries of the US and reaches Africa on the one hand and Brazil on the other. Only the loyalty of a person, tempered by citizenship, is confined to one's political community – the state. Loyalty is no longer terminal but shared.

Concomitant with the above, a fourth process is in evidence; a shift from a sole emphasis on equality to equality and identity. Project homogenization launched by the nation-state assured equality to minorities of all hues in lieu of shedding their group identity and as a reward for assimilating with the cultural mainstream. And several nation-states of Europe succeeded in the project. While Wales, Scotland, and Ireland underplayed the importance of their cultural identity initially, and took advantage of equality within the United Kingdom and an expanding empire, they had started asserting their identity by the 1950s (see Oommen 1997: 137–40). But in the case of the new multicultural polities of Africa and Asia, there is a shift of emphasis from sequentiality to simultaneity. That is, the nations, ethnies, and minorities in the federal polities of these continents are increasingly insisting on equality and identity simultaneously.

The fifth conceptual clarification that I want to make relates to the controversy between the primordialists and constructionists. The primordialists treat national and ethnic identities as latent phenomena present everywhere, which are invoked by deprived communities at an opportune moment when they experience an erosion of existing privileges, or when they attempt to overcome long-standing denials of privileges. The contextual invocation of identities does not satisfy the constructionists, who insist that these identities and their cultural content are invariably the result of particular historical conjunctures (see, for example, Anderson 1983; Hobsbawm and Ranger 1983). It is suggested that identities such as Yoruba, Zulu, and so on (in the African context) are nineteenth-century European creations (see Comaroff 1991: 666–67). It is also the case that identities such as European and Hindu are creations, the first by the Greeks and the second by the Muslims. The important point here is not who has "created" these identities and when, but why these labels stuck, while others (e.g., barbarians, primitives) did not. I would suggest that it is because they struck a familiar chord, fulfilled an emotional need and provided a shorthand device to communicate certain aspects shared alike by all the people under reference, be it a common homeland, religion, language, or civilization. Thus, some of the constructed identities become acceptable precisely because they contain a primordial element, which is construed as positive by the collectivity concerned. The posited dichotomy between the primordialists and the constructionists is therefore a false one.

We need concepts to make sense of the complex and often confusing empirical reality. But the ways in which nationality and ethnicity are defined have led to contrary results. What we need is a reformulation, and this is to be done *vis-à-vis* another concept, namely, citizenship. Ethnicity, nationality, and citizenship are all identities, but their bases differ. Citizenship is an instrument of equality in democratic states, but ethnicity and nationality are often invoked by states to confer or deny equality and citizenship. This is the rationale behind viewing these concepts in a relational vein.

The terms ethnic and ethnicity are most favored and popular in the USA, as they should be, because they aptly capture and convey the social situation there; the USA is a conglomeration of varieties of people "uprooted" or "dislodged" from different nations. As Yancey *et al.* (1976: 401) correctly observe: "Ethnicity may have relatively little to do with Europe, Asia or Africa, but more to do with the requirements of survival and structure of opportunity in this country," that is, the United States of America. But the equivalent concepts that are suited to describe the overall situation in Europe are nation (and nationality), given the strong attachment people have to their homelands. This is equally true of Asia, although of course these terms are not widely used. And this reluctance should be understood in terms of the prevailing situation in Asian countries. Most Asian states incorporate several nations, and the process of state-formation is not yet complete, nor the states stable, largely because of their multinational composition. Therefore, to assert one's identity in national terms is to spell danger to the state. National identity is often delegitimized to uphold the integrity of the state (Oommen 1990a: 163–82). Further, assertions of identity based on religion, language, region, tribe, and so on are viewed as "communal," "parochial," and even "antinational."

It may also be noted here that the term nation-state is coined out of the limited West European experience. Terms such as "ethnonationalism" have also been in circulation for quite some time (see, for example, Richmond 1987: 3–18; Connor 1994; Fenton and May 2002) to refer to nationalism based on primordial loyalties. Similarly, Worsley writes:

Nationalism is also a form of ethnicity but it is a specific form. It is the institutionalisation of one particular ethnic identity by attaching it to the state. Ethnic groups do not necessarily act together except when they have special interests to secure. When those interests are to obtain a state of its own (or part of a state) the group becomes a nationality. (1984: 247)

This conceptualization, too, suffers from several difficulties. First, it attributes a specificity to ethnic groups which in fact is common to all groups. No group action, whatever may be the basis of constituting it, takes place unless it has a special interest to pursue. Second, it shares with most other conceptualizations the false assumption that the linkage between nation and state is axiomatic. Third, while it recognizes instrumental ethnicity, it denies symbolic ethnicity. It seems to me that it is the combination of instrumental ethnicity emanating out of material deprivation, and symbolic ethnicity based on the anxiety to preserve one's cultural identity, that gives birth to the motive force for state formation. Deprivations emanating out of inequality or denial of identity in isolation will not lead to the crystalization of the demand for a separate state. However, such a demand is plausible only if the ethnic group can constitute itself into a nation, the prerequisites of which are common territory and language.

In order to get rid of the prevailing confusion, we need to conceptualize ethnicity as an interactional, as against an attributional notion. We must view ethnicity as a product of conquest, colonization, and immigration and the consequent disengagement between culture and territory. It is the transformation of the "outs" into the "ins" that leads to the process of ethnies becoming nations.

Part 2

The points made in Part 1 have been essentially five. First, nation-states could not accomplish cultural homogenization in its entirety and hence collective rights are relevant even in them. Second, in the cases of multinational and multicultural states, preservation of collective identities along with individual equality need to be pursued deliberately. Third, national self-determination is irrelevant for multicultural polities as the constituting ethnies are territorially dispersed. In the case of contemporary multinational polities, although self-determination is relevant most of the constituting units do not invoke it; they are state-renouncing nations. Fourth, new nationalisms emerging and crystalizing all over the world, situated as they are in federal polities, simultaneously pursue individual rights and collective identities. Fifth, the posited dichotomy between the primordialists and the constructionists is a false one. With these points in mind let us look at the specificities which obtain in South Asia.

The nationalist expectation that all the elements of the Indian subcontinent would conjointly fight against the British and subsequently work together to create a new and prosperous free India had come to naught by the early decades of the twentieth century. Through the 1916 Lucknow Pact, the British colonial administration accorded equal status to all religions, placing the two principal religious communities – Hindus and Muslims – in acute competition. Recognizing the substantial disparity between Hindus and Muslims in whitecollar employment, the Indian National Congress tried to accommodate Muslims through the 1923 Bengal Pact. The 1932 Communal Award proposed by the British reinforced the growing perception that Hindus and Muslims had two different and irreconcilable identities. The distance from this to the formulation of the "two nation theory" of Mohammed Ali Jinnah, which he first articulated in 1940, was rather short (Jinnah 1960; see also Zavos 2002). The Hindu counterpart of this was enunciated at about the same time (see Golwalker 1939; Savarkar 1949). Thus viewed, the partition of India into two "nations" in 1947 was a logical culmination of a long process. What it is important to note for the present purpose is that this division was in recognition of religious group rights. However, the problem remains basic and fundamental even more than half-a-century after the division of British India. This points not only to the artificiality of the criterion of division but also to the unsustainability of conceding certain collective rights.

The partition of the Indian subcontinent led to one of the biggest population transfers in human history; some 15 million people have been uprooted. While 6 million Muslims left India, 9 million Hindus and Sikhs

factions in both movements are secessionists, others are autonomists – although both insists on collective rights. This is also true of the Punjabi-Sikh movement, although the secessionists are currently reduced in strength as the autonomists have made substantial gains in recent times. Tamil nationalists in Sri Lanka perceive Singhala-Buddhists as a hegemon, but while one faction is secessionist and insists on a sovereign state for Tamils, others opt for different degrees of autonomy within a federal set-up. The three minority nations of Pakistan – Sindh, Baluchistan, and Pashtunistan – view the Punjab as an internal colonizer; in fact they think Pakistan has become "Punjabistan." But the secessionists are particularly vociferous in Sindh. The grand old man of Sindhi nationalism, G. M. Syed, is candid. He maintains:

Sindh has always been there, Pakistan is a passing show. Sindh is a fact, Pakistan is a fiction. Sindhis are a nation, but Muslims are not a nation. Sindhi language is 2000 years old, Urdu is only 250 years old . . . The Sindhis have long been fooled in the name of Islam. (Quoted in Malkani 1984: 134)

However, state-seeking new nationalists of South Asia are ever willing to shed their secessionist orientation. While a minority even abandon their nationalist orientation and become assimilationists, the majority only aspire to be autonomists; they insist only on certain collective rights within a federal polity. This is in utter contrast to the state-seeking nationalism of the colonial times wherein there could not have been any compromise on the nature of the goal pursued – dissociation from the colonial power.

The second variety of state-centered new nationalism is state sponsored; it should properly be called patriotism as it seeks to mobilize the resources of one state against another state – an "enemy" state. Interstate rivalry is the fodder on which this variety of nationalism is fed wherein states are defined and viewed as nations, and nationalism is nurtured through the hatred toward an external and despised "Other." Understandably, chauvinism and jingoism are likely manifestations of this variety of nationalism. If intrastate tension is the feature of state-seeking new nationalism, interstate conflict is the necessary accompaniment of state-sponsored new nationalism. State-led classical nationalism attempted to transform a state-nation into a nation-state; state-sponsored new nationalism takes the nation as axiomatic. However, in so far as the states in conflict are not socioculturally homogeneous, and indeed have populations which share the same characteristics – religion, language, physical features – the conflicts have serious intrastate consequences. This is the situation in South Asia and this is the context in which collective rights become relevant. But in order to render the collective rights of minorities irrelevant, assimilationist nationalism is put on the agenda – Islamic nationalism in Pakistan and Bangladesh, Buddhist nationalism in Sri Lanka, and Hindu nationalism in India are examples of this.

In South Asia, interstate rivalry has been at its apex between India and Pakistan. There have been two wars, and a war-like situation, the recent Kargil conflict. Nuclearization is viewed by both states as projects of national security; questioning excessive expenditure for defense purposes is instantly labeled antinational; the soldiers killed in conflicts become martyrs; the usually un-cared-for defense personnel instantly become charismatic objects; even those who evade tax may contribute "liberally" to the National Defense Fund and can become "nationalists." Amidst this heightened national temperature, the Muslims in India and Hindus and Sikhs in Pakistan become objects of suspicion; they are required to prove their loyalty to the respective nations/states. This puts an enormous strain on these minority populations and on their constitutionally guaranteed freedom of expression, a test to which the members of the majority community is never subjected. Not only the collective rights of these religious minorities (e.g. congregational worship, pilgrimages, religious processions) are in jeopardy, but also markers of their collective identity (dress pattern, food habits, hairstyles) may become "security risks." State-sponsored nationalism endangers the collective rights of those minorities who share cultural characteristics of the majority of the "enemy state." Admittedly, the necessary legal mechanisms and citizen protections ought to be instituted for safeguarding the collective rights of the relevant minorities.

Of the two varieties of state-renouncing nationalism, one manifests itself in the demand for establishing coterminality between political-administrative units and cultural boundaries in multinational federal polities. Internation equality along with preservation of cultural identity are the goals of this variety of state-renouncing nationalism. However, while renouncing sovereign states, these nations invariably insist on their "provincial" states. The movement for the linguistic reorganization of India in the place of the artificial administrative units set up by the British is an example of this kind of nationalism. Most of the large linguistic collectivities in India and Pakistan have their own "states" if they have their own homeland. In the case of Sri Lanka, the goal of autonomists among Tamils is precisely this, while secessionists demand an exclusive sovereign state for Tamils. Even in the case of Bangladesh, which is predominantly populated by Bengali Muslims, the non-Bengalis insist on cultural autonomy. The Chakma leader, Manabendra Narayan Larma, articulated the demand for the recognition of the cultural identity of Chakmas, who are predominantly Buddhists and inhabit the Chittagong Hill Tract, thus:

"Under no definition or logic can a Chakma be Bengalee or a Bengalee be a Chakma . . . As citizens of Bangladesh we are all Bangladeshis but we also have a separate ethnic identity, which unfortunately the Awami League leaders do not want to understand" (quoted in Hussain 1986: 201).

While the major linguistic groups (i.e. nations) in India and Pakistan have their own provincial states, this is not true of the tribal communities or the subaltern nations. If the demand for their provincial states are conceded it is usually in order to tone down their demand for sovereign states. But such subaltern nations invariably have their homelands on interstate borders and hence command considerable political clout and striking power. Thus the numerically smaller Nagas (1.2 million) and Mizos (0.7 million) have their own separate provincial states, but the demands by the much larger encysted tribes of central India for separate provincial states are not likely to be conceded. In fact, some of the central Indian tribes are much larger in size: Santals, 6 million; Bhils, 6 million; Gonds, 3 million; and Oraons, 2 million, according to the 1991 census of India. It may be pertinent to recall here that 54 percent of member states of the United Nations have a population of 5 million or less and 27 percent have 1 million or less. Subaltern nations such as the Santals and Bhils, which have as great a population as the largest 45 percent of nation-states, are denied the right to national self-determination. They are even denied their collective rights to protect and preserve their cultural identity, as their legitimate demand for provincial states is not conceded. To deny these and many such other communities their collective rights, be it in South Asia or elsewhere, is nothing less than culturocide (Oommen 1990b: 43–66), the systematic liquidation of cultural groups. Renunciation of the sovereign state by a nation should not be invoked as the rationale to deny its collective rights. Further, we should not think that demands for collective rights within multinational and polyethnic states are illegitimate or unsustainable. In fact, it is exactly this value orientation and theorization that prompts the proliferation of nation-states, quite a few of which are unviable as economic entities and political enterprises.

One of the contentions in multinational federal polities is the relative importance to be assigned to the central government and provincial governments. Those who argue for a strong center see themselves as "nationalists," and those who prefer strong provincial governments are dubbed as "regionalists" who uphold parochial interests. But it is often forgotten that what are designated as "regions" are "nations" in a multinational polity and the "regionalists" are only arguing for their collective rights as nations. Conversely, those who prefer a central government with limited but crucial areas of operation (defense, foreign policy, fiscal policy), and substantial decentralization of political authority to provincial governments, define themselves as "democrats" and dub those who insist on a strong center as "authoritarians." These varying perceptions are rooted in the underlying conceptual differences between them; the "nationalists" consider the federal polity as the "nation" and the "regionalists" view the regions as nations. The former indirectly deny collective rights and the latter implicitly endorse collective rights.

The "statist" often says "I am an Indian first and last," decimating his other identities. The "nationalist" would say "I am an Indian but also a Malayali or Maharashtrian," acknowledging the notion of a multiple identity set. It is interesting to recall here the perceptive answer Wali Khan, the doyen of Pashtun nationalism, gave in 1974 when questioned whether he was a Muslim, a Pakistani, or Pashtun first? He answered that he was a "six-thousand-year-old Pashtun, a thousand-year-old Muslim and a 27-year-old Pakistani" (quoted in Harrison 1987: 285). To acknowledge one's multiple identity is to unfold the relevance of one's collective rights in different contexts. To insist that one identity displaces other identities and/or one of the identities has primacy over others, irrespective of contexts, ignores the complexity of reality on the ground. There is no primary identity or terminal loyalty; all are contextual. Pursuantly, membership in different collectivities entails different sets of collective rights.

The second type of state-renouncing nationalism surfaces in the context of ethnification and minoritization. Ethnicity is a product of dissociation between culture and territory. Ethnies are constrained to renounce exclusive states for themselves because they are territorially dispersed; they lack a spatial anchorage. Ethnies are of several backgrounds – refugees and exiles who flee to freedom or safety and immigrants who seek better pastures. Once in the new habitat, often a search for roots begins; they become aware of the need to maintain their cultural specificities, particularly religion and language. This search becomes acute if they are persecuted and discriminated against at the point of arrival and/or the conditions for nurturing cultural specificities become adverse.

The Sindhi Hindus who left their ancestral homeland are dispersed all over urban India. Their vociferous demand for according constitutional recognition to the Sindhi language persisted for two decades until it was conceded in 1967. This collective cultural right is about the only means now available to maintain their specificity, although the third-generation Sindhi migrant has practically forgotten the language (see Daswani 1996; Khubchandani 1997). That is, constitutional protection of cultural/linguistic rights is no guarantee of sustenance of cultural/linguistic identity (cf. May 2001). The story is exactly the opposite in the case of Mohajirs, the Urdu-speaking Muslims who migrated to Pakistan from North India. Through their political alignment with the largest and the most powerful nationality of Pakistan, the Punjabis, and due to its presumed linkage with Islam, Urdu became the official language of Pakistan. This facilitated not only the preservation of the cultural identity of Urdu speakers but also their domination. And yet they remain an ethnie in Pakistan, which is evident from the fact that these immigrants were initially labeled as Pahangirs or Hindustanis, a clear connotation of their outsider status. To escape this stigmatization, they adopted the label Muhajir, invoking its association with the prophetic tradition of *hijrat* (Ahmed 1988: 33–34). That is, dominant status in itself will not "nationalize" a group if it is territorially displaced. Even the Muhajir claim as the "fifth nationality" of Pakistan (the other four being Punjabi, Sindhi, Baluchi, and Pushtoon) is not conceded by the Pakistani state or society.

The case in Bangladesh of "Bihari Muslims," the Hindi-speaking Muslims from North India, is the third case of an ethnie in South Asia. As Urdu-speaking Muslims, the "Bihari Muslims" too thought that their Muslimness was a sufficient condition to comfortably graft them on to the eastern wing of Pakistan. Although their deterritorialization was a disadvantage right from the beginning, their religion provided a partial compensation. But with the transformation of East Pakistan into Bangladesh, linguistic identity gained salience and the intensity of Bihari Muslims' ethnification increased. They were not only uprooted from their ancestral homeland in India but subsequently also from their adopted homeland (Bangladesh). This clearly points to the need to uphold collective rights in the case of ethnic collectivities. Ethnies are often deterritorialized through utterly undemocratic sociopolitical processes; to deny them collective rights is to add insult to injury.

Finally, there are those who continue to live in their ancestral homeland but who underwent instant minoritization due to the redrawing of state boundaries. Consequent on the division of territory and subsequent immigration, those Muslims who remained in India and those Sikhs and Hindus who remained in Pakistan became minorities instantly. It is important to note here that, in so far as the dislocation happened within the national territory, not only was there no ethnification, there was no minoritization either. For example, although the Punjabi Muslims and Punjabi Sikhs exchanged their residence, as long as they remained within the Punjab they could still retain their nationality and dominance.

Thus those Sikhs who came from the Pakistan Punjab and remained in the Indian Punjab were not culturally uprooted like the Sikhs who went to other parts of India, where they became refugees, outsiders, and ethnies. Similarly, the Hindu Bengalis from East Pakistan who settled in West Bengal did not face the kind of cultural loss experienced by those Bengalis who settled outside Bengal. Once again, if the settlers become a majority in their adopted homeland, as in the case of Bengalis in Tripura in India, they could shed their minority and ethnic status and become nationals. But minoritization cannot be the basis for denying collective rights as those peoples subjected to this process are often mere victims of history.

Part 3

I have distinguished between two types of new nationalisms – state-centered and state-renouncing – and two subtypes of each of them in this chapter. Advocacy of collective rights has different meanings and connotations in each of these. State-seeking nationalism, under the rubric of state-centered nationalism, is an assertion of collective rights in the form of national self-determination; it is a manifestation of intrastate tension. It is an effort to transform a part (one or more of the nations in a multinational polity) into a whole, a sovereign nation-state. For the state from which the disengagement is sought, secession is invariably viewed as an illegitimate act; for the nation which seeks separation it is an emancipatory project from an internal colonizer, who is a hegemon. The legitimacy of collective rights in this context is, therefore, a matter of social location and consequent perception.

The other subtype of state-centered nationalism, anchored as it is to interstate rivalry, often degenerates into chauvinism and jingoism. In multinational polities the cultural mainstream, which is based on religion or language and often a combination of the two, becomes the ultimate carrier of the national spirit. Their collective rights come to be thought of as national rights. Conversely, the collective rights of minorities become "anti-national," particularly when and if the minorities share the cultural attributes of the cultural mainstream of the neighboring "enemy" country. For example, the demand by religious minorities for separate civil codes, or the demand by linguistic minorities for recognition of their languages for educational and administrative purposes, is often labeled as "antinational" (cf. May 2001). Here, the collective rights of minorities are delegitimized, depending upon the intensity of interstate rivalry and/or the similarity or difference of the collective identity of the minority groups in question with the majority in the neighboring countries. This

May, S. (2001) *Language and Minority Rights: Ethnicity, Nationalism and the Politics of Language*. London: Longman.

Murphy, M. (2001) "The limits of culture in the politics of self-determination." *Ethnicities* 1 (3): 367–88.

Mutesa II, K. E. (1967) *The Desecration of My Kingdom*. London: Constable.

Nielsson, G. P. (1985) "States and 'nation-groups': a global taxonomy." In Edward A. Tiryakian and Ronald Rogowski (eds.), *New Nationalisms of the Developed West*. Boston: Allen and Unwin, pp. 27–56.

Oommen, T. K. (1989) "Ethnicity, immigration and cultural pluralism: India and the United States of America." In M. L. Kohn (ed.), *Cross-National Research in Sociology*. Newbury Park: Sage Publications, pp. 279–305.

(1990a) *Protest and Change: Studies in Social Movements*. New Delhi: Sage Publishers.

(1990b) *State and Society in India: Studies in Nation-Building*. New Delhi: Sage.

(1997). *Citizenship, Nationality and Ethnicity: Reconciling Competing Identities*. Cambridge: Polity.

(2002) *Pluralism, Equality and Identity: Comparative Studies*. New Delhi: Oxford University Press.

Pi-Sunyer, O. (1985) "Catalan nationalism: some theoretical and historical considerations." In E. A. Tiryakian and R. Ropgwski (eds.), pp. 254–76.

Richmond, A. H. (1987) "Ethnic nationalism: social science paradigms." *International Social Science Journal* 39 (1): 3–18.

Sacks, J. (1997) *The Politics of Hope*. London: Jonathan Cape.

Savarkar, V. D. (1949) *Hindutva*. New Delhi: Bharti Sahitya Sadan.

Scott, C. (1998) *Seeing Like a State*. New Haven: Yale University Press.

Smith, A. D. (1983) *Theories of Nationalism*. London: Duckworth.

(1998) *Nationalism and Modernism*. London: Routledge.

Smith, M. G. (1965) *The Plural Society in British West Indies*. Berkeley: University of California Press.

Tilly, C. (1993) *European Revolutions, 1942–1992*. Oxford: Blackwell.

Van den Berghe, P. L. (1983) "Australia, Canada and the United States: ethnic melting pots or plural societies." *ANZJS* 19 (2): 238–52.

Worsley, P. (1984) *The Three Worlds: Culture and World Development*. Chicago: Chicago University Press.

Yancey, L.W. E. Ericksen, and J. Richard (1976) "Emerging ethnicities: a review and reformulation." *American Sociological Review* 41 (3): 391–403.

Zavos, J. (2002) "Identity politics and nationalisms in Colonial India." In S. Fenton and S. May (eds.), *Ethnonational Identities*. London: Palgrave Macmillan, pp. 109–28.

7   Justice and security in the accommodation of minority nationalism

Will Kymlicka

Minority nationalism is a universal phenomenon. As Walker Connor notes, countries affected by it

> are to be found in Africa (for example, Ethiopia), Asia (Sri Lanka), Eastern Europe (Romania), Western Europe (France), North America (Guatemala), South America (Guyana), and Oceania (New Zealand). The list includes countries that are old (United Kingdom) as well as new (Bangladesh), large (Indonesia) as well as small (Fiji), rich (Canada) as well as poor (Pakistan), authoritarian (Sudan) as well as democratic (Belgium), Marxist-Leninist (China) as well as militantly anti-Marxist (Turkey). The list also includes countries which are Buddhist (Burma), Christian (Spain), Moslem (Iran), Hindu (India), and Judaic (Israel).
>
> (Connor 1999: 163–64)

In all of these countries, national minorities are battling with the state – peacefully or violently – over issues of political representation, language rights, self-government, control over resources, and internal migration.

While the challenge of minority nationalism arises in all parts of the globe, the state's response to it varies tremendously from region to region. In this chapter, I want to compare the accommodation of minority nationalism in two regions: the Western democracies and the postcommunist countries of Eastern and Central Europe (hereafter ECE). The response to minority nationalism in these two regions is very different. To oversimplify, we can say that in the West, there is a trend toward accepting the legitimacy of minority nationalism, and toward accommodating it through some form of territorial autonomy. In the ECE, by contrast, minority nationalism is often viewed as illegitimate, and the idea of territorial autonomy is strongly resisted.

What explains these differing responses to minority nationalism? There are many factors at play here, but I will focus on one of them, namely, that the claims of national minorities are judged by different criteria. In the West, they are assessed primarily in terms of *justice*. The goal is to find an accommodation that is more or less fair to both majority and minority, and an increasing number of states accept that justice requires some form

144

of self-government for minorities. In the ECE, the claims of minorities are primarily assessed in term of *security*. The goal is to ensure that minorities are unable to threaten the existence or territorial integrity of the state, and most ECE states believe that self-government for minorities poses such a threat.

This is an oversimplification, of course, and I will discuss some of the exceptions and complications below. But it immediately raises a problem for those of us who take a personal or professional interest in the fate of minorities in ECE. As I discuss below, there have been several attempts by Western organizations to develop international norms regarding minority rights, and ECE countries are closely monitored for how well they adhere to these norms. Indeed, respecting international norms of minority rights has been made one of the preconditions for ECE countries to be admitted into the EU or NATO.

But what are we in the West trying to achieve with these standards? Are we trying to ensure security for newly independent and/or newly democratizing states, or are we trying to ensure justice for vulnerable minorities within those states? The simple answer is that Western organizations hope to achieve both of these goals – to simultaneously promote both security for states and justice for minorities. Indeed, the assumption that justice and security go together is an article of faith for almost everyone who works in the field.[1]

But the claim that justice for minorities promotes state security may not be true, at least not in the way its proponents imagine. I think that considerations of justice and security often point in different directions. More accurately – and this is the crux of my argument – the *discourses* of justice and security pull in different directions. It makes all the difference in the world whether states view minority claims through the lens of fairness and justice, or through the lens of national security and loyalty. As I discuss below, in ECE, the discourse on minority rights is highly "securitized," and I think it is impossible under these conditions to ensure justice or tolerance for minorities.

If that is right, it suggests that justice for minorities can only occur if we can "desecuritize" the discourse of minority rights in ECE countries – i.e. if we manage to get people to think of minority claims in terms of justice/fairness rather than loyalty/security. The problem is that we have no clear idea how to do this. Indeed, I suspect that the current approach of Western organizations – in both their informal diplomacy and formal legal codes of minority rights – is failing to confront this question.

My focus will be on Eastern Europe, but the underlying question is universal. The conflict between discourses of justice and security also arises in Africa, Asia, or Latin America. Eastern Europe is not at all exceptional in its preoccupations with security – that is the norm around the world. It is the West that stands out in having somehow managed to move minority rights from the "security" box to the "justice" box. The crucial question, then, is whether the conditions that have made it possible for Western countries to desecuritize the discourse on minority rights can be replicated elsewhere. One optimistic view is that democratization and economic development are the crucial conditions for this shift, and so the "minorities problem" will resolve itself as non-Western countries develop. My own view, however, is that the conditions which make possible the shift from a discourse of security to a discourse of justice are not a simple or straightforward function of economic development or democratization, and may be quite complex and elusive.

That is the background to my argument. The chapter itself has three parts. I begin by briefly describing the current situation of minority rights in the West in the first part; then I examine the "securitized" discourse in ECE, and I conclude with some suggestions about what Western organizations could do to desecuritize these debates.

Multination federalism in the West

Many Western democracies contain groups which think of themselves as "nations," and which mobilize along nationalist lines to gain or maintain self-government. This includes both substate national groups, such as the Catalans, Basques, Flemish, Scots, Welsh, Corsicans, Puerto Ricans, and Québécois, and indigenous peoples, like the Sami, Inuit, Maori, Maya, Australian Aboriginal peoples and American Indians.

In the past, the desire of these groups for self-government was typically suppressed, often brutally. But, over the past century, an increasing number of Western democracies have grudgingly accepted the legitimacy of these demands, and have accommodated them through some form of territorial autonomy. In some countries, this shift to territorial autonomy has been achieved by adopting a federal system, since federalism allows the creation of regional political units, controlled by the national minority, with substantial (and constitutionally protected) powers of self-government. Countries that have adopted federalism to accommodate minority nations include Switzerland (for the French- and Italian-speaking minorities), Canada (for the Québécois), Belgium (for the Flemish), and Spain (for the Catalans, Basques, and Galicians).

In other countries, or for other national groups, there may be geographic or demographic reasons why federalism in the technical sense will not work. In these cases, we see the emergence of various quasi-federal forms of territorial autonomy. For example, Britain has recently adopted a quasi-federal system of devolution to Scotland and Wales, which now have their own legislative assemblies. And while Puerto Rico is not part of the US federal system (i.e. it is not one of the fifty states), it has a special self-governing status within the United States as a "Commonwealth." Similarly, while Italy and Finland are not federations, they have adopted special forms of territorial autonomy for the Austrians in South Tyrol, and for the Swedes in the Aland Islands. In all of these cases, territorial autonomy enables national minorities to establish and govern their own public institutions, often operating in their own language, including schools, universities, courts, and regional parliaments. This trend towards quasi-federal forms of autonomy is even clearer in the context of indigenous peoples: Indian tribes in the United States and Canada are recognized as having rights of self-government, and are acquiring (or reacquiring) control over education, heath care, policing, child welfare, natural resources, and so on. Similarly, the Scandinavian countries have created Sami Parliaments; the Maori in New Zealand have increased autonomy.

In all of these countries, the goal of eliminating minority national identities has been abandoned, and it is now accepted that these groups will continue to see themselves as separate and self-governing nations within the larger state into the indefinite future. As a result, an increasing number of Western democracies that contain national minorities accept that they are "multination" states, rather than "nation-states" (cf. Oommen, this volume). They accept that they contain two or more nations within their borders, and recognize that each constituent nation has an equally valid claim to the language rights and self-government powers necessary to maintain itself as a distinct societal culture. And this multinational character is often explicitly affirmed in the country's constitution.

Following Philip Resnick (1994), I will call these "multination federations." They are not all federations in the technical sense, but they all embody a model of the state in which national minorities are federated to the state through some form of territorial autonomy, and in which internal boundaries have been drawn, and powers distributed, in such a way as to ensure that each national group is able to maintain itself as a distinct and self-governing societal culture.

Unlike many forms of multiculturalism which are often disparaged as tokenist or folkloric, this model for accommodating minority nationalism involves a serious realignment of political power and economic resources. The precise range of rights and powers accorded national minorities varies from country to country, but they typically include the following three elements: (a) territorial autonomy; (b) the minority's language is accorded the status of an official language in that territory – either as a coequal official language with the majority language or indeed as the primary or sole official language; (c) the self-governing region has control over education all the way from primary (elementary) through to post-secondary education, including universities in their own language where numbers warrant.

These three features are found wherever there are large national minorities in the West, like the Québécois, Puerto Ricans, Catalans, and Walloons, each of whom has over 2.5 million members. But it is equally true of smaller national minorities, like the Swedes in Finland (285,000); German speakers in South Tyrol (303,000); or the Italian speakers in Switzerland (500,000). All of these groups have territorial autonomy, official language status, and schools (including universities) in their own language. Under these conditions, it is not an exaggeration to view the state as a union of two or more equal partners.

This trend towards multination federalism is very widespread in the West. Amongst the Western democracies with sizeable national minorities, only France and Greece resist any notion of territorial autonomy for their historic minorities, and even France is moving in this direction in its negotiations regarding Corsica. To be sure, the details often remain controversial even in those countries with well-established forms of multination federalism. Critics sometimes fear that self-government for national minorities may violate the basic principles of liberal democracy, such as the principle of equal citizenship, or the protection of individual civil and political rights. However, in reality, virtually all existing forms of minority self-government in the West are firmly subject to constitutional guarantees of the rule of law, individual rights, and democratic procedures. Indeed, proponents of multination federalism argue that it can actually enhance the freedom and equality of citizens, by putting minority and majority on a more equal footing. As a result, there seems to be a growing consensus that some form of territorial autonomy and language rights for indigenous peoples and national minorities is justifiable in terms of liberal-democratic justice.[2]

The discourse of minority rights in ECE

Both the practice and the discourse of minority rights in ECE is very different. There is enormous resistance in virtually every ECE country to the idea of federalism or other forms of territorial autonomy for national minorities. Russia is the only country that voluntarily adopted a form of multination federalism that grants significant territorial autonomy to several national minorities.[3] In all other countries, territorial autonomy has been strongly resisted.

In some cases, preexisting forms of minority autonomy were scrapped: Serbia revoked the autonomy of Kosovo/Vojvodina; Georgia revoked the autonomy of Abkhazia and Ossetia; Azerbaijan revoked the autonomy of Ngorno-Karabakh. Indeed the revoking of minority autonomy was often one of the first things that these countries chose to do with their newfound freedom after the collapse of communism.[4] In other cases, requests to restore historic forms of autonomy were rejected (e.g. Romania refused to restore the autonomy to Transylvania which had been revoked in 1968). In yet other cases, requests to create new forms of autonomy were dismissed (e.g. Estonia rejected a referendum supporting autonomy for Russian-dominated Narva; Kazakhstan rejected autonomy for ethnic Russians in the north; Ukraine rejected a referendum supporting autonomy for ethnic Romanian areas; Lithuania rejected requests for autonomy by ethnic Poles; Macedonia rejected a referendum for autonomy for Albanian-dominated Western Macedonia in 1992).[5] And, in yet other cases, countries have redrawn boundaries to make it impossible for autonomy to be adopted in the future (e.g. Slovakia redrew its internal boundaries so that ethnic Hungarians would not form a majority within any of the internal administrative districts, and hence would have no platform to claim autonomy; Croatia redrew internal boundaries in Krajina and west Slavonia to dilute Serbian-populated areas).[6]

The only cases in ECE (outside Russia) where territorial autonomy has been accepted are cases where the national minority simply grabbed political power and established de facto autonomy without the consent of the central government. In these situations, the only alternative to recognizing de facto autonomy was military intervention and potential civil war. This was the situation in TransDneister in Moldova; Abkhazia in Georgia; Krajina in Croatia; Crimea in Ukraine; and Ngorno-Karabakh in Azerbaijan. Even here, most countries preferred civil war to negotiating autonomy, and only accepted autonomy if and when they weren't able to win militarily.[7]

This almost blind resistance to territorial autonomy is reflected in the recent history of Krajina, a Serbian-populated area of Croatia that has been the subject of a brutal civil war. Many commentators believe that autonomy for the Serbs was the only option that might have avoided this bloodshed (Varady 1997). However, Serb demands for territorial autonomy were considered too much for the Croats to accept after independence, and they offered only minimal forms of cultural autonomy without political self-government. So the local Serbs took up arms, backed by the Serbian-dominated Yugoslav army, and simply took over political power in the region. At this point, Croatia offered territorial autonomy to

Krajina, but this was now considered too little by the Serbs, who would settle for nothing less than secession and incorporation into Serbia. When the Croat army retook Krajina, the Serbs reconsidered and accepted the Croat offer of autonomy, but by then the victorious Croats had withdrawn the offer of autonomy, and have since proceeded to dispossess the local Serbs of their rights and property, and to resettle Bosnian Croats in areas of former Serb settlement. Both sides preferred civil war, secession, and ethnic cleansing to negotiating autonomy.

What explains this overwhelming resistance to the general principle of recognizing minority nationalism, and to the more specific idea of federalism, or other forms of minority autonomy? One popular explanation, particularly amongst journalists, is that nationalism in the West is "civic" nationalism, and hence more accommodating of minorities, whereas nationalism in the ECE is "ethnic" nationalism, and hence more aggressive towards minorities (e.g. Ignatieff 1993). I do not think this is a helpful answer. Attempts to test empirically the proposition that nationalism in ECE is more "ethnic" than in the West haven't come up with much supporting evidence (Kuzio 1999). But in any event, the civic/ethnic distinction does not explain how states respond to minority nationalism. So-called "civic" nations, such as France and the United States, have historically been reluctant to accord territorial autonomy to national minorities, and there is nothing in the logic of civic nationalism that requires national minorities to be accorded self-government. Indeed, many defenders of civic nationalism oppose self-government claims precisely on the grounds that minority nationalism is "ethnic" nationalism, and hence has no place in a civic nation. Conversely, there is nothing in the logic of "ethnic" nationalism that precludes according self-government to other ethnic nations, and there are many historic examples of two or more "ethnic" nations sharing power in a single state.[8]

To explain the resistance to multination federalism in ECE, we need to look elsewhere. Some people in ECE oppose multination federalism on the same grounds critics raise in the West: i.e. concerns about its impact on liberal-democratic principles of equality and freedom. But such arguments are comparatively rare in the ECE debate, and are often buried underneath other, more important arguments that are not found in the West. I will look at three such objections that are distinctive to the ECE debate: what I will call the "transition priority" objection; the "historic justice" objection; and the "security" objection.

(1) The Transition Priority objection: One obvious difference between East and West is that ECE countries are in a state of political and economic transition: politically, they are shifting from communist dictatorships to liberal democracies, and economically, from planned economies

to market economies. This raises the question as to where minority rights fit into a broader trajectory of transition. Should ECE states deal with "the minority question" before tackling these political and economic transformations, or afterwards?

In the West, the process of accommodating minority nationalism has taken place within states that have reasonably well-functioning market economies and democratic political systems. The challenge was to pluralize already functioning liberal-democratic economic and political systems. Elsewhere in the world, however, the challenge of minority nationalism is magnified by the fact that it is occurring simultaneously with other radical transformations of the state and economy.

In conditions of transition, given the multiple demands on the state's time and resources, priorities need to be established. And many people argue that priority should be given to establishing the rule of law and economic development, before turning to issues of minority rights. Even if the idea of multination federalism is a desirable one in the long term, in the short term ECE states need to give priority to liberalization and democratization before addressing pluralization. They should defer the potentially divisive issues of language and culture for now, and focus on the common interests that majority and minority have in democracy and development.

Indeed, one could argue that discussing minority rights is almost pointless without some minimal development of the state's capacity to implement policy and to enforce the law. This minimal condition is not met in many ECE states. As Doroszewska notes, the Western model of multination federalism assumes that states are able to adopt and implement laws and policies, to uphold the rule of law, and to enforce rights. It assumes that states have the political will to solve problems resulting from their ethnocultural diversity; that there exists some sort of national "majority" which defines the state's policy toward national "minority"; and finally, that the state has a vision of what this policy should or should not be, and makes the appropriate decisions to meet these objectives (Doroszewska 2002).

Doroszewska argues that these assumptions are "unwarranted" in many ECE countries, where quasicriminal ruling elites are simply interested in privatizing public wealth, and not interested in social or minority issues.

Talking about minority rights is perhaps idle where there is no coherent framework of state power capable of adopting and implementing policies and upholding laws and rights. Discussing the merits of Western models of minority rights may seem pointless when some post-Soviet states are not even able to collect taxes and investigate crimes.

This is an important objection, and I used to have considerable sympathy for it. However, I have grown less sympathetic, for two reasons. First, this argument is almost always invoked in a hypocritical way. For, in fact, the very first priority of most ECE governments has been to deal with issues of language and culture, by adopting laws which give symbolic recognition and legal protection to the majority's language and culture. For example, official language laws were often the very first laws passed in ECE states after 1989, well before issues of economic privatization or democratic reforms. So the state viewed the protection of the majority's language and culture as of the utmost importance – it was only the protection of the minority's language and culture that they wanted to postpone.

Moreover, the effect of these laws – often an intended effect – is to make it more difficult to accept minority claims later on. For example, the privileging of majority languages and cultures, and the elimination of minority autonomy, were often enshrined in the constitution, so that they would be difficult to revise later on. Thus the first sentence of the postcommunist Romanian constitution says Romania is a "unitary and indivisible" state, thereby ruling out any form of federalism. Similarly, the Bulgarian constitution explicitly rules out the granting of territorial autonomy to any group for any reason (and indeed says that there are no minorities in Bulgaria, even though ethnic Turks are 10 percent of the population).

The point of putting such statements in the constitution is not to defer claims to official bilingualism or territorial autonomy, but rather to permanently take them off the political agenda. Indeed, the aim is to make the renouncing of such claims a litmus test for the loyalty of minorities. Any minority leader who even suggests federalism is, by definition, disloyal to the constitution, and hence can be ignored, denied a seat at the political table, and perhaps put under police surveillance as a security threat.

Minorities in ECE are often told that they should support "democratic reformers" within the majority, and defer their minority rights claims until these democrats have successfully defeated the former communists and democratized the state. Such a voluntary deferral of minority rights claims is supposed to help prove the loyalty and democratic credentials of the minority, and make the majority more sympathetic to their claims over the long term. No doubt this may be a sound strategy in some cases. However, much depends on the views of these "reformers." In Serbia, for example, the "democratic opposition" throughout the 1990s was systematically hostile to minority claims.[9] There is no reason to believe that once in power such reformers will miraculously convert to minority rights, rather than seeking to permanently entrench a highly centralized, majoritarian vision of democracy.

If anything, the fact that these countries are undergoing a transition is precisely a reason to tackle, rather than ignore, issues of minority rights. As Horowitz notes, "times of transition are often times of ethnic tension. When it looks as if the shape of the polity is being settled once and for all, apprehensions are likely to grow" (Horowitz 1985: 190). And this is what we see now in many ECE states. "The shape of the polity" is already being fixed as a unitary, centralized nation-state, and minorities will have to find whatever bits of power and resources they can find within such a structure. There will be little chance of reopening questions about bilingualism or federalism that were "deferred" in the name of democratic consolidation. It is a dangerous idea to defer minority rights if in the meantime notions of a highly centralized unitary nation-state are being permanently entrenched in the constitution (often by "democratic reformers").

Second, even if we agree that economic development and democratic reforms are the most urgent issues, and that the first priority for many ECE countries is to increase their state capacity, is the best way to achieve these goals to defer minority rights? What is the relationship between adopting minority rights and improving the taxcollecting and law-enforcing capacity of the state? Some people seem to think that the "premature" adoption of minority rights would make it more difficult to achieve democratic state consolidation. On this view, granting language rights or territorial autonomy to minorities would detract from efforts to build state capacity, and so we need to defer the former until the latter is well established. But how would denying autonomy to the Russians in Crimea make it easier for Ukraine to collect taxes? How does denying language rights to Hungarians in Slovakia make it easier for the Slovak government to investigate crimes, stop corruption, and enforce the rule of law? Why suppose that the only way to improve state capacity is to deny minorities their autonomy or language rights?

Dealing with minority issues may in fact be a precondition for the modernization of the state. For one thing, the only viable way to build state capacity in modern societies is to do so consensually, and this requires the voluntary participation of citizens (Schopflin 2002). Moreover, refusing to address minority issues can play into the hands of radicals and authoritarians amongst both the majority and minority. Since minorities will feel excluded from statebuilding, they will be visibly dissatisfied, which will reinforce majority fears that the minority is disloyal, and hence reinforce the power of intolerant majority nationalists, who say that democracy and liberalism must be subordinate to issues of national security. It will also reinforce the illiberal and authoritarian tendencies within the minority. Denied their legitimate rights by the majority, they exercise ever-tighter control over what little power they do possess. Deferring minority rights in the name of promoting democratic consolidation is, therefore, likely to be counterproductive.

Here again, this may vary from country to country. But it seems to me that Russia and Ukraine would be worse off today if they had not come to an accommodation with their national minorities, and that Serbia and Slovakia would be better off today if they had come to such an accommodation earlier on. We can also find indirect support for this in the West. As I noted earlier, in most cases in the West, multination federalism was only adopted after democratic consolidation had occurred. But one important exception is Spain, and virtually every commentator on the transition from dictatorship to democracy after the death of Franco agrees that the decision to federalize the country in order to accommodate Catalan and Basque nationalism aided in the consolidation of democracy. Why should the same not hold in the transition from dictatorship to democracy in ECE?

So I think the transition priority argument is more complex than many suppose. Still, it is an important issue not found in the West.

(2) The historic injustice objection: another distinctive aspect of the debate in ECE is the appeal to historic injustice. Some people say that this focus on historical rights and wrongs is unique to Eastern Europe, and that Western democracies have managed to get beyond this "backward-looking" obsession with history and to focus instead on "forward-looking" coexistence.

It is certainly true that feelings about historic injustice run deep in many ECE countries. (It is a cliché, but partly true, that if you ask a Serb about the rights of the Albanians in Kosovo, he/she is likely to say "you need to understand what happened in 1389.") But I think the same is true in many Western countries as well. Appeals to historical injustice are increasingly common in the West. Consider the recent explosion of writing on the issue of reparations to African Americans for the historic wrongs of slavery and segregation (Robinson 2000). Claims for the rectification of historic injustice are also a vital part of contemporary mobilization by indigenous peoples in New Zealand, Australia, and Canada, and even of some immigrant groups – e.g. Japanese-Canadians seeking apologies and compensation for their detention in the Second World War (James 1999).

However, issues of historic injustice operate very differently in the West. In the West, it is almost always the minority that invokes this argument, seeking apology and compensation from the state which has historically mistreated it. Hence the argument from historic injustice operates to strengthen minority rights claims, and to buttress the argument for greater equality between majority and minority. It is invoked to pressure the majority to say "never again will we try to expel, subordinate or oppress you."

In ECE, however, it is typically the majority that feels that it has been the victim of oppression, often at the hands of their minorities, acting in collaboration with foreign enemies. Hence the majority wants the minority to express guilt, and to offer an apology, as a way of saying that never again will the minority be disloyal to the state. We see this in the Czech Republic regarding the German minority; in Slovakia and Romania re the Hungarian minority; in the Baltics re the Russian minority; in Croatia re the Serbian minority; in Bulgaria re the Turkish minority, to name a few.

In all of these cases, minorities are seen (rightly or wrongly) as allies or collaborators with external powers that have historically oppressed the majority group. Hungarians in Romania and Slovakia may be a relatively small minority (10–15 percent of the population in each country), but Slovakians and Romanians perceive them as the allies of their former Habsburg oppressors, and indeed as the physical residue of that unjust imperialism. The Russians who settled in Estonia and Latvia after the Second World War are seen by the state, not as a weak and disenfranchised minority group, but as a tool of their former Soviet oppressors. The Muslim Albanians in Serbia and Macedonia, or the Muslim Turks in Bulgaria, are seen as a reminder of, and collaborator with, centuries of oppression under the Ottomans.[10]

In short, the sort of historic injustice that is central to the ECE debates, unlike in the West, is the historical oppression of the majority group by its minorities in collaboration with a kin state or foreign power. This, I think, is truly distinctive to Eastern Europe, not found in the West (except perhaps in Ireland and Cyprus).[11] The result is the phenomenon known as "minoritized majorities" – majorities which think and act as if they were the minorities.[12]

In this context, arguments about historic injustice work against minority rights claims. Indeed, taken to their logical conclusion, they may suggest that minorities have no right to exist on the territory of the state, if their presence there is related to such an historic injustice. After all, were it not for unjust Russian and Soviet imperialism, there would be few Russians in the Baltics. Were it not for unjust Ottoman imperialism, there would be few Turks in Bulgaria and few Albanians in Serbia. If the goal is to remedy the wrongs created by these historic injustices, why not try to undo the Russification of the Baltics, either by expelling the Russians or by insisting that they assimilate to Estonian and Latvian culture? Why not try to undo the Turkification of Bulgaria under the Ottomans, either by expelling the Turks or by insisting they assimilate to Bulgarian culture?[13]

In short, whereas arguments about rectifying historic injustice in the West operate to strengthen the minority's claim for a more equal distribution of rights and resources between majority and minority, in ECE they can be invoked to weaken the minority's claims, and indeed to question the very legitimacy of the minority's existence.

Why are majorities in ECE so keen to recall these historic injustices, and to get minorities to acknowledge their role in them? For the same reason that minorities in the West advance claims about historic injustice – namely, the fear that it can happen again. Majorities in ECE fear that minorities, either by themselves or in collaboration with their kin states or other international forces, could again reduce the majority to a condition of subservience and oppression. This is why it is so important to the majority that the former wrongdoers (and their descendents and allies) agree that never again will this happen.

(3) The loyalty/security objection: this leads to what I believe is the most important argument in the ECE discourse – namely, the loyalty/security objection. The history of imperialism, collaboration, and border changes have encouraged three interrelated assumptions which are now widely accepted by ECE countries: (a) that minorities are disloyal, not just in the sense that they lack loyalty to the state (that is equally true of secessionists in Québec or Scotland), but in the stronger sense that they collaborated with former oppressors, and continue to collaborate with current enemies or potential enemies;[14] therefore (b), a strong and stable state requires weak and disempowered minorities. Put another way, ethnic relations are seen as a zero-sum game: anything that benefits the minority is seen as a threat to the majority; and therefore (c), the treatment of minorities is above all a question of national security.[15]

In short, the discourse on state/minority issues in ECE has been "securitized," to use Ole Waever's terminology (Waever 1995). It's important to emphasize how widespread this phenomenon is. Claims about security arise in the most unlikely places. One of the most striking recent examples is Greece's claim that the use of the name "Macedonia" by its neighboring state is a threat to Greece's very existence. (Greece did not object to the fact that the former Yugoslav republic of Macedonia was becoming an independent state; but they insisted that it was a threat to Greece to call this country "Macedonia".)

Foreign observers are puzzled as to how the use of the name Macedonia by a poor and defenseless country could pose any threat to Greece, a much more powerful state and a member of NATO, the strongest military alliance in history. But Greek political elites felt it served their interests to present this as an issue of national security, rather than simply one of culture or politics.

Similarly, the government of Macedonia, for its part, has declared that it would be a threat to the very existence of the state if the Albanian minority in Macedonia were to have a university operating in their own language (and hence they bulldozed the buildings of the private University of Tetovo, killing two people in the process).[16] Here again, independent observers have difficulty seeing how a privately funded Albanian-language university can threaten the existence of a state, but Macedonian political elites have managed to persuade most of their citizens that this is indeed a matter of national security, rather than one of culture or education or economics.

As these examples show, the decision to securitize an issue reflects a deliberate political strategy by particular political actors. An issue only becomes securitized if certain political elites decide to describe it in these terms – as an existential threat to the state and its dominant national group – and succeed in persuading enough others of this description. Why would political elites adopt this strategy? Securitizing an issue has two important implications. First, since these issues are said to have the potential to undercut the state, they trump normal democratic processes of debate and negotiation. After all, the first task of the state is to secure its existence, and only then can it afford to discuss and negotiate. As Waever puts it, by securitizing issues, political leaders claim that these issues

must be addressed prior to all others because, if they are not, the state will cease to exist as a sovereign unit and all other questions will become irrelevant. . . . Operationally, however, this means: In naming a certain development as a security problem, the "state" can claim a special right . . . By uttering "security", a state representative moves a particular development into a specific area, and thereby claims a special right to use whatever means are necessary to block it. (Waever 1995: 54–55)

Second, securitizing an issue also trumps issues of justice. The whole question of what justice requires between majority and minority is submerged, since national security takes precedence over justice, and since disloyal minorities have no legitimate claims anyway. This helps to explain why there is little scholarly or public debate in ECE about what principles of justice should regulate the accommodation of ethnocultural diversity. In the fervid debate over the Albanian-language university in Macedonia, for example, it is difficult to find anyone asking what fairness requires in the sphere of higher education in multinational and multilingual states, or how mother-tongue higher education relates to liberal principles of freedom and equality. Security trumps justice, and disloyal minorities forfeit any claims of justice anyway.

The only exception to this filtering out of justice arguments is arguments about the historic injustices that the majority has suffered, and which the minority is perceived to be responsible for. This sort of justice claim passes through the securitization filter, since it provides the historical evidence to support the securitization of the issue in the first place. So the historic injustice and securitization arguments feed off each other, and both operate to exclude any claims of justice which the minority might advance. Under conditions of securitization, "justice" means that the majority should be compensated for the historic wrongs it has suffered from its disloyal minorities; it does not mean that minorities have any claim to a fairer or more equal distribution of power, rights, and resources.[17]

In short, when minority issues are securitized, the space for moral argument and democratic debate drastically shrinks. I believe that this displacement of justice by security is what most clearly distinguishes the minority rights debate in the ECE from the West.[18] Indeed, the low level of securitization of minority issues in the West is, on reflection, quite remarkable. After all, several countries in the West contain active secessionist movements – in Québec, Flanders, Scotland, Puerto Rico, and Catalonia. In all of these cases, there are political parties that contest the very existence of the state, and so threaten the security of the state. And in some cases, these secessionist parties have even come to power, or shared power in coalitions.

Yet in all of these cases, Western political actors have not securitized issues of minority nationalism. The claims of these movements are addressed, like other minority rights claims, through a discourse of justice – i.e. in terms of freedom, equality, and solidarity. And they are resolved through normal democratic procedures and negotiations. In other words, secessionist politics in the West is normal politics. It is seen as normal and natural that secessionist politicians are speaking on television, sitting on parliamentary committees, and campaigning in the streets. No one thinks that the active participation of secessionist politicians is a reason for suspending normal democratic procedures or debates, or for trumping claims of justice.[19]

The difference here with ECE is striking. In Macedonia, the minority's modest demand for a private university is securitized as a threat to the existence of the state. In Canada, the minority's demand to break up the state is viewed as normal politics. This contrast between a justice-based debate in the West and a security-based debate in ECE is manifested in many ways. For example, in both regions there is an active debate over the concept of "collective rights," but the debate is very different. In the West, the concern with collective rights is that they can be invoked to override individual rights – an issue of justice. In ECE, by contrast, the main objection to the idea of collective rights is that they can be invoked as a basis of secession or irredentism – an issue of national security.

So the minority debate in ECE is subject to pervasive securitization. It is this fact, rather than the fact of transition, which most sharply distinguishes minority debates in the East and West.[20] Whereas ECE states securitize even modest claims for minority rights, such as official language status or mother-tongue universities, Western states do not securitize even radical claims for secession. I believe that the success of multination federalism in the West is intrinsically linked to this crossparty consensus not to "play the security card" when dealing with minority nationalist issues. The health of a democracy depends on the self-restraint of political leaders in playing this card, and the skepticism of citizens when elites do try to play it.

One way to think of this is to say that there is a threshold at which the security card gets played. In order to avoid state repression, minorities need to keep their demands below this threshold, while simultaneously trying to negotiate that threshold upwards.[21] But where is this threshold? We can list some typical minority demands in descending order of strength:

1. secessionist violence/terrorism

— — — — ——

2. democratic secessionist mobilization
3. territorial autonomy
4. minority-language higher education
5. veto rights
6. collective rights
7. official language status

— — — — ——

8. minority-language elementary schools
9. minority-language street signs

In the West, the threshold today is very high – in between 1 and 2. In effect, minority nationalism only becomes securitized when it involves terrorism, as in Northern Ireland or the Basque Country. So long as it remains peaceful and democratic, then minority nationalism is not securitized, even if it is explicitly aimed at secession. In ECE, by contrast, the threshold today is very low – between 7 and 8. Any claim for territorial autonomy, minority-language higher education, collective rights or official language status triggers the security card. Only very weak claims, such as mother-tongue elementary schools, can safely be left to the normal processes of democratic politics.

I believe that the securitization of minority nationalism in ECE is detrimental not just to the minorities, but to democracy itself, and to the existence of a peaceful civil society. There is a clear correlation between democratization and minority nationalism. Those ECE countries without significant minority nationalisms have democratized successfully (Czech Republic, Hungary, Slovenia, Poland); those countries with powerful minority nationalisms are having a more difficult time (Slovakia; Ukraine; Romania; Serbia; Macedonia; Georgia). The minority issue is not the only factor here, but I believe it is an important one.

In an essay first published in 1946, Istvan Bibo provided a thoughtful analysis of this problem. He argued that the experience of nineteenth-century Hungary taught leaders that their minorities might use their democratic freedom to secede. Ever since, ECE states have feared the exercise of democratic freedoms by minorities. As a result, they have consistently tried to suppress, dilute, or contain these democratic freedoms, sometimes by embracing fascism or other forms of authoritarianism (i.e. by suppressing everyone's freedom), sometimes by disempowering minorities (i.e. by suppressing the minority's freedom). But, in either case, the result is a stunted and fearful form of democracy. As he puts it:

> In a paralyzing state of fear which asserts that freedom's progress endangers the interests of the nation, one cannot take full advantage of the benefits offered by democracy. Being a democrat means, primarily, not to be afraid: not to be afraid of those who have different opinions, speak different languages, or belong to other races. The countries of Central and Eastern Europe were afraid because they were not fully developed mature democracies, and they could not become fully developed mature democracies because they were afraid. (Bibo 1991: 42)

I believe that this remains true today. Most ECE states with minority nationalisms have the shell of liberal democracy, but remain afraid of the full and free exercise of democratic freedoms.

Secession and the desecuritizing of minority rights

If this analysis is correct, then we need to think about ways to desecuritize minority issues. One approach would be to sit back and allow the "natural" historical evolution to occur. On this view, every state must go through various stages of nationbuilding, including a virulent early phase where minority issues are securitized. But, over time, ethnic relations will eventually settle into a stable and peaceful pattern. This virulent stage of nationbuilding may involve coercive assimilation, discrimination, and ethnic cleansing, but eventually either the minorities will be crushed, expelled, or assimilated, and cease to pose a security threat, or they will be strong enough to resist, and then the state will have to enter into negotiations with them, resulting in some more or less stable form of coexistence and minority rights.

This, of couse, is what happened in the West. Many national minorities were successfully crushed in the West, through forced assimilation (the Basques and Bretons in France) and ethnic cleansing (the American Indians). Others were strong enough to resist these efforts (the Québécois in Canada; Flemish in Belgium), and eventually were able to negotiate the sort of multination federalism discussed earlier. All of the antiminority policies witnessed in the ECE in the last decade have their precedents in the West when Western states were newly independent or newly democratizing. Indeed, Taras Kuzio claims that most ECE countries are actually more liberal than Western states were at comparable stages of nationbuilding (Kuzio 1999).

On this view, then, ethnic relations will eventually be desecuritized in ECE, and we may indeed end up with multination federalism in some countries, but only as a result of the natural stages of nationbuilding. One can't skip the stages to go directly to a multination state.

I do not think this is a viable approach. Minorities today are better educated and organized than minorities in the nineteenth century, and have stronger international allies. Moreover, we now live in an era of human rights and of international law. State policies that were tolerated or ignored in the nineteenth century are intolerable today, and are monitored by a dense network of international organizations.

So the international community will be involved in ethnic relations in ECE. Sitting back and doing nothing is no longer an option. But what can the international community do to help desecuritize these issues? How can it raise the threshold for minority claims, and to what level should it be raised?

There are several options here. One is to accept that the fear of secession is so great in ECE that it cannot be desecuritized. So the best that can be done is to try to draw a watertight separation between secession and other minority rights claims, such as territorial autonomy (hereafter TA), and to persuade ECE states that adopting TA will not and indeed could not lead to secession. The idea here would be to encourage states to think about TA in an open-minded way, without challenging their view that secession is unthinkable and that secessionist mobilization is intolerable. The goal would be to persuade ECE states to put TA on the political agenda, while agreeing with these states that secession cannot be a legitimate topic of public debate or political mobilization.

This could be done in a variety of ways. In particular, the international community can provide strong assurances regarding secession. It can make solemn pledges guaranteeing the integrity of state borders in ECE, and can insist as part of its TA proposals that the minority agree to some loyalty clause which affirms their acceptance of state borders. And it can insist that kin states renounce all irredentist territorial claims on neighboring states, and indeed pressure these states to sign bilateral treaties guaranteeing the borders.[22] With these guarantees against secession in place, the international community can then encourage states to think in a more open-minded way about TA, and about the role it can play in promoting greater trust, cooperation, and stability in multination states.

Much of this has already been done in ECE, and yet it has had little success in persuading ECE states to consider TA in an openminded way. These states obviously do not trust international guarantees regarding state borders, and understandably so. For one thing, the international community has a rather mixed record on this issue. In some cases (like Abkhazia, Chechnya, and Trans-Dneister), it has indeed refused to recognize *de facto* secessions, and continues to support the principle of the integrity of state borders. But in other cases, notably in the former Soviet Union and Yugoslavia, it was very quick to recognize secessions. ECE states assume, perhaps rightly, that Western powers will sacrifice the principle of the integrity of state borders if they have some larger geopolitical reason for doing so.

More importantly, even if the international community does hold firm to this principle, it doesn't solve the problem of what to do with a territory where the local majority has clearly and democratically affirmed a desire to secede. Imagine that a national minority achieves TA, and begins to conduct democratic elections for the new territorial government. At first, none of the political parties may be explicitly secessionist, partly in order to ensure international cooperation with the new TA regime. But certainly some parties will be pushing for greater autonomy. And over time (perhaps in response to some manifestation of majority intolerance), some people will begin to discuss the merits of secession. Perhaps they won't call it secession, but rather some form of "confederation," or "sovereignty association" or "associated statehood," in which the seceding territory maintains some nominal link with the larger state, while becoming *de facto* independent. And let's imagine that a party promoting some such form of (quasi)-secession is created, and after a few elections eventually becomes the governing party. As part of its platform, it holds a referendum on its proposals for confederation or sovereignty association. Perhaps this referendum is defeated at first (as every such referendum has been defeated in the West), but there is always the chance that it will win, and then the territorial government declares (quasi)independence.

Now what? What does the state do? Let's imagine the international community keeps its promise, and refuses to recognize the declaration of independence. Still the territory has proclaimed independence, and perhaps is beginning to implement this on the ground. Let's say it is refusing to pay taxes to the central government, adopts and enforces laws which violate the state's constitution, adopts its own currency, and refuses to have its citizens drafted into the state army. In principle, the state could send in the army to crush this secessionism – that is, civil war. But even assuming that the state army could win such a civil war (which was not true in several ECE states), the fact is that the international community is unlikely to accept this sort of response. The international community may not favor secession, but nor does it favor military suppression of democratically elected and nonviolent secessionist governments. They will favor "negotiation," the end result of which may be to accept *de facto* independence, even if the fiction of state unity is maintained.

The state could try to short-circuit this scenario by passing a law that secessionist parties cannot run for office. But how do we know which parties are secessionist, and who is to judge? Are parties supporting "confederation" secessionist? Will we send the secret police to attend party rallies to find out what the party really wants? Or perhaps the state could pass a law forbidding the holding of a referendum on secession. But even if we could define such a law, there is still the problem of enforcing it. Let's imagine that the territorial government says that it will hold the referendum anyway: will the state send in the army to break up the balloting stations?

There is no obvious way for a free and democratic country to prevent a self-governing minority from electing secessionist parties, and from holding referendums on secession. This, at any rate, appears to be the lesson from the Western multination federations, all of whom have grudgingly accepted the legitimacy of secessionist political mobilization. The state can only prevent this by undemocratic and illiberal means. And even if these means worked, they would undermine the whole point of the exercise. After all, the point of having TA was to give the minority some sense of secure self-government. The minority will not feel any security if the larger state decides which minority parties are free to run for office, and which questions can be put to a referendum.[23] If the minority needs the majority's permission for every proposed law, political party, or referendum, it is not a meaningful form of self-government. Notice that even those members of the minority who are not in favor of secession are nonetheless typically in favor of the right of secessionist parties to run for office. That the state allows such parties to run is considered proof that it is genuinely committed to democracy and autonomy.

My point is not that federalism inevitably leads to secession. Just the opposite. I believe that democratic federalism reduces the likelihood of secession. But I think democratic federalism only works (or best works) to inhibit secession when secessionist political mobilization is allowed. (Indeed, federalism is only democratic if it allows this.) Minorities will only find TA an acceptable form of self-government if they have the right to freely debate their future, including freely debating a range of options from assimilation to secession. If the state decides for them which options they can debate, and which parties they can vote for, the minority has neither freedom nor democracy, and this will just increase their desire for true independence.

On my view, then, in order to get the full benefits of federalism, we need to accept the legitimacy of secessionist parties, and that entails accepting the possibility (however slim) of a democratically mandated secession. Federalism of this form reduces the chance of secession actually taking place, but it legitimizes the presence of secessionists in the political debate, and institutionalizes the possibility of choosing secession. Successful multination federalism requires desecuritizing democratic secessionist mobilization, and viewing it as simply part of normal politics. Attempts to promote federalism while prohibiting secessionist mobilization are likely to be undemocratic, illiberal, and in the end counterproductive.

In short, multination federalism is unlikely to work where the state views secession as unthinkable, and secessionist mobilization as intolerable. Defenders of TA in ECE have typically tried to promote TA without challenging this fear of secession. They want to put TA on the agenda, while keeping secession off the agenda. But I doubt this strategy will work. In the Western experience, accepting TA has gone hand in hand with accepting the legitimacy of secessionist mobilization, and accepting the possibility of a democratically mandated referendum on secession. ECE states can see this perfectly well. They know that Western-style TA has not "solved the problem of secession," and that international guarantees about state borders will not solve it either. They know that if Québec, Scotland, Puerto Rico, or Catalonia votes one day for secession, there is little that the state, or the international community, can do to prevent it.

If this is correct, the option of setting the threshold between TA and secession will not work. We therefore face a difficult choice: we can either try to push the threshold upwards, and pressure ECE states to desecuritize democratic secessionist mobilization, or push it downwards, and pressure minorities to advance only claims that will not generate security fears.

I believe that the international community has essentially adopted the second approach. Various Western organizations are pressuring national minorities to withdraw claims for territorial autonomy, and promoting instead what is often called "nonterritorial autonomy" or "personal autonomy."[24] The idea here is to allow minorities to have some modest control over their own institutions, such as schools, media, and theatres, without creating any territorial base for potential secessionism.

This idea of nonterritorial autonomy is the flavor of the month in international organizations, and amongst many academic commentators as well. This is said to be the best way of protecting minorities without triggering the security card.[25] I have argued elsewhere, however, that these models of nonterritorial autonomy cannot achieve justice for large, territorially concentrated national minorities. This is why Western democracies have moved toward the model of multination federalism. Had nonterritorial models been sufficient, multination federalism would not have been adopted in the West. It's worth noting, in this respect, that while many commentators extol the virtues of nonterritorial autonomy in ECE, no one suggests that Spain, Canada, Belgium, UK, or Switzerland should scrap their forms of multination federalism for nonterritorial autonomy. No one seriously contemplates the idea that the Catalans, Scots, or Québécois would (or should) be satisfied with nonterritorial autonomy. So why should comparably sized minorities in ECE? I believe that some federal or quasi-federal form of TA is the only just or feasible solution in many multination states.[26]

But even if nonterritorial models are sufficient in many cases, it is surely unacceptable if this defines the threshold for political debate. Even if TA is unnecessary in many cases, it is surely necessary that groups be able to advocate it democratically, and debate its merits publicly. Justice may not require that minorities be granted TA, but democracy requires that minorities be able to discuss TA without being accused of disloyalty, or without being subject to police surveillance. If our concern is with democracy in ECE, as well as minority rights, we need to push that threshold higher up.

This suggests we need to consider a different strategy. Given the perceived link between TA and secession, any attempt to make room for an open debate on TA must also mean making room for an open debate on secession. We need, in short, to desecuritize democratic secessionist mobilization. We must, therefore, challenge the assumption that eliminating secession from the political agenda should be the first goal of the state, a goal which trumps democratic procedures or claims of justice.

We should try to show that secession is not necessarily a crime against humanity, and that the goal of a democratic political system shouldn't be to make it unthinkable. States and state borders are not sacred. The first goal of a state should be to promote democracy, human rights, justice, and the well-being of citizens, not to somehow insist that every citizen view themselves as bound to the existing state "in perpetuity" – a goal which can only be achieved through undemocratic and unjust means in a multination state.[27] A state can only fully enjoy the benefits of democracy and federalism if it is willing to live with the risk of secession.

This indeed is the conclusion that Bibo reached in his 1946 essay. I quoted earlier his claim that ECE states were unable to "take full advantage of the benefits offered by democracy" because they feared the exercise of democratic freedoms by national minorities, and his view that being a democrat means "not to be afraid of those who have different opinions, speak different languages, or belong to other races." He went on to argue that "Under these conditions, a clear-sighted, brave and democratic public opinion can pursue only one course of action: it can offer minorities the greatest opportunities within the existing framework and use its own initiatives to satisfy the boldest minority demands, accepting even the risk of secession" (Bibo 1991: 50).

Of course, as Bibo notes, this sort of "brave and democratic" approach is only possible if we reduce the stakes of secession. I believe that the acceptance of secessionist mobilization in the West is tied to the fact that secession would not threaten the survival of the majority nation. Secession may involve the painful loss of territory, but it is not seen as a threat to the very survival of the majority nation or state. If Quebec, Scotland, Catalonia, or Puerto Rico were to secede, Canada, Britain, Spain, and the United States would still exist as viable and prosperous democracies. In ECE, by contrast, it is widely believed that "the secession of foreign-speaking or minority territories forebodes national death." According to Bibo, accepting the risk of secession was not possible in ECE because of a "political consciousness burdened by fear of survival" (Bibo 1991: 50, 55).[28]

The increased acceptance of secessionist mobilization in the West is also tied to the fact that secession would not necessarily dramatically affect the rights or interests of people in the seceding territory. If Quebec, Scotland, Puerto Rico, or Catalonia were to secede, there would be few changes in the legal rights of people within those regions, or the distribution of power between groups, or in the language of public institutions. Whether these groups have self-government within a larger state, or exist as separate states, they will in either case promote their national language and culture within the constraints of a liberal-democratic constitution which ensures respect for the rights of internal minorities. The seceding group does not gain much by going from a multination federation to an independent state, and internal minorities do not lose much.

In ECE, by contrast, secession is often viewed almost as a matter of life and death. Since politics in unitary nation-states is typically seen as a zero-sum, winner-take-all battle, it is of the utmost importance whether you are a majority or a minority in the state. If you are the majority, it is your language and culture which monopolizes public space and which is a precondition for access to jobs and professional advancement, and every important political decision is made in a forum where you form a majority. If you are the minority, you are faced with political disempowerment (i.e. no important decisions are made in a forum where you are the majority), cultural marginalization, and long-term assimilation. It is no wonder, therefore, that secession is viewed with such dread by ECE states.

If ECE states are ever to accept the risk of secession (and hence accept the risk of a democratic TA), we need to reduce these stakes of secession. We need to find a way of assuring states that the loss of a minority territory does not "forebode national death," and of assuring potential internal minorities that secession does not mean that they will lose their rights or jobs or identities. I believe that such a change in attitudes toward secession is needed, in the long term, if we are ever to have the genuine accommodation of ethnocultural diversity in ECE states. To summarize a complicated argument, I think that the fair accommodation of diversity requires that states be willing to consider claims for TA or other forms of powersharing; and that states will only consider these claims in an openminded way if they are willing to accept the legitimacy of secessionist mobilization; and they will only accept the legitimacy of democratic secessionist mobilization if they no longer see secession as tantamount to national death.

This, at any rate, is the lesson I draw from the Western experience. I believe that multination federalism has worked well in the West to ensure ethnocultural justice, and to reduce the likelihood of secession. But it has been able to achieve this in part because citizens accept the legitimacy of secessionist mobilization. And they accept this legitimacy because the stakes of secession have been dramatically reduced, both for the majority group in the rump state and for internal minorities.[29]

I think there is much the international community can do to reduce the stakes of secession, and thereby increase the willingness of states to adopt forms of democratic TA. But it involves a rather different approach than that currently taken by the international community. At present, the focus is on trying to provide guarantees against secession, not on reducing the stakes of secession. In my view, the goal shouldn't be to provide iron-clad guarantees of existing state borders (which cannot be done in a free and democratic society), but rather to provide firm guarantees that the rights of internal minorities will be protected in the event that state borders change, and that the majority group will survive as a nation even if it loses some minority-inhabited territory.

This sort of change in attitude can only be a very long-term process. And many people think it is unrealistic. Some even view the attempt to help minorities by lowering the stakes of secession as "perverse." According to Horowitz, for example, "it seems perverse to start at the rear end of the problem – with secession – rather than to encourage domestic measures of inter-ethnic accommodation" (Horowitz 1997). Similarly, Norman says that we need to spend more time on how to work out ways of strengthening political marriages rather than facilitating political divorces (Norman 1998: 40). If I am right, however, under the existing circumstances of ECE, the only way to create democratic room to strengthen political marriages is to lower the stakes of political divorce.

NOTES

1. For the ubiquity of this assumption, see Norman 2001.
2. For a defense of the claim that multination federalism meets, and may enhance, liberal-democratic principles, see Kymlicka 2001: ch. 5.
3. It is an interesting question why Russia is an exception. However, it is important to note that multination federalism is not in fact widely accepted in Russia. Most Russian leaders and intellectuals do not like what they call "ethnic federalism," and would prefer to replace it with a German-style form of administrative federalism, in which national minorities do not exercise territorial self-government. Their acceptance of the existing system is almost entirely strategic and transitional. So Russia is not as different from other ECE countries as first appears.
4. On the revoking of autonomy in Georgia, see Vasilyeva 1996; on Nagorno-Karabakh, see Dudwick 1996; on Kosovo, see Troebst 1998; Ramet 1997: 148–54.
5. For a discussion of how post-Soviet countries have approached claims to territorial autonomy, see Kolsto 2002. On the referendum in Estonia, see Laitin 1998: 95; on autonomy in Ukraine see Solchanyk 1994; Marples and Duke 1995; Jaworsky 1998; Packer 1998.
6. On the gerrymandering in Slovakia, see Ramet 1997: 134; Hungarian Coalition 1997: 12, 22. A more extreme policy to forestall autonomy involves promoting settlement of the majority group in the area of minority concentration, so as to swamp the national minority, and make it a minority even within its traditional territory, and hence incapable of exercising autonomy no matter how boundaries are drawn. In the 1980s, the Romanian dictator Ceaucescu was "bulldozing Hungarian villages and colonizing Romanians in their place"

(Cornwall 1996: 19; Ramet 1997: 69). More recently, Serbia tried to encourage massive Serbian "recolonization" of Kosovo, by guaranteeing unemployed Serbs free land and higher wages if they moved to Kosovo (Miall 1999: 135; Ramet 1997: 149–54). For a discussion of such "state-directed population movements," see McGarry 1998.

7. Ukraine was the only country that chose to accept autonomy rather than start a civil war (Marples and Duke 1995), although even it threatened that the declaration of Russian autonomy in Crimea would lead to war (Laitin 1998: 100). The other four countries decided on military intervention. Georgia, Moldova, and Azerbaijan lost the war, and so are negotiating autonomy for Abkhazia, Trans-Dneister, and Ngorno-Karabakh. (On the autonomy negotiations in Georgia, see Coppieters 2000; Vasilyeva 1996; in Moldova, see Chinn and Roper 1995; Socor 1994; Thompson 1998; ECMI 1998; in Azerbaijan, see Dudwick 1996.) Croatia won their war against the Serbs in Krajina, and promptly expelled them, to make sure there would be no chance of Serbian autonomy in the future. The initial position of the Bosnian government of Alija Izetbegovic was also for a centralized unitary state, with no provisions for minority autonomy, and the current cantonal arrangements are the result of an inconclusive civil war.

8. On the multiple confusions involved in standard discussions of civic/ethnic nationalism, see Kymlicka 2001: chs. 12–15.

9. Hence it was a serious mistake to think that removing Milosevic would resolve the crisis in Kosovo. Some people argue that if Albanians in Kosovo had not boycotted the December 1992 election, and supported the main opposition party, they could have helped defeat Milosevic. But the main opposition to Milosevic was equally hostile to the idea of territorial autonomy for Kosovo (Guzina 2000).

10. The flip side is that many of these "post-imperial" minorities, were once not only autonomous, but even privileged rulers over the majority group, and so have gone from privileged overlords to subordinate minorities. This has involved a dramatic reduction in status, as well as in rights and powers, which is not easy for them to accept.

11. For the centrality of this "triadic relationship" between states, minorities, and kin-states in ECE, see Brubaker 1996. By contrast, most Western national minorities do not have a kin-state, and no history of collaborating with foreign invaders or empires. For example, the task of maintaining unity in Switzerland is made easier because the French-speaking part of Switzerland "has never, at any point of its history (bar a few years of Napoleonic rule with partial annexation) been part of France; the French-speaking Swiss are in no way descendants or cousins of the French . . . Similarly, German-speaking Switzerland has never been part of Germany, and Italian-speaking Switzerland has never been part of Italy" (Grin 1999: 5).

12. The phrase was coined, I believe, by Tove Skutnabb-Kangas. For an application to the Baltics, see Druviete 1997.

13. This is precisely what Bulgaria tried to do in the 1980s, for example by forcing all the Turks to adopt ethnic Bulgarian names. Bulgaria argued that the coerced assimilation of the Turks was simply reversing the unjust pressure

that the Ottomans put on Slavs to convert to Islam and to assimilate to Turkish culture (Tomova 1998).

14. This pervasive rhetoric of loyalty/disloyalty is exacerbated in some countries by a local version of Huntington's "clash of civilizations" thesis (Huntington 1996). On this view, the world is divided into distinct "civilizations," grounded essentially in religion, that are in more or less inherent conflict. So the conflict between the Serbs and Albanians over Kosovo is not just a conflict between languages, cultures, or nations, but also between civilizations – an Orthodox Christian civilization and a Muslim civilization. Two civilizations cannot coexist as equal partners in a single state. One civilization must be dominant, and the other subordinate (and hence prone to disloyalty). This clash of civilizations view is also invoked, not only in conflicts between Christians and Muslims, but also between Orthodox and Catholics (e.g. in Romania), or between Protestants and Orthodox (e.g. in Estonia). Where people accept this premise about the clash of civilizations, there is no room for questions about fairness or justice to minorities. Relations between conflicting civilizations are a matter of power and security, not justice.

15. For discussions of this disloyalty/security/fifth-column view, see Andreescu 1997 (re Hungarians in Romania); Mihalikova 1998: 154–57 (re Hungarians in Slovakia); Nelson 1998; Solchanyk 1994 and Jaworsky 1998 (re Russians in Ukraine); Offe 1993: 23–24; Strazzari 1998 (re Albanians in Macedonia); Pettai 1998 (re Russians in the Baltics).

16. For the unhappy tale of the Albanian university in Tetovo, see Pritchard 2000.

17. For example, the Justification section of the 1995 Law on the State Language in Slovakia consists mainly in recounting various Habsburg laws and policies from the nineteenth century that suppressed the use of Slovak and promoted Magyarization. There is no attempt to discuss what would be a fair accommodation of the diverse interests of the majority and minorities. (The Justification is reproduced and discussed in Minority Protection Association 1995.)

18. Except again for Northern Ireland and Cyprus, which have historically been highly securitized.

19. In the past, secessionist parties were banned or kept under secret police surveillance; secessionist professors were sometimes fired from their jobs, and so on. But today, secessionist politics is normal politics.

20. I used to think that the most important distinguishing fact about postcommunist countries is precisely that they are postcommunist – i.e., they are undergoing economic and political transition. I now think that the most distinctive factor is that they are postimperial (post-Ottoman, post-Habsburg, or post-Soviet) – i.e. that majority–minority relations are operating in a context of "minoritized majorities" who have historically been oppressed by their own minorities or the allies of these minorities.

21. As Waever puts is, the task for minority leaders is "to turn threats into challenges: to move developments from the sphere of existential fear to one where they could be handled by ordinary means, as politics, economy, culture, and so on" (Waever 1995: 55). In short, the goal is to negotiate limitations

on the use of the security card. Or in Waever's terms, the motto for defenders of democracy should be "less security, more politics!" (56).

22. For the role of bilateral treaties in desecuritizing minority issues, see Gal 1999.

23. This is one reason why federalism in India has failed to reduce Kashmiri secessionist sentiments. In the name of national security, the central government intervenes constantly to replace elected state governments, repeal state laws, and so on. Federalism only works to reduce secessionist sentiments if it allows for genuine self-government.

24. For the OSCE's discouraging of TA, see Zaagman 1999; Packer 1998; Chandler 1999. For other Western organizations, see Dunay 1997; Heintz 1998. I discuss the attitudes of these organizations in Kymlicka 2002: 369–87.

25. For examples of the enthusiasm for nonterritorial autonomy in ECE, see Liebich 1995; Karklins 2000; Offe 1993; Goble 2000. These models are often said to be inspired by the ideas of Otto Bauer and Karl Renner, who proposed it for the Habsburg Empire (Bauer 2000).

26. For arguments on why ideas of nonterritorial autonomy are insufficient, see Kymlicka 2002: 361–65. See also Stepan 1999 and Young 1994, both of whom argue that federalism is the only option for many cases of minority nationalism.

27. Rawls argues that a liberal-democratic theory of justice should be premised on the idea that people are bound to a state "in perpetuity." I believe that this is an unrealistic and inappropriate goal, particularly in multination states. See Kymlicka 2001: ch. 5.

28. "In Western and Northern Europe the political rise or decline of one's country, the growth or diminution of its role as a great power, and the gaining or losing of colonial empires could have been mere episodes, distant adventures, beautiful or sad memories; in the long run, however, countries could survive these without fundamental trauma, because they had something that could not be taken away or questioned." In Eastern Europe, by contrast, there was "an existential fear for one's community" (Bibo 1991: 39).

29. I should make clear that I am not here endorsing the idea that minorities have a moral right of secession whenever they want to (the so-called "primary right" theory of secession). It might well be unjust for minorities who have generous minority rights within a system of multination federalism to secede simply because they want to have an independent state. It might be that secession is only morally justifiable when it is invoked as a remedy for some injustice, as defenders of the "remedial right" theory of secession argue. I am not here taking any stand on this ongoing debate about the moral right of secession between primary right and remedial right theorists (on this debate, see Moore 1998). I am rather arguing that any viable scheme for accommodating minority nationalism must make room for democratic secessionist mobilization, and view it as normal politics. The secessionist aspiration may be morally unjustifiable, according to the best normative theory of secession, if the minority's just claims are already being met within the existing state. But there are many unjust aspirations that are advanced in democratic politics (e.g. claims by the rich for tax cuts). I am arguing about what is a legitimate

issue to be put on the political agenda for public debate and political mobilization, not about what is the morally best answer to these debates.

REFERENCES

Andreescu, Gabriel (1997) "Recommendation 1201 and a security (stability) network in Central and Eastern Europe." *International Studies (Bucharest)* 3: 50–63.

Bauer, Otto (2000 [1907]) *The Question of Nationalities and Social Democracy.* Minneapolis: University of Minnesota Press.

Bibó, István (1991 [1946]) "The distress of East European small states." In Karoly Nagy (ed.), *Democracy, Revolution, Self-Determination: Selected Writings.* Boulder: Social Science Monographs.

Brubaker, Rogers (1996) *Nationalism Reframed.* Cambridge: Cambridge University Press.

Chandler, David (1999) "The OSCE and the internationalisation of national minority rights." In Karl Cordell (ed.), *Ethnicity and Democratisation in the New Europe.* London: Routledge.

Chinn J. and Roper S. (1995) "Ethnic mobilisation and reactive nationalism: the case of Moldova." *Nationalities Papers* 23 (2): 291–326.

Connor, Walker (1999) "National self-determination and tomorrow's political map." In Alan Cairns *et al.*, (eds.), *Citizenship, Diversity and Pluralism.* Montreal: McGill-Queen's University Press.

Coppieters, Bruno *et al.* (eds.) (2000) *Federal Practice: Exploring Alternatives for Georgia and Abkhazia.* Brussels: VUB University Press.

Cornwall, Mark (1996) "Minority rights and wrongs in Eastern Europe in the twentieth century." *The Historian* 50: 16–20.

Doroszewska, Ursula (2002) "Rethinking the state and national security in Eastern Europe," in Kymlicka and Opalski: pp. 126–34.

Druviete, Ina (1997) "Linguistic human rights in the Baltic states." *International Journal of the Sociology of Language* 127: 161–85.

Dudwick, Nora (1996) "Nagorno Karabakh and the politics of sovereignty." In Ronald Suny (ed.), *Transcaucasia, Nationalism and Social Change.* Ann Arbor: University of Michigan Press.

Dunay, Pal (1997) "Concerns and opportunities: the development of Romanian-Hungarian relations and national minorities." In Gunther Bachler (ed.), *Federalism Against Ethnicity.* Zurich: Verlag Ruegger.

ECMI (1998) "From ethnopolitical conflict to inter-ethnic accord in Moldova." European Centre for Minority Issues, Report No. 1, Flensburg, Germany.

Gal, Kinga (1999) *Bilateral Agreements in Central and Eastern Europe: A New Inter-State Framework for Minority Protection.* Flensburg: European Centre for Minority Issues, Working Paper No. 4.

Goble, Paul (2000) "A new kind of autonomy." *RFE/RL Russian Federation Report* 2/17 (10 May).

Grin, Francois (1999) "Language policy in multilingual Switzerland: Overview and recent developments." ECMI Brief No. 2, European Centre for Minority Issues, Flensburg, Germany.

Guzina, Dejan (2000) "Nationalism in the context of an illiberal multination state: the case of Serbia" (Ph.D. thesis, Department of Political Science, Carleton University, Ottawa).

Heintz, Hans-Joachim (1998) "On the legal understanding of autonomy." In Markku Suksi (ed.), *Autonomy: Applications and Implications*. The Hague: Kluwer.

Horowitz, Donald (1985) *Ethnic Groups in Conflict*. Berkeley: University of California Press.

(1997) "Self-determination: politics, philosophy law." In Will Kymlicka and Ian Shapiro (eds.), *Ethnicity and Group Rights*. New York: NYU Press.

Hungarian Coalition in Slovakia (1997) "The Hungarians in Slovakia." Information Centre of the Hungarian Coalition in Slovakia, Bratislava.

Huntington, Samuel (1996) *The Clash of Civilizations and the Remaking of World Order*. New York: Simon and Schuster.

Ignatieff, Michael (1993) *Blood and Belonging: Journeys Into the New Nationalism.* New York: Farrar, Straus and Giroux.

James, Matt (1999) "Redress politics and Canadian citizenship." In Harvey Lazar and Tom McIntosh (eds.), *How Canadians Connect*. Kingston: Institute of Intergovernmental Relations, Queen's University.

Jaworsky, John (1998) "Nationalities policy and potential for interethnic conflict in Ukraine." In Opalski (ed.), pp. 104–27.

Karklins, Rasma (2000) "Ethnopluralism: panacea for East Central Europe?," *Nationalities Papers* 28 (2): 219–41.

Kolsto, Pal (2002) "Territorial autonomy as a minority rights regime in postcommunist countries." In Kymlicka and Opalski (eds.), pp. 200–19.

Kuzio, Taras (1999) "Nationalising states or nationbuilding? A critical review of the theoretical literature and empirical evidence." Paper presented for the annual convention of the Association for the Study of Nationalities, New York, April 1999.

Kymlicka, Will (2001) *Politics in the Vernacular: Essays on Nationalism, Multiculturalism and Citizenship*. Oxford: Oxford University Press.

(2002) "Western political theory and ethnic relations in Eastern Europe" and "Reply and conclusions." In Kymlicka and Opalski (eds.), pp. 13–105, 345–413.

Kymlicka, Will and Opalski, Magda (eds.) (2002) *Can Liberal Pluralism Be Exported?* Oxford: Oxford University Press.

Laitin, David (1998) *Identity in Formation: The Russian-Speaking Populations in the Near Abroad*. Ithaca: Cornell University Press.

Liebich, Andre (1995) "Nations, states and minorities: why is Eastern Europe different?," *Dissent* (Summer): 313–17.

Marples, David and David Duke (1995) "Ukraine, Russia and the question of Crimea." *Nationalities Papers* 23 (2): 261–89.

McGarry, John (1998) "Demographic engineering: the state-directed movement of ethnic groups as a technique of conflict regulation." *Ethnic and Racial Studies* 21 (4): 615–38.

Miall, Hugh (1999) "The Albanian communities in the postcommunist transition." In K. Cordell (ed.), *Ethnicity and Democratisation in the New Europe*. London: Routledge.

Mihalikova, Silvia (1998) "The Hungarian minority in Slovakia: conflict over autonomy." In Opalski (ed.), pp. 148–64.

Minority Protection Association (1995) *The Slovak State Language Law and the Minorities: Critical Analyses and Remarks.* Budapest: Minority Protection Association.

Moore, Margaret (ed.) (1998) *National Self-Determination and Secession.* Oxford: Oxford University Press.

Nelson, Daniel (1998) "Hungary and its neighbours: security and ethnic minorities." *Nationalities Papers* 26 (2): 314–30.

Norman, Wayne (1998) "The ethics of secession as the regulation of secessionist politics," in Margaret Moore (ed.), *National Self-Determination and Secession.* Oxford: Oxford University Press.

 (2001) "Justice and stability in multinational societies." In Alain Gagnon and James Tully (eds.), *Multinational Democracies.* Cambridge: Cambridge University Press.

Offe, Claus (1993) "Ethnic politics in East European transitions." In Jody Jensen and Ferenc Miszlivetz (eds.), *Paradoxes of Transition.* Szombathely: Savaria University Press.

Opalski, Magda (ed.) (1998) *Managing Diversity in Plural Societies: Minorities, Migration and Nation Building in Postcommunist Europe.* Ottawa: Forum Eastern Europe.

Packer, John (1998) "Autonomy within the OSCE: the case of Crimea." In Markku Suksi (ed.), *Autonomy: Applications and Implications.* The Hague: Kluwer.

Pettai, Vello (1998) "Emerging ethnic democracy in Estonia and Latvia." In Opalski (ed.), pp. 15–32.

Pritchard, Eleonar (2000) "A university of their own." *Central Europe Review* 2 (24) (19 June).

Ramet, Sabrina (1997) *Whose Democracy? Nationalism, Religion, and the Doctrine of Collective Rights in Post-1989 Eastern Europe.* London: Rowman and Littlefield.

Resnick, Philip (1994) "Toward a multination federalism." In Leslie Seidle (ed.), *Seeking a New Canadian Partnership.* Montreal: Institute for Research on Public Policy.

Robinson, Randall (2000) *The Debt: What America Owes to Blacks.* New York: Dutton.

Schopflin, George (2002) "Liberal pluralism and post-communism." In Kymlicka and Opalski (eds.), pp. 109–25.

Socor, Vladimir (1994) "Gagauz autonomy in Moldova: a precedent for Eastern Europe?." *RFE/RL Research Report* 3 (33) (26 August): 20–28.

Solchanyk, Roman (1994) "The politics of state-building: centre–periphery relations in post-Soviet Ukraine." *Europe-Asia Studies* 46 (1): 47–68.

Stepan, Alfred (1999) "Federalism and democracy: beyond the US model." *Journal of Democracy* 10 (4): 19–34.

Strazzari, Francesco (1998) "Macedonia: state and identity in an unstable regional environment." In Opalski (ed.), pp. 165–90.

Thompson, Paula (1998) "The Gagauz in Moldova and their road to autonomy," in Opalski (ed.), pp. 128–47.

Tomova, Ilona (1998) "The migration process in Bulgaria." In Opalski (ed.), pp. 229–39.

Troebst, Stefan (1998) *Conflict in Kosovo: Failure of Prevention.* Flensburg: European Centre for Minority Issues.

Varady, Tibor (1997) "Majorities, minorities, law and ethnicity: refletions on the Yugoslav case." *Human Rights Quarterly* 19: 9–54.

Vasilyeva, Olga (1996) *The Foreign Policy Orientation of Georgia.* Ebenhausen: Stiftung Wissenchaft und Politik.

Waever, Ole (1995) "Securitization and desecuritization." In Ronnie D. Lipschutz (ed.), *On Security.* New York: Columbia University Press.

Young, Crawford, 1994. *Ethnic Diversity and Public Policy: An Overview.* UNRISD, Occasional Paper No. 8.

Zaagman, Rob (1999) *Conflict Prevention in the Baltic States: The OSCE High Commissioner on National Minorities in Estonia, Latvia and Lithuania.* ECMI Monograph No. 1. Flensburg: European Centre for Minority Issues.

8   Two concepts of self-determination

Iris Marion Young

In a speech he gave before a 1995 meeting of the Open-Ended Inter-Sessional Working Group on Indigenous Peoples' Rights, established in accordance with the United Nations Commission on Human Rights, Craig Scott appealed to a meaning of self-determination as relationship and connection rather than its more common understanding as separation and independence.

> If one listens, one can often hear the message that the right of a people to self-determination is not a right for peoples to determine their status without consideration of the rights of other peoples with whom they are presently connected and with whom they will continue to be connected in the future. For we must realize that peoples, no less than individuals, exist and thrive only in dialogue with each other. Self-determination necessarily involves engagement with and responsibility to others (which includes responsibility for the implications of one's preferred choices for others) . . . We need to begin to think of self-determination in terms of peoples existing in relationship with each other. It is the process of negotiating the nature of such relationships which is part of, indeed at the very core of, what it means to be a self-determining people.[1]

Scott's plea is very suggestive, but he neither develops a critical account of the concept of self-determination from which he distinguishes his own, nor does he explain the meaning, justification, and implications of the concept he proposes.

In this chapter, I articulate these two interpretations of a principle of the self-determination of peoples, and argue for a relational interpretation along the lines that Scott proposes. Like Scott, my motive in this conceptual work is to contribute to an understanding of the specific claims of indigenous peoples to self-determination. I believe the concept of self-determination I advocate, however, applies to all peoples and relationships among peoples.

First, I briefly review the current status of a principle of self-determination in international law and recent developments of indigenous peoples. Then I elaborate the historically dominant interpretation of a principle of self-determination for peoples, which continues to hold the minds of many who write on the subject. This concept of self-determination equates it with sovereign independence, where the self-determining entity claims a right of nonintervention and noninterference. Drawing particularly on feminist critiques of a concept of the autonomy of the person as independence and noninterference, I argue that this first concept of self-determination ignores the relations of interdependence peoples have with one another, especially in a global economic system. Again following the lead of feminist theories of autonomy, I argue for a relational concept of the self-determination of peoples. I draw on Philip Pettit's theory of freedom as nondomination to argue that peoples can be self-determining only if the relations in which they stand to others are nondominating. To ensure nondomination their relations must be regulated both by institutions in which they all participate and by ongoing negotiations among them.

Self-determination and international politics

Neither the United Nations Charter nor the 1948 Declaration of Human Rights mentions a right of self-determination. The General Assembly resolution 1541 appears to be the origin of the post-Second World War discourse of self-determination. Passed with the project of decolonization in view, that resolution defines self-government as entailing either independence, free association with an independent state, or the integration of a people with an independent state on the basis of equality. It implicitly entails the "salt water" test for ascertaining whether a people deserves recognition of their right to self-determination: they have a distinct territory separated by long global distances from a colonial power from which they claim independence. Recognition of self-determination in these cases entails recognition of separate independent sovereign states if that is what the former colonies wish.

Between the era of postcolonial independence and the early 1990s the international community showed great reluctance to apply a principle of self-determination to disputes among peoples in territorial contiguity. In two decades fewer than ten new states were established and recognized under such a principle. As international law on human rights has evolved, some scholars argue that many of the issues of freedom and self-governance that people in the world raise can be treated under individual human rights principles, without invoking a collective principle of self-determination – such as rights of minorities against discrimination and persecution, rights to participate in the governance of the state, rights of cultural practice and preservation.

Some international agreements since the 1950s, however, elaborate further a principle of self-determination for peoples. The Covenant on Economic, Social and Cultural Rights and Covenant on Civil and Political Rights, which was drafted in 1966 and went into force in 1976, states a principle of self-determination in Article 1. All peoples have the right to self-determination, which means freely to determine their political status and pursue economic, social, and cultural development. The Helsinki Final Act of 1975, the Conference on Security and Cooperation in Europe, also reaffirms the right of a people to be free from external influence in choosing their own form of government.[2]

A principle of self-determination for peoples, then, has been increasingly recognized as applying to all peoples, and not only those in the territories of the former European colonies of Africa and Asia. Continued and wider affirmation of a principle of self-determination in international documents encourages indigenous groups and other displaced, oppressed, or dominated groups to press claims against states that claim to have jurisdiction over them both directly and in international forums. Hotly contested, of course, is just what counts as a "people" who have a legitimate claim to self-determination. This is a crucial question which I believe cannot be settled by means of a once and for all definition. Peoples are not natural kinds, clearly identifiable and distinguishable by a set of essential attributes. Although I shall not argue this here, I believe that the relations among peoples and their degrees of distinctness are more fluid, relational, and dependent on context than such a substantial logic suggests.[3]

Instead of addressing the important and contentious question of what a people is, here I will assume that there are some groups in the world today whose status as distinct peoples is largely uncontested, but which do not have states of their own and make claims for greater self-determination. Among such groups are at least some of those called indigenous peoples.

I bracket the question of what is a people in order to focus on the question of what counts as self-determination. For while a principle of self-determination appears to have acquired a wider scope in international law in recent decades, it appears at the same time to have lost clarity and precision as a concept. Since the era when former colonies obtained state independence, the international community has been very reluctant to allow a principle of self-determination to ground or endorse claims of separation, secession, and the formation of new states. The breakup of the Soviet Union and Yugoslavia into separate sovereign states is a grand exception, mainly explicable by a cynical desire in the West to weaken a former world power once and for all. Claims by minority groups that they are wrongly dominated by dominant groups in nation-states seem to be getting more hearing in international political discussions. At the same time the dominant opinion among global powers gives a strong priority to the preservation of existing state territories. Thus the opinion seems to be widely held among scholars and practitioners of international law that if certain peoples have rights to self-determination, this does not entail rights to secede from existing nation-states and establish their own independent sovereign states with exclusive rights over a contiguous territory. Such clarity on what self-determination does not imply today, however, produces confusion about what it does imply. It is to this question that I aim to contribute moral and political theoretical arguments of clarification.

The claims of indigenous peoples

For more than twenty years, United Nations commissions have met to discuss the claims and status of the world's indigenous peoples. This work has culminated in the UN Draft Declaration of the Rights of Indigenous Peoples, which was discussed at the 1995 meeting I cited above. Indigenous activists hope that this Declaration or a close sister will be approved by a majority of the world's states and peoples by the end of the UN decade on the indigenous in 2004.[4]

At issue in world forums and in documents such as the Draft Declaration are both the definition of indigenous peoples and to whom the definition applies. Just who counts as indigenous is fairly clear in the case of the American settler colonies and in the settler colonies of Australia and New Zealand. They are the people who inhabited the land for centuries before the European settlers came, and who live today in some continuity with the premodern ways of life of their ancestors. The United Nations, however, also recognizes some other peoples in Europe, Asia, and Africa as indigenous, a designation which some states contest for some of "their" minorities. Still other groups, which the United Nations does not recognize as indigenous, would like to be so recognized. Just who should and should not count as indigenous people, as distinct from simply ethnic groups, is a contentious issue. Although this question is also important, I will bracket it as well. I will assume that descendants of the pre-Columbian inhabitants of North and South America count as indigenous peoples, as well as the Aboriginal people of New Zealand and Australia. While I believe there are others who ought to have rights of indigenous people, in this chapter I will not develop criteria for classifying a people as indigenous and apply these criteria. Although I begin my thinking about the principle of self-determination by reflecting on the claims of (at least some) indigenous people, ultimately I believe that the conception of self-determination which I recommend ought to apply to all peoples. Thus for the argument of this chapter it is neither necessary to find an iron-clad definition of *indigenous* nor to sort out which peoples are and which are not indigenous.

The UN Draft Declaration specifies that indigenous peoples have a right to autonomy or self-government in matters relating to their internal and local affairs, including culture, employment, social welfare, economic activities, land and resources, management and environment.[5] Nothing in the Declaration implies that indigenous peoples have a right to form separate states, and few if any indigenous people actually seek to form separate states. Most seek explicit recognition as distinct peoples by the states that claim to have jurisdiction over them, and wider terms of autonomy and negotiation with those states and with the other peoples living within those states. They claim or seek significant self-government rights, not only with respect to cultural issues, but with respect to land and access to resources. They claim to have rights to be distinct political entities with which other political entities, such as states, must negotiate agreements and over which they cannot simply impose their will and their law.[6]

Although indigenous peoples rarely seek to be separate states, they nevertheless claim that their legitimate rights of self-determination are nowhere completely recognized and respected. Every region of the world has its own stories and struggles of indigenous people in relation to the states that have emerged from colonization, and a full review of these claims and struggles would take me away from the conceptual work that is the main task of this chapter. Thus I will focus on the example of indigenous related to the United States. Native Americans have a relatively long history of self-government institutions recognized by the US government; in the last twenty years Native self-government has been more actual than ever before. Nevertheless, Native Americans typically claim that the US government has never recognized their rights to self-determination, and that they are not so recognized today. The US Congress reserves the right to recognize a group as a tribe, a status which accords it self-government rights. At any time, the Congress believes itself to have the power to rescind tribal status, and it has done so in the past, most notably during the period in the 1950s when the Indian Termination Act was in effect. Congress continues to act as though it has ultimate legislative authority over Native Americans. In the Indian Gaming Act of 1988, Congress for the first time ever required Native peoples to negotiate with US state governments regarding the use of Indian lands.

Some US public officials believe that Indians should not have distinct and recognized self-government and legal jurisdiction, and have led efforts to cripple Indian sovereignty. In the fall 1997, for example,

Senator Slade Gorton (R – Washington) led a move to make the allocation of funds to tribal governments conditional on their waiving their current immunity from civil lawsuits filed in US courts. This effort, hidden within the bill allocating funds to the National Endowment for the Arts and for national parks, was defeated. Even if it had passed it would likely not have stood up to treaty-based court challenge. It nevertheless shows how thin the line may be between self-government and subjection for Native Americans today.

My interest in rethinking the concept of the self-determination of peoples, then, begins from this apparent paradox. Indigenous peoples claim not to have full recognition of rights of self-determination, but most do not claim that allowing them to constitute separate states is necessary for such recognition. The dominant meaning of the concept of self-determination today would seem to require sovereign statehood. What is a meaning of the concept of self-determination that would correspond to the claims of indigenous peoples? I will argue that a concept of self-determination as relational autonomy in the context of non-domination best corresponds to these indigenous claims.

Self-determination as noninterference

Although some international political and legal developments of recent decades have brought it into question, the most widely accepted and clearly articulated meaning of self-determination defines it as independent *sovereignty*. An authority is sovereign, in the sense I have in mind, when it has final authority over the regulation of all activities within a territory, and when no authority outside that territory has the legitimate right to cancel or override them.[7]

This concept of self-determination interprets freedom as noninterference. On this model, self-determination means that a people or government has the authority to exercise complete control over what goes on inside its jurisdiction, and no outside agent has the right to make claims upon or interfere with what the self-determining agent does. Reciprocally, the self-determining people have no claim on what others do with respect to issues within their jurisdictions, and no right to interfere in the business of the others. Just as it denies rights of interference by outsiders in a jurisdiction, this concept entails that each self-determining entity has no inherent obligations with respect to outsiders.

Only states have a status approaching self-determination as noninterference in today's world. When the principle of self-determination was systematized in the early twentieth century and then again after the Second World War, world leaders created or authorized the formation of states according to criteria of viability and independence. For a state to be sovereign or self-determining, and thus to have a right of non-interference, it was thought, it must be large enough to stand against other states if necessary, and have the right amount and kind of resources so that its people can thrive economically without depending on out-siders. Thus the world powers that created states after the First World War were concerned that no state be land locked and that states recog-nized as sovereign have sufficient natural resources to sustain an indepen-dent economy. The powers creating states in the decades after the Second World War also brought these standards of viability for independent living to bear on their work, usually seeking to make states large, though not always succeeding. Some today who worry about applying a principle of self-determination to peoples, such as indigenous peoples, continue to take the ability to be economically independent as a condition of such exercise of self-determination.

Some political theorists argue that state sovereignty considered as final authority and the enjoyment of noninterference is eroding today, and may have never existed to the extent that concept supposes.[8] Some think that global capitalism and international law increasingly circumscribe the independence and sovereignty of states.[9] Here I am less concerned with whether any peoples or governments actually have self-determination as noninterference, however, than with evaluating the normative adequacy of the concept, especially in light of indigenous peoples' claims. I argue below that noninterference is not a normatively adequate interpretation of a principle of self-determination.

My argument relies on two different but I believe compatible efforts to theorize a concept of individual autonomy which criticize the primacy of noninterference and offer alternative accounts. The first comes from feminist political theory and the second from neorepublican theory. Both theories suggest that the idea of freedom as noninterference does not properly take account of social relationships and possibilities for domina-tion. The form of their arguments can be extended, moreover, from the relation among individuals to relations among peoples.

The concept of freedom as noninterference presupposes that agents have a domain of action that is their own which is independent of need for relationship with or influence by others. The status of autonomous cit-izenship presupposes this private sphere of individual property. From this base of independence, on this account, individual agents enter relation-ships with others through voluntary agreements. Except where obliga-tions are generated through such agreements, the freedom of individuals ought not to be interfered with unless they are directly and actively inter-fering with the freedom of others. The ideal of self-determination, on this view, consists in an agent being left alone to conduct his or her affairs over his or her own independent sphere.

Critics of liberal individualism since Hegel have argued that this image of the free individual as ontologically and morally independent fails to recognize that subjects are constituted through relationships, and that agents are embedded in institutional relations that make them interdependent in many ways. Relational feminist critics of the equation of freedom with noninterference draw on both these insights. In contrast to an account of the subject as constituted through bounding itself from others, a relational account of the subject says that the individual person is constituted through his or her communicative and interactive relations with others. The individual person acquires a sense of self from being recognized by others with whom he or she has relationships; she acts in reference to a complex web of social relations and social effects that both constrain and enable her.[10]

On this account, the idea that a person's autonomy consists in control over a domain of activity independent of others and from which they are excluded except through mutual agreements is a dangerous fiction. This concept of self-determination as noninterference values independence, and thereby devalues any persons not deemed independent by its account. Historically this meant that only propertyholding heads of households could expect to have their freedom recognized. Women and workers could not be fully self-determining citizens, because their position in the division of labor rendered them dependent on the property holders. Feminist criticism argues, however, that in fact the male head of household and property holder is no more independent than the women or workers he rules. The appearance of his independence is produced by a system of domination in which he is able to command and benefit from the labor of others. This frees him from bodily and menial tasks of self-care and routine production, and helps increase his property, so that he can spend his time at politics or business deals. In fact, the more powerful agents are as embedded in interdependent social relations as the less powerful agents. Feminists argue that contemporary discourse of the freedom of individuals understood as noninterference continues to assume falsely that all or most persons are or ought to be independent in the sense that they can rely on their own sphere of activity to support them and need nothing from others.

Feminist theory thus offers an alternative concept of autonomy, which takes account of the interdependence of agents and their embeddedness in relationships at the same time that it continues to value individual choices. In this concept, all agents are owed equal respect as autonomous agents, which means that they are able choose their ends and have capacity and support to pursue those ends. They are owed this because they are agents, and not because they inhabit a separate sphere from others. The social constitution of agents and their acting in relations of interdependence means the ability to be separate in that way is rare if it appears at all. Thus an adequate conception of autonomy should promote the capacity of individuals to pursue their own ends in the context of relationships in which others may do the same. While this concept of autonomy entails a presumption of noninterference, especially with the choice of ends, it does not imply a social scheme in which atomized agents simply mind their own business and leave each other alone. Instead, it entails recognizing that agents are related in many ways they have not chosen, by virtue of kinship, history, proximity, or the unintended consequences of action. In these relationships agents are able either to thwart one another or support one another. Relational autonomy consists partly, then, in the structuring of relationships so that they support the maximal pursuit of individual ends.

In his reinterpretation of ideals of classical republicanism, Philip Pettit offers a similar criticism of the idea of freedom as noninterference.[11] Interference means that one agent blocks or redirects the action of another in a way that worsens that agent's choice situation by changing the range of options. On Pettit's account, noninterference, while related to freedom, is not equivalent to it. Instead, freedom should be understood as nondomination. An agent dominates another when he or she has power over that other and is thus able to interfere with the other *arbitrarily*. Interference is arbitrary when it is chosen or rejected without consideration of the interests or opinions of those affected. An agent may dominate another, however, without ever interfering with that person. Domination consists in standing in a set of relations which makes an agent *able* to interfere arbitrarily with the actions of others.

Thus freedom is not equivalent to noninterference both because an unfree person may not experience interference, and because a free person may be interfered with. In both cases the primary criterion of freedom is nondomination. Thus when a person has a personal or institutional power that makes him or her able to interfere with my action arbitrarily, I am not free, even if in fact the dominating agent has not directly interfered with my actions. Conversely, a person whose actions are interfered with for the sake of reducing or eliminating such relations of domination is not unfree. On Pettit's account, it is appropriate for governing agents to interfere in actions in order to promote institutions that minimize domination. Interference is not arbitrary if its purpose is to minimize domination, and if it is done in a way that takes the interests and voices of affected parties into account. Like the feminist concept of relational autonomy, then, the concept of freedom as nondomination refers to a set of social relations. "Non-domination is the position that someone enjoys when they live in the presence of other people and when, by virtue of social design, none of those others dominates them" (p. 67).

In sum, both the feminist and neorepublican criticisms of the identification of freedom with noninterference are mindful of the relations in which people stand. A concept of freedom as noninterference aims to bound the agent from those relations, and imagines an independent sphere of action unaffected by and not affecting others. Because people are deeply embedded in relationships many of which they have not chosen, however, they are affected by and do affect one another in their actions, even when they do not intend this mutual effect. Such interdependence is part of what enables domination, the ability for some to interfere arbitrarily with the actions of others. Freedom then means regulating and negotiating the relationships of people so that all are able to be secure in the knowledge that their interests, opinions, and desires for action are taken into account.

Relational interpretation of self-determination

We are now in a position to fill out Craig Scott's claim, that I quoted above, that we should think of the self-determination of peoples in the context of relationships. For the moment I will keep the discussion focused on the situation of indigenous people in the Americas and the antipodes. Because of a long and dominative history of settlement, exchange, treaty, conquest, removal, and sometimes recognition, indigenous and nonindigenous peoples are now interrelated in their territories. Webs of economic and communicative exchange, moreover, place the multicultural people of a particular region in relations of interdependence with others far away. In such a situation of interdependence, it is difficult for a people to be independent in the sense that they require nothing from outsiders and their activity has no effect on others.

I propose that the critique of the idea of freedom as noninterference and an alternative concept of relational autonomy and nondomination is not only relevant to thinking about the meaning of freedom for individuals. It can be usefully extended to an interpretation of the self-determination of a people. Extending any ideas of individual freedom and autonomy to peoples, of course, raises conceptual and political issues of what is the "self" of a people analogous to individual will and desire, by which it can makes sense to apply a concept of self-determination to a people at all. Extending political theoretical concepts of individual freedom to a people appears to reify or personify a social aggregate as a unity with a set of common interests, agency, and will of its own.[12] In fact, however, no such unified entity exists. Any tribe, city, nation, or other designated group is a collection of individuals with diverse interests and affinities, prone to disagreements and internal conflicts. One rarely finds a set of interests agreed upon by all members of a group that can guide their autonomous government. When we talk about self-determination for people, moreover, we encounter the further problem that it is sometimes ambiguous who belongs to a particular group, and that many individuals have reasonable claim to belong to more than one. Since a group has neither unanimity nor bounded unity of membership, what sense does it make to recognize its right to self-determination.

It is certainly true that group membership is sometimes plural, ambiguous, and overlapping, and that groups cannot be defined by a single set of shared attributes or interests. This is why it is sometimes difficult to say decisively that a particular collection of individuals counts as a distinct people. Such difficulties do not negate the fact, however, that historical and cultural groups have often been and continue to be dominated and exploited by other groups often using state power to do so. Nor do these ambiguities negate the fact that freedom as self-government and cultural autonomy is important to many people who consider themselves as belonging to distinct peoples.

Any collection of people that constitutes itself as a political community must worry about how to respond to conflict and dissent within the community, and whether the decisions and actions carried out in the name of a group can be said to *belong* to the group. For this reason the "self" of a group that claims a right to self-determination needs more explication than does the "self" of individual persons, though the latter concept is hardly clear and distinct. Insofar as a collective has a set of institutions through which that people make decisions and implement them, then the group sometimes expresses unity in the sense of agency. Whatever conflicts and disagreements may have led up to that point, once decisions have been made and action taken through collective institutions, the group itself can be said to act. Such a discourse of group agency and representation of agency to wider publics need not falsely personify the group or suppress differences among its members. Most governments claim to act for "the people," and their claims are more or less legitimate to the extent that the individuals in the society accept the government and its actions as theirs, and even more legitimate if they have had real influence in its decisionmaking processes. This capacity for agency is the only secular political meaning that the "self" of collective self-determination can have.

Self-determination for indigenous peoples, as well as other peoples, should not mean noninterference. An interpretation of self-determination modeled on state sovereign independence equates a principle of self-determination with noninterference. For the most part, indigenous peoples do not wish to be states in that sense, and while they claim autonomy they do not claim such a blanket principle of noninterference. Their claims for self-determination, I suggest, are better understood as a quest for an institutional context of nondomination.[13]

On such an interpretation, self-determination for peoples means that they have a right to their own governance institutions through which they decide on their goals and interpret their way of life. Other people ought not to constrain, dominate, or interfere with those decisions and interpretations for the sake of their own ends, or according to their judgment of what way of life is best, or in order to subordinate a people to a larger "national" unit. Peoples, that is, ought to be free from domination. Because a people stands in interdependent relations with others, however, a people cannot ignore the claims and interests of those others when their actions potentially affect them. Insofar as outsiders are affected by the activities of a self-determining people, those others have a legitimate claim to have their interests and needs taken into account even though they are outside the government jurisdiction. Conversely, outsiders should recognize that when they themselves affect a people, the latter can legitimately claim that they should have their interests taken into account insofar as they may be adversely affected. Insofar as their activities affect one another, peoples are in relationship and ought to negotiate the terms and effects of the relationship.

Self-determining peoples morally cannot do whatever they want without interference from others. Their territorial, economic, or communicative relationships with others generate conflicts and collective problems that oblige them to acknowledge the legitimate interests of others as well as promote their own. Pettit argues that states can legitimately interfere with the actions of individuals in order to foster institutions that minimize domination. A similar argument applies to actions and relations of collectivities. In a densely interdependent world, peoples require political institutions that lay down procedures for coordinating action, resolving conflicts, and negotiating relationships.

The self-determination of peoples, then, has the following elements. First, self-determination means a presumption of noninterference. A people has the prima facie right to set its own governance procedures and make its own decisions about its activities, without interference from others. Second, insofar as the activities of a group may adversely affect others, or generate conflict, self-determination entails the right of those others to make claims on the group, negotiate the terms of their relationships, and mutually adjust their effects. Third, a world of self-determining peoples thus requires recognized and settled institutions and procedures through which peoples negotiate, adjudicate conflicts, and enforce agreements.

Self-determination does not imply independence, but rather that peoples dwell together within political institutions which minimize domination among peoples. It would take another essay to address the question of just what form such intergovernmental political institutions should take; some forms of federalism do and should apply. Finally, the self-determination of peoples requires that the peoples have the right to participate *as peoples* in designing and implementing intergovernmental institutions aimed at minimizing domination.

I have argued for a principle of self-determination understood as relational autonomy in the context of nondomination, instead of a principle of self-determination understood simply as noninterference. This argument applies as much to large nation-states as to small indigenous groups. Those entities that today are considered self-determining independent states in principle ought to have no more right of noninterference than should smaller groups. Self-determination for those entities now called sovereign states should mean nondomination. While this means a presumption of noninterference, outsiders may have a claim on their activities.

Understanding freedom as nondomination implies shifting the idea of state sovereignty into a different context. Sovereign independence is neither a necessary nor a sufficient condition of self-determination understood as nondomination. As I have developed it above, a self-governing people need not be able to say that it is entirely independent of others in order to be self-determining; indeed, I have argued that such an idea of independence is largely illusory. For these reasons self-governing peoples ought to recognize their connections with others, and make claims on others when the actions of those others affect them, just as the others have a legitimate right to make claims on them when their interdependent relations threaten to harm them.

Those same relations of interdependence mean, however, that sovereign independence is not a sufficient condition of self-determination understood as nondomination. The people living within many formally independent states stand in relation to other states, or powerful private actors such as multinational corporations, where those others are able to interfere arbitrarily with the actions in order to promote interests of their own. For some people formal sovereignty is little protection against such dominative relations. The institutions of formal state sovereignty, however, allow many agents to absolve themselves of responsibility to support self-governing peoples who nevertheless stand in relations of domination.

Thus the interpretation of self-determination as nondomination ultimately implies limiting the rights of existing nation-states and setting these into different more cooperatively regulated relationships. Just as promoting freedom for individuals involves regulating relationships in order to prevent domination, so promoting self-determination for peoples involves regulating international relations to prevent the domination of peoples.

Applying a principle of self-determination as nondomination to existing states, then, as well as to peoples not currently organized as states, has profound implications for the freedom of the former. States ought not to have rights to interfere arbitrarily in the activities of those peoples in relation to whom they claim special jurisdictional relation. In the pragmatic context of political argument within both nation-state and international politics, many indigenous groups do not challenge the idea that the autonomy rights they claim are or will be within the framework of nation-states. Some appear to recognize that nation-states presume a right of noninterference in their dealings with "their" autonomous minorities.[14] If self-determination for peoples means not noninterference but nondomination, however, then nation-states cannot have a right of noninterference in their dealings with indigenous minorities and other ethnic minorities. Small, resource poor, relatively weak peoples are more likely to experience domination by larger and more organized peoples living next to or among them than by others far away. The nation-state that claims jurisdiction with respect to a relatively autonomous people is likely sometimes to dominate that people. If a self-determining people has no public forum to which it can go to press claims of such wrongful domination against a nation-state, and if no agents outside the state have the authority and power to affect a state's relation to that people, then that people cannot be said to be self-determining.

Thus a principle of self-determination for indigenous peoples can have little meaning unless it accompanies a limitation on and ultimately a transformation of the rights and powers of existing nation-states and the assumptions of recognition and noninterference that still largely govern the relation between states.[15] There are good reasons to preserve the coordination capacities that many existing states have and to strengthen these capacities where they are weak. Nevertheless, the capacities of diverse peoples to coordinate action to promote peace, distributive justice, or ecological value can in principle be maintained and enlarged within institutions that also aim to minimize the domination that states are able to exercise over individuals and groups.

Illustration: the Goshutes *vs.* Utah

Let me illustrate the difference between a concept of self-determination as noninterference and a concept of self-determination as autonomy in regulated relations by reflecting on a particular conflict between a Native American tribe and some residents of the state of Utah.

The Skull Valley Band of Goshutes have offered to lease part of their reservation as the temporary storage ground for high-level civil nuclear waste. The state of Utah's territory surrounds this small reservation, and state officials have vowed to block the border of the reservation from shipments of nuclear waste. The Skull Valley Band of Goshutes asserts that they have sovereign authority over the reservation territory and the activities within it, and that the state of Utah has no jurisdiction over this activity. The state of Utah, on behalf of counties near the reservation, claims that they have the responsibility to protect the health and welfare of the citizens of Utah. Since the storage of nuclear waste carries risks of potential harm that people in counties surrounding the reservation would bear, along with those living on the reservation, the state of Utah feels obliged to assert its power.[16]

So far as I understand the law of tribes and the United States, the Goshutes do have a right to make this decision through their own government mechanism, and to issue their own guidelines to a waste storage operation that wishes to lease their land. They are obliged neither to consult the state of Utah nor to abide by the regulations of the US Environmental Protection Agency. Just this sort of legal independence makes Indian reservations attractive as potential sites for the treatment or storage of hazardous wastes from the point of view of the companies that operate such facilities. Sometimes companies are willing to pay handsomely for the privilege of working with Indian groups in order to bypass what some regard as unnecessarily complex and time-consuming state and federal regulatory processes. For their part, some Indian groups such as the Skull Valley Band find in such leasing arrangements one of only a few opportunities to generate significant income with which they can improve the lives of their members and develop reservation infrastructure.

The Goshutes, I have said, do have self-determination rights in this situation. They are a distinct and historically colonized people with a right to preserve their cultural distinctness and enlarge their well-being as a group through their own forms of collective action. On the interpretation of this right of self-determination that I reject, they may simply deny that the state of Utah and US federal government have a right to interfere with their decision to lease the land for a nuclear waste storage site. On this interpretation, they can rightfully say that this decision is entirely their business and is none of the business of the state of Utah.

There is no denying, however, that the siting of a nuclear waste storage facility has potential consequences for people living in Utah counties near the reservation. They can be just as adversely affected as those on the reservation if the facility leaks radioactive material into the ground, water, or air. On my account of self-determination, the Goshutes and the citizens of Utah are in a close and ongoing relationship. This relationship, in this case partly defined by geographical proximity, obliges the Goshutes to take the interests of potentially affected citizens of Utah into account.

The apparent approach of the state of Utah to this controversy, however, is to challenge any right to self-determination. The state of Utah apparently would like to have the power to override the Goshute decision, to impose state government power and regulations over this group. It seems that between the two groups we face the alternatives of either recognizing the right of the Indian band to do what it wishes with its territory, or recognizing the right of a larger entity around it to exercise final authority over that territory.

More generally, the United States Congress has begun hearings on the question of whether US tribal sovereignty should not be revised or eliminated. There are many in the United States who believe that disputes such as this nuclear siting dispute are best addressed by eliminating jurisdictional difference. All the people in a contiguous territory in this case, ought to be subject to the same laws and procedures of decisionmaking. On this account, a state ought to be the overriding, unifying, and final authority, with no independent entities "within" it. When that state is recognized by the international community as an independent sovereign state, such as the United States or New Zealand, then that sovereign state has a right of self-determination understood as noninterference. Such a right of noninterference applies particularly to the right of that state to make its own decisions about how it will rule over "its" minorities who claim rights of self-determination in relation to it. All states recognized as independent sovereign states in international law today have, at the moment, such a right of noninterference with respect to "their" indigenous peoples. Hearings considering the question of whether to continue the current system of tribal self-determination assume that the United States has such a right.

From the point of view of indigenous people, even those that presently have significant autonomy rights in relation to the states that claim jurisdiction over them, this right of states is illegitimate. The only recourse they have within the logic of national sovereigntists is to assert for themselves the right of autonomy as noninterference. Political stand-off, then, is the typical result of this position.

Self-determination understood as relational autonomy, on the other hand, conceives the normative and jurisdictional issues in this dispute as follows. The Skull Valley Band of the Goshutes should be recognized as a self-determining people. This implies that they have self-government rights and through that government they can make decisions about the use of land and resources under their jurisdiction which they think will benefit their members. Thus they may decide to lease land for nuclear waste storage. They do not have an unlimited right of noninterference, however, concerning their activities. Communities outside the tribe who claim potential adverse effects on themselves because of tribal decisions have a *claim* upon those activities, and the Goshutes are morally obliged to hear that claim. Intergovernmental relations ought to be so structured that, when self-governing entities stand in relationships of contiguity or mutual effect, there are settled procedures of discussion and negotiation about conflicts, side-effects of their activities, and shared problems. Because parties in a dispute frequently polarize or fail to respect each other, such procedures should include a role for public oversight and arbitration by outside parties with less stake in the dispute. Such procedures of negotiation, however, are very different from being subject to the authority of a state under which more local governments including the indigenous governments stand, and which finally decides the rules.[17]

Final question: the rights of individuals

I have argued that international law ought to continue to recognize a principle of self-determination for peoples, and should interpret this principle differently from the traditional principle of noninterference and independence. I have argued for an alternative interpretation of self-determination as relational autonomy in the context of institutions that aim to prevent domination. Some critics suspect claims to self-determination, and recognizing such claims, because they worry that this gives license to a group to oppress individuals or subgroups within the group. If a people has a right to govern its affairs in its own way, some object, then this allows discriminatory or oppressive practices and policies toward women, or members of particular religious groups, or castes within the group to go unchallenged. This sort of objection has little force, however, if we accept a concept of self-determination conceived as relational autonomy in the context of institutions that minimize domination.

My articulation of a principle of self-determination as involving non-domination instead of noninterference above focused on the relationship between a group and those outside the group. If we give priority to a principle of nondomination, however, then it should also apply to the relation between a group and its members. The self-determination of a people should not extend so far as to permit the domination of some of its members by others. For reasons other than those of mutual effect, namely reasons of individual human right, outsiders sometimes have a responsibility to interfere with the self-governing actions of a group in order to prevent severe human rights violations. This claim introduces a whole new set of contentious questions, however, about how human rights are defined, who should decide when they have been seriously violated by a government against its members, and the proper agents and procedures of intervention. These important questions are beyond the scope of this chapter. A relational concept of self-determination for peoples does not entail that members of the group can do anything they want to other members without interference from those outside. It does entail, however, that insofar as there are global rules defining individual rights, and agents to enforce them, that all peoples should have the right to be represented *as peoples* in the fora that define and defend those rights. Thus the sort of global regulatory institutions I have said are ultimately necessary to prevent domination between peoples should be constituted by the participation of all the peoples regulated by them.

NOTES

This chapter was first published in Austin Sarat (ed.), *Human Rights and International Politics*, University of Michigan Press, 2001.
1. Craig Scott, "Indigenous self-determination and decolonization of the international imagination: a plea," *Human Rights Quarterly* 18 (1996): 819.
2. On the state of international law, see Hurst Hannum, "Self-determination in the post-colonial era," in Donald Clark and Robert Williamson (eds.), *Self-Determination: International Perspectives*, New York: St. Martin's Press, 1996, pp. 12–44; see also Hannum, *Autonomy, Sovereignty, and Self-Determination: The Accommodation of Conflicting Rights*, Philadelphia: University of Pennsylvania Press, 1990.
3. I develop some of this argument in another paper "Self-determination and global democracy," in Ian Shapiro and Stephen Macedo, *NOMOS: Designing Democratic Institutions*, New York: New York University Press, 1999; see also I. M. Young, *Inclusion and Democracy*, Oxford: Oxford University Press, 2000, ch. 7.
4. See Russell Lawrence Barsh, "Indigenous peoples and the U.N. Commission on Human Rights: a case of the immovable object and the irresistible force," *Human Rights Quarterly* 18 (1996): 782–813.
5. Erica-Irene A. Daes, "The right of indigenous peoples to self-determination in the contemporary world order," in Clark and Williamson (eds.), *Self-Determination*, p. 55.

6. Recent discussions affirm that the principle of self-determination does not imply that indigenous peoples wish to or have a right to secede from existing states to form new sovereign states. Much discussion of the meaning of the principle turns on implementation of land rights and self-governance rights within a state. See *Report of the Working Group Established in Accordance with Commission on Human Rights Resolution 1995/32.* United Nations Economic and Social Council, December 6, 1999.

7. For definitions of sovereignty, see Christopher Morris, *An Essay on the Modern State*, Cambridge: Cambridge University Press, 1998, p. 166; Thomas Pogge, "Cosmopolitanism and sovereignty." *Ethics* 103 (Oct. 1992): 48–75.

8. See Daniel Philpott, "Sovereignty: an introduction and brief History," *Journal of International Affairs* 2 (Winter 1995): 353–68.

9. See David Held, *Democracy and the Global Order*, Cambridge: Polity Press, 1995, chs. 5 and 6; Ruth Lapidoth, "Sovereignty in transition," *Journal of International Affairs* 45 (2) (Winter 1992): 325–46.

10. See Anna Yeatman, "Beyond natural right: the conditions for universal citizenship," in Yeatman, *Postmodern Revisionings of the Political*, New York: Routledge, 1994, pp. 57–79; "Feminism and citizenship," in Nick Stevenson (ed.), *Cultural Citizenship*. London: Sage, 1998; "Relational individualism," manuscript; see also Jennifer Nedelsky, "Relational autonomy," *Yale Women's Law Journal* (1989); "Law, boundaries, and the bounded self," in Robert Post (ed.), *Law and the Order of Culture*; for an application of this feminist revision of autonomy to international relations theory see Karen Knop, "Re/Statements: feminism and state sovereignty in international law," *Transnational Law and Contemporary Problems* 3 (2) (Fall 1993): 293–344; see also Jean Elshtain, "The sovereign state," *Notre Dame Law Review* 66 (1991): 1355–84.

11. Philip Pettit, *Republicanism*, Oxford: Oxford University Press, 1997.

12. See Russell Hardin, *One for All*, Chicago: University of Chicago Press, 1995, for a critique of the notion of collective common interests in the context of nationalist politics.

13. For one effort toward this sort of conceptualization in the context of the relation of Maori and Pakeha in New Zealand, see Roger Maaka and Augie Fleras, "Engaging with indigeneity: Tino Rangatiratanga in Aotearoa," in Duncan Ivison, Paul Patton, and Will Sanders, *Political Theory and the Rights of Indigenous Peoples*. Cambridge: Cambridge University Press, 2000, pp. 89–112.

14. See, for example, Hector Diaz Polanco, *Indigenous Peoples in Latin America: The Quest for Self-Determination*, Lucia Rayas (trans.), Boulder: Westview Press, 1997, especially Part II.

15. See Franke Wilmer, *The Indigenous Voice in World Politics*. London: Sage, 1993.

16. Timothy Egan, "New prosperity brings new conflict to Indian country," *New York Times*, March 8, 1998, Nation/Metro sec. See also "Other nuclear waste facilities being considered in Utah," *Salt Lake Tribune*, February 20, 2000; "Utah County's Toxic Tradition is under Threat," *New York Times*, October 20, 2002; "US Withholds Approval for Nuclear Wastage Storage on Indian Reservation," *New York Times*, March 11, 2003.

17. Will Kymlicka, *Multicultural Citizenship*. Oxford: Oxford University Press, 1995; Kymlicka argues that national minorities, including indigenous peoples, ought to have recognized self-government rights, and that such rights limit nation-state sovereignty over them without making them separate sovereign states. Kymlicka does not specify the details of the meaning of self-government in a context of negotiated federated relationships as much as one would like, but it is clear that he has something like this in mind.

Part III

New directions

9 Redistribution or recognition?
A misguided debate

Bhikhu Parekh

In recent years cultural issues in one form or another have come to dominate the public agenda. Gays and Lesbians, women, ethnic and cultural minorities, religious communities, indigenous peoples, and others demand that society should recognize their identities, respect their differences, and take full account of these in its laws, political institutions, and public policies. This, what is generally called the politics of recognition, has attracted considerable opposition from every conceivable direction. For conservatives, it undermines national unity and social cohesion and is a recipe for chaos. For some liberals, it is collectivist, threatens individual liberty and personal autonomy, and subverts the great universalist heritage of the Enlightenment. For socialists and social democrats, it diverts attention from the great and urgent issues of social and economic justice. And for Marxists, it detracts from the class struggle, weakens working-class solidarity, and plays into the hands of the dominant class. In this chapter I concentrate on the last two groups, especially the socialists and social democrats. Following the current usage, I shall call their view the politics of redistribution.[1]

The concern with redistribution has a long history going back to the early Greek democrats, and includes influential Christian thinkers, millenarian movements, socialists, Marxists, and egalitarian liberals. Drawing their inspiration from differently grounded egalitarian conceptions of justice, its advocates argue that all human beings have equal worth, dignity, or value, and are equally entitled to lead meaningful and fulfilling lives. They should therefore as a matter of justice enjoy equal access to the rights, opportunities, material resources, and basic capabilities needed to lead such lives. In an unequal society this requires getting the privileged groups to share, by means of persuasion, pressure, or coercion, their resources with the poor and the unprivileged, and involves some form of redistribution.[2]

Although the pursuit of equality involves redistribution, the two are not identical. Equality involves helping the poor and otherwise ill-equipped groups to acquire such basic capacities and skills as are needed to plan

199

their lives and make sensible use of the opportunities and goods available to them, and these capacities and skills are not a matter of redistribution even in the extended use of the term. Equality also involves equality of respect, public affirmation of equal human worth and dignity, and this too has nothing to do with redistribution. Redistribution primarily refers to material resources which can be transferred from one group to another. Even in this sense, redistribution can fall far short of equality. It may enable marginalized groups to lead decent lives without radically reducing the prevailing inequalities in different areas of life. Although I shall concentrate on the politics of redistribution, we need to bear in mind that it forms only a part of the wider pursuit of equality.

The politics of recognition has a different philosophical basis and orientation. In one form or another it too has a long history.[3] Classical Athens, the Roman Empire, and medieval kingdoms respected the cultural beliefs and practices of their minorities, resident aliens, subject peoples, and religious groups. They generally dealt with these groups according to their own customs and laws and did not demand, and were sometimes resisted when they demanded, conformity to the established practices and values of the dominant community. Although their differences were respected and recognized, they were never, however, accepted as equals. They generally lived on the margins of society, did not enjoy equal citizenship, and the respect given to them was contingent on the traditions and the goodwill of the dominant community.

The liberal view of the individual and society that began to gain ascendancy from the seventeenth century onwards represented a radically different approach. It took individuals not communities and groups as its basic moral and political units, and asserted their equality. *Qua* human beings they had equal worth, shared certain fundamental interests in common, and had an equal right to pursue them. Individuals did differ culturally, religiously, ethically, and so on, but these differences were seen either as contingent and not central to their humanity, or as politically irrelevant. They were therefore treated as a personal matter for individuals, and the liberal state was expected to concern itself only with the protection of the shared common interests of its citizens.[4]

Contemporary forms of politics of recognition grow out of and both share and criticize the liberal approach to cultural and other differences. They accept the liberal principles of equality and justice but take a different view of the nature of the individual, and give the principles a different content and scope. For the advocates of the politics of recognition, human beings are culturally embedded in the sense that their identity is profoundly shaped by and integrally tied up with their culture. Even if we do not go as far as saying that they are determined or even constituted by it, they argue, we cannot deny that it is a source of their system of meaning, values, and ideals, forms part of their fundamental human interest, and matters to them deeply. Their culture cannot therefore be abstracted away from them and confined to the so-called personal or private sphere of life. It permeates all areas of their lives, including the political, and the state has a duty to recognize and respect it. Advocates of the politics of recognition argue that although the liberal state claims to abstract away all differences, in fact it does not and cannot. Since it necessarily needs some conception of the good life to structure its institutions and shape its laws and policies, it unwittingly adopts, institutionalizes and enforces the categories, practices, and values of the dominant culture. In so doing, it discriminates against other cultures, and creates a climate inhospitable to their flourishing or even survival. The liberal proposal to accommodate this criticism by requiring the state to practice strict cultural neutrality does not satisfy the advocates of the politics of recognition, both because such neutrality in their view is inherently impossible and cannot deliver on its promise, and because it does not meet their demand for the public recognition of differences.

Advocates of the politics of recognition therefore insist that rather than privatize cultural, religious, and other differences, the state should take full public account of them in its laws, institutions, practices, and policies. It should, of course, treat all its citizens equally but equality should not mean identical or uniform treatment. Laws may legitimately grant exemptions to some groups and not to others; political institutions may find ways of giving adequate representation or greater autonomy to marginalized or alienated groups; public policies may focus on or give greater resources to those whose cultures are under severe external threat; the state may reassess the existing symbols of national identity to acknowledge the presence of new or long-neglected groups; and so on.[5]

The politics of recognition as outlined above has been a subject of considerable criticism at the hands of many of the advocates of redistribution.[6] First, it is obsessed with culture. It assumes that culture is far more important than the economy, and that all or at least all significant conflicts are cultural in origin and can only be resolved in cultural terms. It thus privileges identity over justice and is indifferent to the question of redistribution. Second, the state cannot and should not recognize or have anything to do with identity, be it cultural, religious, ethnic, or any other. Identities are subject to change and constant reassessment. If the state were to recognize them, it would necessarily formalize and freeze them and arrest their development. They also vary from individual to individual so that the state would have to devise such a complex system of differential treatment that it would undermine equality. It is precisely because identities are important to the individual that they should be kept out of the state's reach. Third, since the politics of recognition is preoccupied with difference, it undermines the solidarity of the oppressed and the marginalized, and makes it impossible for them to unite and act together. What is more, it is committed to some form of relativism, and cannot provide a crosscultural ethic needed to underpin a radical political and moral theory. Fourth, the politics of recognition plays into the hands of the dominant class, which is all too happy to allow the Sikh his turban, the American Indians their peyote, the Muslims their halal meal, and so on, as long as the inequalities of wealth and power are left unchallenged. The politics of recognition diverts attention from the struggle for economic equality and social justice, dissipates moral and political energy, and leaves the prevailing social order more or less intact. Finally, it judges the state on the basis of its ability to respect and accommodate cultural demands rather than to secure social justice and equal life-chances. By shifting the basis of legitimacy in this way, it subverts one of the most powerful weapons in the armory of the critics of an unjust social and political order.

We can readily agree that some advocates of the politics of recognition are open to these and related criticisms. The criticisms, however, are exaggerated. Many identity-based groups such as women, blacks, and gays have often fought for equality of rights, opportunities, and resources, and have formed alliances with their redistributivist counterparts. Some of them do remain obsessed with cultural issues, but such distortions occur in every new movement and cannot be used to delegitimize or dismiss it. The real question is whether the politics of recognition addresses important issues that are neglected by the politics of redistribution, and whether it is inherently incompatible with the latter. My answer is in the negative. I wish to argue that the two forms of politics stress different and complementary aspects of equality, and that each necessarily needs the other to give it depth and energy.[7]

Why the politics of redistribution and recognition are complementary

The advocates of redistribution take an extremely narrow view of justice and assume that the equality of rights, opportunities, life-chances, etc. is the only or the most important desideratum in a good society. Imagine a society in which economic and other inequalities are drastically reduced or even eliminated and its members are equally able to lead the lives of their choice, but they all lead the same kind of life, have the same tastes, and think along broadly similar lines. It is naive to think that this cannot happen in an egalitarian society, for there is nothing about such a society that militates against moral and cultural uniformity. Indeed Tocqueville thought this an endemic danger in it, and some perceptive critics of modern society have argued that we are already moving in this direction. What is missing in our imaginary society is the diversity of ways of thought, life, tastes, moral perspectives, ideals, and so on, in short, moral and cultural diversity. The great moral, aesthetic, political, democratic, and other benefits of such a diversity have long been emphasized by liberal and other writers and need no repetition. The advocates of recognition fully appreciate this and offer one way of nurturing diversity. We may disagree with their answer, but cannot deny that their general objective is commendable.

The point of this argument is reinforced by looking at our imaginary society from a different angle. Suppose it achieves redistributive justice but takes demeaning views of gays, lesbians, women, blacks, and religious minorities. It insists on only one correct way to live, behave, marry, conduct political discourse, find sexual fulfilment, organize the family, and so on, and attaches different forms and degrees of social, legal, and other sanctions to deviant behavior. Its members enjoy economic and social equality, but not the equality to define and publicly express their identity. Women are free to express their femininity in the private sphere but are expected to conduct themselves as, and cultivate the qualities of, men in the public sphere. And while the gays are free to practice homosexuality, they are expected to keep it quiet and make no public assertions of it. Such individuals are bound to feel that they are oppressed in the sense that they are made to feel ashamed of who and what they are, that their lives are fragmented in a way that others' are not, that they are denied equal public respect and freedom of self-expression, that they cannot be at ease with themselves and are coerced into conforming to someone else's ideas of how they should live, and that they are unable fully to participate in the collective life of their society except on terms dictated by others. As Charles Taylor puts it, the nonrecognition or misrecognition of their identity imprisons people into a reduced mode of being and gives rise to deep unhappiness and a sense of powerlessness. Oppression and inequality can take many forms, the economic being only one of them. The politics of redistribution focuses on some of these, that of recognition on others.[8]

If redistribution was all that ultimately mattered, it would be difficult to see why one should not dismantle the indigenous peoples' ways of life, or those of the Gypsies and other traditional communities. Indigenous peoples generally live in poverty, and since their way of life is partly responsible for this, one might argue that it should be dismantled, albeit gradually and peacefully. They also generally sit on vast resources of land, minerals, timber, etc., and it might be argued that we should acquire and use them to increase the general level of prosperity. We rightly think that such policies are wrong. The politics of redistribution cannot tell us why this is so; that of recognition provides at least a partial answer.

We might go further and ask why redistribution is a worthwhile goal and why inequalities are undesirable even after the basic needs of all are met. Few champions of redistribution have offered a satisfactory answer. Rawls' widely shared view that inequality is justified only if it works to the advantage of the worse off permits a vast degree of it. Indeed many of the conservative and libertarian defenses of the current inequalities often use arguments not dissimilar to Rawls'. Furthermore, since Rawls generally defines disadvantage in material terms, he is unable to appreciate that inequalities are unacceptable even when they benefit the worse off. As R. H. Tawney argued, inequality beyond a certain point is morally and politically corrosive, the former because it breeds arrogance and complacency in some and obsequiousness, inferiority, and marginality in others, the latter because it breaks up society into self-contained groups and militates against the common experiences, concerns, and aspirations that are necessary to sustain a program of redistributive justice, including Rawls'.[9]

Tawney's argument can be reinforced by highlighting the cultural consequences of inequality. Vast economic, social, and other inequalities concentrate economic, cultural, and political power in the hands of a small group of people and enable them to set the moral tone of the wider society. The dominant group confers prestige on certain forms of life and ways of doing things, encourages certain types of ambition and motivation, privileges certain values, goals and careers, and by means of a complex blend of inducements and sanctions shapes the choices and lives of their fellow citizens. Great inequalities tend to homogenize society, stifle a wide variety of valuable identities, and discourage a diversity of perspectives and ways of life. Unlike the advocates of redistribution, those of recognition grasp this point. They stress the importance of diversity, and demand its public recognition as one way of nurturing it. When properly interpreted, the politics of recognition can provide a powerful critique of inequality that deepens and complements that offered by the redistributivists.

In the light of our discussion, we can conclude that distributive justice is not enough. We also need cultural diversity and the freedom to explore, assess, reconstitute, and express our identities in an environment free from obsession with uniformity. And that requires that the state should under appropriate circumstances recognize, respect, cherish, and support the legitimate identities of its citizens. This is not to say that all identities need public recognition. Some do, some don't, depending on the nature of the identity involved and the wider social context. Some identities can flourish or even survive only when protected from the public gaze; others are devalued or remain precarious when privatized. While we may therefore rightly question the plea for the indiscriminate public recognition of all identities made by some of the advocates of recognition, we cannot deny their basic point that the state should not as a matter of principle remain indifferent to the claims of identities. Since the good society must aim at both redistributive justice and conditions conducive to diversity, the politics of redistribution and recognition are equally important and need to be integrated into a coherent theory of politics. Both are concerned with freedom and equality, differing largely in the aspects they concentrate on. When analyzing a state, the politics of redistribution inquires into its class character and the ways in which this is obscured and reproduced. By contrast, the politics of recognition inquires into its cultural character, the identities it institutionalizes, the groups it excludes or marginalizes, and the subtle ways in which all this is veiled and perpetuated. Far from being in conflict, the two forms of politics offer complementary insights into the structure of social and political life and its mechanisms of exclusion and marginalization.[10]

Dialectic of recognition and redistribution

I have so far argued that the politics of recognition and redistribution are complementary. One could go further and argue that each necessarily needs the other to give it depth and energy, and to realize its objectives. I hope to show this first by looking at the politics of redistribution, and then at that of recognition.

Economic inequalities have many causes. One of them is the low self-esteem and poor motivation, drive, and discipline of groups who have long been oppressed, marginalized, or denigrated. They and their histories and cultures are generally devalued and even treated with contempt. They are told that as a people they have contributed nothing worthwhile to humankind, that they have no great achievements to their credit, and that these limitations reflect their inferior capacities. When such negative images are repeated over time and become part of society's literature, arts, textbooks, and informal conversation, they are internalized by its members, including the victims who develop what W. E. B. DuBois calls a "double-consciousness," "always looking at one's self through the eyes of others," and become caricatures of others' caricatures of them. They have poor self-respect, low self-esteem, and sometimes even suffer from self-hatred. They aim low, rule out certain careers as not for people like them, easily reconcile themselves to their failures, are poorly motivated, and lack inspiring role models and a supportive social network. Predictably, they achieve little, remain trapped in lowly positions, are drawn to unlawful activities, and pose threats to others, all of which further reinforces and is readily used by the wider society to prove their inferiority. When Malcolm X was in his teens, he told his teacher that he wanted to be a lawyer. The teacher replied: "A lawyer – that's no realistic goal for a nigger. You need to think about something you *can* be. You are good with your hands – making things. Why don't you plan on carpentry?"[11] Malcolm X's experience is repeated in the lives of countless black men, women, and other inferiorized groups. Some like him do of course manage, by sheer will power, good luck or unexpected stimulus and support, to break out of the vicious cycle, but many do not, and even the former sometimes carry the scars of their struggle.

Long-oppressed and marginalized groups cannot escape from their economic predicament unless they feel convinced that this is not their fate or natural condition or all they are worth, and that it is within their power to change it. This requires building up their self-respect, self-esteem, and personal and collective pride. This is one of the reasons why African Americans in the 1960s began to take great interest in their history and culture, to highlight their great historical periods and contributions, and to assert their racial identity and equality. A similar process has also occurred in the history of erstwhile colonies and other inferiorized and humiliated groups, each seeking ways of countering its negative self-image, building up its collective self-confidence, and asserting its equality with the dominant groups. These are obviously complex processes and involve much myth-making and distorted history. Such excesses, however, are inevitable and usually self-correcting, and do not undermine either the validity of the spirit that inspires them or the benefits of the psychological and other changes that they produce. After all, a good deal of Euro-American history too was and is built on such falsehoods and distortions, and many in the West feel deeply threatened even today by attempts to question these. Like personal identities, collective identity has a complex logic. During the early stages of identity formation, every group relies on myths and exaggerations to build up its self-esteem and internal unity. But once these are achieved, it generally develops the confidence to challenge these distortions and take a critical view of itself. Redistribution is not a purely economic and political phenomenon, because economic and social equality cannot be given on a platter. It has to be striven for and, what is no less important, sustained, and that requires deep psychological, moral, and cultural changes among the oppressed. Since the politics of recognition is an integral part of this process of cultural change, the politics of redistribution needs its support.

People value their identity for many different reasons.[12] It is the basis of their sense of self-worth and social standing. It bonds them to those sharing it, and gives them both a sense of common belonging and the collective empowerment that accompanies it. Their identity also gives them a moral anchor, a sense of direction, and a body of ideals and values. As the world becomes increasingly globalized, rootless, and impersonal, cultural, religious, ethnic, and other identities become important sources of stability, giving their members the confidence to change with the times without suffering a moral panic. This is why they demand not only equality and justice but also a recognition of and respect for their identities. A theory of politics that ignores this basic fact has only a limited popular appeal and chance of success. The politics of redistribution therefore needs to link up with the politics of recognition and mobilize the energies it generates to realize its redistributivist goals. It is partly because it has so far failed to do so that it has alienated important groups and is left without a constituency.[13] The advocates of redistribution are right to fear that preoccupation with identity and recognition can lead to fragmentation, but wrong not to appreciate that ignoring it altogether has its own obvious dangers. The answer lies in linking up with the politics of recognition, correcting its excesses, channeling its energies, and forming alliances around a common set of objectives.

There is also another way in which the politics of redistribution depends on the politics of recognition. Redistribution requires principles to decide who is entitled to make what claims. The principles can only be arrived at by means of a democratic dialogue, which generates them, tests their validity, and gives them legitimacy. The dialogue is justly structured and conducted only when all the relevant points of view are valued and heard and allowed to speak in their distinct voices. If it were to require all participants to speak in a single language, it would not only fail to render other languages their due but also enshrine the domination of the group or culture it represents. No single language can adequately articulate the full range of diverse experiences of and insights into the structures of injustice. Religious, cultural, and ethnic communities, women and others should therefore be able to bring to the public agenda their respective views and experiences, which they can best do only if they speak in their own voices. And if some of these voices are inaudible, we need to seek them out, empower them, and ensure their adequate representation in the deliberative bodies. This is precisely where the politics of recognition comes in. It ensures that all legitimate identities are heard, are able to participate as equals and help evolve principles of justice enjoying cross-cultural consensus and legitimacy. Without the politics of recognition, the politics of redistribution either cannot get off the ground or enjoy popular support.

I have so far argued that the politics of redistribution calls for the politics of recognition. The converse is just as true. Communities and their cultures tend to be devalued for a variety of reasons, their economic inequality and powerlessness being one of the most important of them. When individuals and communities are poor or oppressed, they tend to be politically and economically invisible and voiceless, and count for little. Their poverty and inequality need to be explained, and the usual strategy is to lay all the blame on their culture, customs, practices, low ambition, temperament, psychological make-up, and poor natural endowment. For centuries the Jews, the Japanese, the Chinese, the Indians, and others were held in low esteem and subjected to patronizing and demeaning stereotypes. As their economic conditions improved and as they became a significant political and economic presence in the world at large, their self-images as well as others' views of them underwent profound changes.

Thanks to the considerable economic success of the Indian immigrants in the UK, they and their culture are viewed in a positive light that bears little relation to the way they were perceived only a few years ago. The racist South African regime felt compelled to classify Jews and the Japanese as honorary whites and to respect and accommodate their cultural and religious identities. During the past few decades, Western countries have begun to show considerable admiration for the Japanese and Chinese societies, and even to ask what the West could learn from them. The West finds virtues in their ways of life that had always been there but which it had hitherto failed to notice because of its condescending attitude to them. In other words, identities are valued, recognized, respected, and cherished when they meet the society's criteria of success, and in ours these are economic and political. Groups at the bottom of the economic and social hierarchy therefore need to fight for justice and equality and become powerful if their identities are to be respected, not superficially, out of goodwill or in response to moral blackmail, but as their due. The politics of recognition remains impotent unless it is embedded in the politics of redistribution.

As we saw earlier, a vastly unequal society has a structural tendency towards homogenization, and tends to stifle cultural diversity. It institutionalizes and throws its weight behind a particular way of life or vision of the good society, and generates the pressure to conform and assimilate. If different moral and cultural visions are to flourish and command respect, they need to counter this trend by fighting for greater economic, political, and social equality, acquiring power and visibility, and demanding secure space for self-expression. Equality disperses and checks economic and political power and encourages the spirit of freedom and self-respect. It both protects differences against oppressive homogenization and nurtures the disposition to explore and express them. Economic, social, and political equality is thus a necessary precondition and basis of cultural diversity, and the politics of recognition ignores it at its peril.

Since greater equality is in the common interest of cultural, ethnic, and other groups, they need to act in concert, a fact they do not always appreciate. Some of them remain content to pursue narrow cultural goals, waste their energies fighting among themselves for their meagre shares of public resources, or allow themselves to be played off against each other by the dominant groups in all too familiar ways. However there is nothing inevitable about this, and there are good examples in Britain, USA, Canada, Australia, and elsewhere of close intergroup cooperation. What is needed is a coherent ideology showing the vital linkages between the politics of recognition and redistribution within the framework of a broad egalitarian vision, and a political leadership capable of building a united front. Since the resulting politics has an economic and a cultural basis and draws its energy from both the struggle for material resources and respect for identity, it has the potential to become a powerful political force.[14]

Agenda for a new theory of justice

Since redistribution and recognition are integrally related and pertain to different but complementary aspects of equality, a well-considered theory of justice needs to address both. Notwithstanding its great internal variety and with some notable exceptions, much of the traditional discussion of justice has concentrated on the question of redistribution, asking how rights, political power, offices, opportunities, and resources should be distributed. Its questions, categories, and assumptions are all structured by this preoccupation. As a result it is theoretically ill-equipped to answer the questions raised by the demands of culture, identity, and difference, which are either not a matter of redistribution at all or cannot be distributed in the same way as material resources and opportunities.[15]

This raises the question as to how we should deal with them. We have several alternatives. We could dismiss them as an unnecessary distraction from the "real" issues of distributive justice. I have shown why this is an incoherent response. Or we could try to fit them into the traditional theory of distributive justice. I have shown why this cannot be done except by so distorting the questions that they lose their focus and point and by so stretching the traditional theory of justice that it becomes incoherent. Or we could ignore the traditional theory of justice altogether and develop an independent theory of identity and recognition. Since the issues of identity and redistribution are closely related, this approach is both incoherent and breaks the vital link between the two sets of concerns. Or we could integrate the two in a bifocal theory of justice that grasps the empirical and normative connections between the economic and cultural issues and is grounded in a richer view of equality. This seems to be the only satisfactory approach.

Briefly, such a theory of justice has the following features. First, it acknowledges that like individuals, groups too can be the subjects of justice and make claims on each other and the wider society. Groups are treated unjustly when they are humiliated, oppressed, negatively stereotyped, or subjected to unequal treatment. Racism, sexism, and homophobia are some examples of this. These forms of injustice cannot be explained and tackled in individualist terms because the individuals involved are subjected to them not as individuals but by virtue of belonging to relevant groups. They therefore call for appropriate forms of collective action, including both a collective struggle and collective remedies.

Second, justice encompasses claims to material resources as well as to those based on identity. Injustice is done not only when individuals are exploited or denied the basic material conditions of the good life but also when they are culturally oppressed or denied the opportunity to speak in their own voices and freely shape and express their identities, subject, of course, to the requirements of a democratically agreed body of moral principles. Recognition and redistribution articulate different forms of equality, and both alike need to be addressed by a theory of justice.

Third, justice is culturally mediated and its guiding principles cannot be defined, interpreted, and applied in a cultural vacuum. Questions about who can be the subjects of justice, what matters fall within its ambit, how to determine the principles of justice, whether they should be based on merit, effort or need, the place of justice in moral life and its relation to other great values have an irreducible cultural core. For many indigenous peoples, the gods and the spirits of ancestors make claims based on justice; we think differently. For animal liberationists, animals or rather the more developed among them are subjects of justice; others think differently. Since views on the good life differ, those on what the subjects of justice are entitled to also vary. The Chinese have one set of ideas on what we owe or is due to each other and our ancestors; other civilizations take a different view. Given their theory of incarnation, Hindus and Buddhists hold views on personal identity and merit that are markedly at variance with those held by Christians, Jews, and secularists.

Since different groups hold different views on almost all aspects of justice, and since we are prone to universalizing ones that appear self-evident to us, a theory of justice can only be based on a consensus developed through a democratic dialogue between different points of view. The philosopher has an important contribution to make, but only as one voice among many. And the greater its sensitivity to the diversity of voices, the less it is likely to be dismissed as partisan propaganda and the more it is likely to command respect. Since new points of view constantly emerge and we gain new insights into the nature and forms of injustice, every theory of justice is tentative and open to revision.

Fourth, justice concerns not only the state but also the society at large and each of its individual members. In the distributivist view of justice, the state remains the focus of attention as it alone is in a position to command and redistribute resources. This is not the case with matters relating to recognition. Individual self-respect, self-esteem, and sense of identity are socially constituted and depend on others' confirmation. The state can certainly help by institutionalizing and protecting the equal dignity and rights of its citizens, but this is not enough. In their day-to-day encounters citizens might treat some individuals or groups with disdain, avoid them, make offensive remarks, and in general make their lives a nightmare. Such forms of behavior do injustice to those involved, even though the law takes no account of them. A society with a sexist, racist, or antisemitic culture daily subjects large numbers of people to humiliating treatment and does them injustice at the deepest level. Since we have for centuries tended to take a statist view of justice and concentrated on law-defined and state-delivered forms of justice, we have ignored the kinds and areas of injustice for which society, culture, or each of us individually is responsible. The politics of recognition has highlighted the multiple agents of injustice, and a well-considered theory of justice needs to take full account of them.

Fifth, although redistribution and recognition, the two major forms and sites of justice, are closely related, they are different in their nature and logic, and cannot be reduced to each other. Economic and social inequalities on the one hand, and misrecognition or nonrecognition on the other, have overlapping but different causes, and are perpetuated by different mechanisms. Redistribution facilitates recognition, but that is not the only reason to value it, for the equality that inspires and results from it is desirable on other grounds as well. Conversely, public recognition of legitimate identities expands the society's sense of solidarity by including the hitherto marginalized groups into a newly constituted collective "we" and assists redistribution, but that is not the only reason to value it. While highlighting the empirical and normative connections between recognition and redistribution and grounding both in a broader concept of equality, a well-considered theory of justice should avoid giving a reductionist account of them.

Finally, unlike the questions raised by redistribution, those raised by recognition cannot all be reduced to matters of justice. Identities conflict, and no society can accommodate all of them. Furthermore, a society is often committed to a particular conception of the good life that defines its identity, and might rightly resist compromising its integrity or rendering it incoherent by conceding cultural demands which, although valuable, cannot be easily integrated into its way of life. Since identities are often contested and subject to redefinition and change, it might be sometimes unwise to institutionalize them or even grant them public recognition. For these and other reasons, appeal to justice is sometimes either irrelevant, not enough, or counterproductive in dealing with issues involving recognition. Other values and considerations come into play, and the demands of justice need to be balanced against them. This calls for a wider moral theory of which the theory of justice is a part. A well-considered theory of justice needs to recognize its own limits and resist the temptation to colonize areas lying beyond its purview.

NOTES

1. There are also other forms of politics than those of redistribution and recognition, but I ignore them in this chapter.
2. If we were starting with a clean historical slate or if equality once established was likely to continue forever, redistribution would not be necessary.
3. Discussions of recognition wrongly assume that it is a modern phenomenon. Many premodern Western and non-Western societies granted it as a matter of fact, although their reasons for doing so were rarely theorized. Indian and Islamic societies were in this respect more articulate.
4. Much of preliberal thought accepted the reality of difference but took a hierarchical view of it. Liberalism stressed equality but equated it with uniformity and took little account of difference. We need to find ways of integrating difference into, and developing a richer concept of, equality.
5. For a valuable discussion of how this can be done, see Will Kymlicka, *Multicultural Citizenship*, Oxford: Clarendon Press, 1995. See also my *Rethinking Multiculturalism*, London: Palgrave, 2000.
6. Brian Barry, *Culture and Equality*, Cambridge: Polity, 2001 and "Muddles of multiculturalism," *New Left Review*, April 2001, are the best polemical examples of this.

7. For a valuable discussion of these issues, see Nancy Fraser, "From redistribution to recognition? Dilemmas of justice in a 'post-socialist' age," in Cynthia Willett (ed.), *Theorising Multiculturalism: A Guide to the Current Debate*, Oxford: Blackwell, 1998. See also her "A rejoinder to Iris Young," *ibid.*; and *Justice Interruptus: Rethinking Key Concepts of a Post-Socialist Age*. London: Routledge, 1997.

8. For excellent discussions, see Charles Taylor, *Sources of the Self*, Cambridge: Cambridge University Press, 1989 and "The politics of recognition," in A. Gutmann (ed.), *Multiculturalism*, Princeton: Princeton University Press, 1994.

9. R. H. Tawney, *Equality*, London: Allen and Unwin, 1952, 4th edition.

10. See Timothy Hinton, "Must Egalitarians choose between Fairness and respect?", *Philosophy and Public Affairs* 30 (2002); and Jonathan Wolff, "Fairness, respect and the egalitarian ethos," *Philosophy and Public Affairs* 2 (1998).

11. Cited in Alex Haley, *The Autobiography of Malcolm X*. New York: Grove Park, 1966. See also W. E. B. Dubois, *The Souls of Black Folk*, Chicago: A. C. McClury, 1903; and Ralph Ellison, *The Invisible Man*, New York: Random House, 1952.

12. For a sensitive account of its ontological basis, see Emmanuel Levinas, *Totality and Infinity: An Essay on Exteriority* (trans.) Alphonso Lingis, Pittsburgh: Duquesna University Press, 1990, pp. 194–95. See also Adriann Pepevzak, *To the Other: Introduction to the Philosophy of E. Levinas*, West Lafeyette, IN: Purdue University Press, 1993.

13. The continuing disputes about the welfare state and affirmative action are some examples of this.

14. See the excellent article by James Tully, "Struggles over recognition and distribution," *Constellations* 7 (2000).

15. See my "Barry and the dangers of liberalism," in Paul Kelley (ed.), *Multiculturalism Reconsidered: Culture and Equality and its Critics*, Cambridge: Polity, 2002.

10   Borders, boundaries, and the politics
of belonging

Nira Yuval-Davis

The title of the recent White Paper prepared by the immigration team of David Blunkett, the current Home Secretary of the British Labor government, is "Secure Border, Safe Haven" (January 2002). In the introduction to the White Paper, Blunkett explains the logic of the title. He sees "a clear, workable" and especially "robust nationality and asylum system" (pointing out that people crossing the Channel Tunnel in container lorries demonstrate how difficult it is to reach the UK) as a precondition of "our need to be secure within our sense of belonging and identity" (Foreword to White Paper). Blunkett is not alone. John Crowley actually defines the arena of the politics of belonging as the "'dirty work' of boundary maintenance (1999: 30)."

What I want to do in this chapter is to discuss questions relating to the politics of belonging and the relationship between them and constructions of boundaries and borders. After discussing the issues involved on a general level, I shall relate them specifically to the debate taking place these days in Britain on the construction of the national collectivity and the relationship between this and the notion of "secure borders."

Since he became UK Home Secretary, David Blunkett has been engaged in finding ways of establishing a "sense of belonging" to the British national collectivity as a precondition for gaining formal British citizenship. The absence of such a sense has been construed as the direct cause of the lack of "social cohesion" and the main reason for the race riots in the north of Britain in 2001 (Cantle Report 2001). About ten years earlier, Norman Tebbit, then a secretary in Margaret Thatcher's Conservative government, developed the (in)famous "cricket test" which demanded people to cheer for the national cricket team in a game played against the team of people's country of origin as a proof that they "really" belong. Part of the political debate in the UK and in many other states, where policies of multiculturalism have been official state policy since the 1970s, is the extent to which the participatory dimension of citizenship can be separated from the emotional dimension of identification. A related question is the extent to which nation-state belonging should

214

claim privileged position in the multilayered constructions of people's associations and affiliations.

This last question has been tackled partially by citizenship studies that have greatly expanded over the last ten or fifteen years. Several important debates have taken place in this field that are relevant to our subject matter here, such as the gendered, classed, and cultured nature of citizenship. One such debate that is especially important to mention has been between the liberals and the republicans, and/or the communitarians, as well as more recently with the transnationals. There is no space to get into the details of the debate (e.g. Avineri and Shalit 1992; Daly 1993; Oldfield 1990; Peled 1992). However, while the liberals construct citizenship as a relationship between individuals and the state, communitarians and republicans, in somewhat different ways, construct citizenship as a way of belonging to a national community. They do not, however, usually differentiate between national and civil societal community and thus naturalize an overlap between them. Given that this overlap in reality virtually never happens, this causes some of the most serious problems in the politics of belonging.

However, the most famous communitarian theorist of citizenship, at least in the UK, T. H. Marshall (1950, 1975, 1981), does not define citizenship in terms of belonging to a state at all but as a "full membership in the community with all its rights and responsibilities." This definition has enabled transnationals like Hall and Held (1989) and later in my own work (Yuval-Davis 1991; 1997a: ch. 4, 1999; Yuval-Davis and Werbner, 1999) to analyze citizenship as a multilayered construct where people are citizens, with rights and obligations, also in other political communities. These polities can be sub-, cross-, and supranational as well as in nation-states – local, ethnic, religious and interstate.

Belonging, however, as Crowley argues (1999: 22), is a "thicker" concept than that of citizenship. It is not just about membership, rights, and duties, but also about the emotions that such memberships evoke. Nor can belonging be reduced to identities and identifications, which are about individual and collective narratives of self and other, presentation and labeling, myths of origin and of destiny.

Belonging is a deep emotional need of people. Countless psychological, and even more psychoanalytical, works have been dedicated to writing about the fears of separation of babies from the womb, from the mother, from the familiar (for most elaborate accounts of this, see, e.g. Otto Rank 1973 [1929]; Bowlby 1969,1973). It is important to emphasize that this need to belong and fear of separation exists even in cases of sexual and other abuse in the family, and even when the environment of the womb itself proves to be far from the perfect haven in which all the needs of the baby are being satisfied (Fodor 1949; Mott 1948; Lake 1966[1]).

Belonging and the yearning to belong, however, have not only been central in psychological discourse. In some way, one could claim that one of the prime concerns of sociological theory since its establishment, and hence in its writings, has been the differential ways in which people belong to collectivities and states – as well as the social, economic, and political effects of instances of the displacement of such belongings as a result of industrialization and/or migration. Some basic classical examples are Tönnies' distinction between *Gemeinschaft* and *Gesellschaft* (1940[1935]), Durkheim's division of mechanical and organic solidarity or Marx's notion of alienation (1975[1844]). Anthony Giddens (1991) has argued that during modernity people's sense of belonging becomes reflexive, and recently Manuel Castells (1996–98) claimed that contemporary society has become the "network society" in which effective belonging has moved from civil societies of nations and states into reconstructed defensive identity communities.

Therefore, neither citizenship nor identity can encapsulate the notion of belonging. Belonging is where the sociology of emotions interfaces with the sociology of power, where identification and participation collude, or at least aspire to or yearn for. Like other hegemonic constructions, belonging tends to become "naturalized" and thus invisible in hegemonic formations. It is only when one's safe and stable connection to the collectivity, the homeland, the state, becomes threatened, that it becomes articulated and reflexive. It is then that individual, collective, and institutional narratives of belonging become politicized. And it is often the Right that exploits the love and hate, fears and hopes that are evoked in these situations in order to build higher walls around the boundaries and borders of the national collectivity and to mobilize the people toward exclusionary politics.

The politics of belonging and the construction of boundaries and borders

Adrian Favell argues (1999: 211) that the "boundary problem" is archetypal to the politics of belonging. Constructing boundaries and borders that differentiate between those who belong, and those who do not, determines and colors the meaning of the particular belonging. It is here that the interrelationships between the politics of belonging and struggles for national self-determination are anchored, and that both collusion and resistance between them are performed and narrated.

Vikki Bell (1999) and Anne-Marie Fortier (2000) discuss the various performative ways in which such boundaries and borders are constructed and reproduced. However, it is important to relate the notion of belonging to the differential positionings from which belongings are imagined and narrated, in terms of gender, class, and stage in the lifecycle, even in relation to the same community and in relation to the same boundaries and borders. The contested and shifting nature of these boundaries and borders may reflect not only dynamic power relations between individuals, collectivities, and institutions but also subjective and situational processes. Depending on the objectives of different ethnic and national projects involving members of the same collectivity or people outside it, the boundary lines can be drawn in very different ways (Anthias and Yuval-Davis 1992; Yuval-Davis 1997a, b).

Political goals and political values in general can affect the ways boundaries of collectivities are constructed by different people as well as their views concerning the extent to which people can be included in a national or ethnic collectivity while continuing to preserve legitimately membership in another one – what is sometimes called a "hyphenated identity." However, it is not just political values that affect the ways people draw collectivity boundaries. It is also their differential positionings and their differential intersectional identities.

It is for this reason that we need to be clear what we mean when we agree with Benedict Anderson that nations are "imagined communities." Nations, according to Anderson, are imagined communities "because the members of even the smallest nation will never know most of their fellow-members, meet them, or even hear of them, yet in the minds of each lives the image of their communion" (Anderson 1991: 6).

Such an abstract form of community is necessarily based on an abstract sense of imagined simultaneity. However, the national imagination also includes former and future generations. The inability, therefore, to meet all members of the nation is not just a result of the size of the nation – it is inherently impossible. Moreover, as Poole comments (1999: 10), Anderson's definition seems to assume that if all the members of the nation could meet face to face, imagination would be redundant. However, any construction of boundaries, of a delineated collectivity, that includes some people – concrete or not – and excludes others, involves an act of active and situated imagination (Stoetzler and Yuval-Davis forthcoming). Could Jews be included in the boundaries of the German nation? Is there "Black in the Union Jack"? Do Québécois form a separate nation from the Canadian one, with their own boundaries? The different situated imaginations that construct these national imagined communities with different boundaries depend on people's positionings, experiences and, probably even more importantly, people's values. They do not come into existence just because of the inability of people to meet all the other members of their nation. On the contrary – this "dirty business of boundary maintenance" which underlies the politics of belonging is all about potentially meeting other people and deciding whether they stand inside or outside the imaginary boundary line of the nation and/or other communities of belonging.

State territorial borders are one major way in which collectivity boundaries are imagined, dividing the people into those who belong to the nation and those who do not. And yet, borders can be experienced – and imagined – in many different ways. As Nugent and Asiwaju argue (1996), there is often a marked difference between the ways official discourse constructs international borders and the ways people who live along the border actually experience them.

The conflict, however, can start already at the level of the official discourse. In one of the chapters that Anderson added to the second edition of his *Imagined Communities* (1991[1983]), he discusses the way Western cartography changed the ways state borders were constructed – as continuous lines that separate absolutely between different countries, nations, and states. Previously, borders were marked in strategic places but there were major border zones in which belonging to a particular political state was ambiguous at best.

Borders play a central role in the discourse of states and nations. Claims for changing borders, "retrieving" pieces of "the homeland," are probably the most popular reasons, why nations go to war, next to defending the "womenandchildren" (Enloe 1990). As Sahlins (1989: 271) claims, borders are "privileged sites for the articulations of national distinctions" – and thus, of national belonging.

This central, but contested, facet of borders is in contrast to the naturalized images of homelands that assume complete congruence (or identity) of people, state, and territory. The spatial location of the homeland is endemic with assumed borders that are often signified by seas, mountain ranges, and rivers. It is an open question (historically variant) whether the national and international legality of those "natural" borders follow from, or rather cause, these naturalized border imaginings. Often the "naturalized" borderlines do not correspond with the boundaries of the ethnic and national communities who live near the borders.

And it is also an open question, with different answers in different historical cases, whether the adherence to such borders relates more to strategic military and economic interests (of the states themselves or of an external superpower as is the case in many postcolonial countries) or whether such borders are inherent to collective imaginings of particular homelands.

As Wilson and Donnan (1998: 4) point out, borderlines simultaneously separate and join states. Such borderlines, in different political situations, would be more or less permeable. But what can be at stake here is not just a variable level of interaction or even enmity between the two states. It can also relate to the extent to which the national collective imaginings in one state embed the same border in a different imaginary environment. Even if it is not imagined as passing in actually two different locations, it is often gazed upon differently and is attributed different meanings on the two sides of the borders. When I met French people shortly before the Channel Tunnel was opened they could not understand why so many people in Britain were so reluctant about the project, when they saw it as a sign of progress and modernization, making the border between France and Britain more like France's other borders. In Britain, however, the Channel Tunnel has been invested with threats of different kinds of invasion of the island – from rabid dogs to asylum seekers. Similarly, the border between Mexico and the USA is imagined very differently on each side of the border (Herzog 1993). It is important to remember, however, that many international borders have not been a formalization of national imaginings of homelands. Rather, they have been a result of negotiations between superpowers, often without any consultation with the national movements involved, controlling a particular part of the globe.

Whatever their origin, national borders acquire highly significant meanings to nation-states, if not in direct relation to myths of national origin, then as an expression of the legitimacy and sovereignty of the state. In this way, national borders become a specific form, spatially bounded, of collectivity boundaries, dividing the world into "us" and "them." Many would argue, as the British Home Secretary, David Blunkett, does, that "secure borders" are a precondition for "secure boundaries" of national collectivity and identity. A myriad of immigration regulations, usually racialized, has been established, since the beginning of the twentieth century, in order to stem people's movements across the globe. There is no space here to discuss the issues in detail (see, e.g. Castles and Miller 1993; Brah et al. 1999). However, it is important to describe some of the dilemmas that confront Western policymakers like Blunkett in today's global and political context.

The ethnic politics of migration

These days there is a growing gap between the political and economic needs of migration to Western countries. At the same time as the political imperative of many Western governments is to block immigration, to establish a "Fortress Europe," to militarize the US/Mexico border, to marginalize and criminalize the so-called "economic migrants," Western economies would not be able to function without them. There is a growing realization (which is reflected, to some extent, in some of the innovations in Blunkett's White Paper) that while the transport and communication revolution might have lessened the need for people in manufacturing and related branches of the economy to be physically around, virtual space cannot solve the need for people in the service and leisure industries that has arisen given demographic changes in the population. There is a demand for both skilled professionals such as doctors, nurses, teachers, and social workers, as well as for unskilled waiters, cleaners, and sex workers. While the discourse is about free movement of capital and blocked movement of humans, there is a continuous process of draining third world countries of their skilled workers, while, at the same time, large percentages of aid budgets are being paid to "consultant" expatriates who live and work very often in separate compounds in third world countries.

This economic reality affects identity politics in both parts of the globe and has brought about the rise of what both Stuart Hall (1996) and Verena Stolcke (1995) call "cultural fundamentalism," although it really should be called "ethnic fundamentalism" because it is all about ethnic boundary maintenance. A lot of attention has been given to the rise of the New Right and White politics in that background, as well as to the rise of Islamic fundamentalism in various third world nationalist movements. The myth of common origin and a fixed immutable, ahistorical, and homogenous construction of the collectivity's culture and/or religion as an encapsulating totality is central to such constructions.

As Stolcke (1995) points out, there is an apparent contradiction in the modern liberal ethos, between an invocation of a shared humanity that involves an idea of generality so that no human being seems to be excluded, and a cultural particularism translated into national terms. A cultural "other," the immigrant or a member of another community who does not share the same myth of common origin, is constructed as an alien and consequently as a potential "enemy" who threatens "our" national and cultural integrity and uniqueness. In yet a further ideological twist, national identity and belonging interpreted as cultural particularity become, thus, insurmountable barriers to do what, as humans, in principle comes naturally, namely, to communicate. Total separation, preferably spatial, is considered to be vital for the common human welfare, in total contradiction to social and economic reality.

Such ethnic fundamentalism can often also be found in "diasporic politics." In spite of a social reality of cultural, social, and often biological hybridity, the need to keep and reproduce identity and belonging can be demonstrated in a variety of ways and can have, as I discussed elsewhere, profound effects on the political and economic realities of the "homelands" (Yuval-Davis 1997b). Communication and transport technologies help to keep and reproduce the connections between "diasporic" people and their communities and countries of origin. Such processes help to reinforce the ethnicization of identity and belonging and the gradual lessening of territorial residence and formal state citizenships in this process.

The ethnicization of the politics of belonging is very salient in large international conferences as, for example, the UN World Conference Against Racism (WCAR) that took place at the beginning of September 2001 in Durban, South Africa. The Palestinian delegation there included Palestinians who were both citizens of Israel and from the Occupied Territories. Africans and people of African descent also worked together as a united caucus. There was an emotional detachment and self-distancing of African Americans, for instance, at the WCAR conference from the official US delegation that cannot be explained simply by its being a republican government.

The ethnicization of identity, however, is multilayered. It does not relate just to specific origins and ethnicities or even religious collectivities. There was an overarching dichotomy at the WCAR conference between those who saw themselves as postcolonials and/or blacks and the West, including East Europeans. Another dichotomy was around questions of culture and religion, around the theme of the "clash of civilizations," polarizing Islamic and Western cultures. In many ways, the Palestinian issue and the occupation and dispossession by the Israelis with the active support of the USA and other Western states, has come to occupy the intersecting heart of these two global dichotomies.

These dichotomies are problematic because the whole underlying sense of bonding and belonging that united people at this level of the politics of belonging in WCAR has been the division of the world into victims and perpetrators of racism. There was no space for ambivalence and contradictory reality. This is why racism in the third world, especially in Africa and the Arab world, had virtually no space at the WCAR conference. And this is why, both for Zionist Jews and anti-Zionists from the third world at the conference, it was important to "prove" that antisemitism exists or doesn't exist in today's world. It is as if the existence of antisemitism and the racialization and oppression of Palestinians by Israel cannot coexist at the same time, as the whole dichotomous construction of racists and anti-racists/=victims of racism, would become spoiled in such a case.

Manuel Castells (1996–98) argues that in today's "postmodern" world there is no more security for people in terms of their life projects, where they live, their work place, their partners in family life, their friends. For these reasons, and also because of the political economy of what he calls "the network society," people get attached to defensive identity communities. These "identity communities" are perceived as primordial, and therefore secure and unchanging, even if largely imagined and sometimes with problematic effects, homogenizing communities, reifying their boundaries and covering up relations of power within them (see also Anthias and Yuval-Davis 1992; 1997a: ch. 3).

These identity politics dynamics constitute central parts of official multicultural policies in various countries as well as of what Charles Taylor has called "the politics of recognition" (1994) and what Nancy Fraser has convincingly described as an additional mode of distributive justice to that of class (Fraser and Honneth 1998; see also Parekh this volume).

It is not incidental that eighty years after the League of Nations and then the United Nations sanctified the principle of national self-determination, the UN convened in the year 2000 its first conference on the issue of self-determination. Nor is it incidental that a large proportion of the cases that were discussed at this conference did not concern national collectivities fighting to establish their own nation-states, like the Palestinians and the Kurds, but other modes of collectivities, such as various cases of Indigenous Peoples' movements, Roma organizations, and African Americans, who call for alternative forms of self-determination (see also Young; Hill-Collins this volume). They are searching for modes of self-determination that would defend them from discriminatory and racialized policies of nation-states and enable them to join supranational decisionmaking bodies such as the European Union and the United Nations as equals rather than as NGOs. At the same time, these modes of self-determination would not oblige them to adhere to the "holy trinity" of people-territory-state characterizing nation-states that they are unable and/or unwilling to conform to.

Whether or not such struggles would succeed, there is a feeling, that comes through strongly in Blunkett's White Paper, that nation-states see themselves threatened by such struggles and by various networks and movements of the global world in general. The construction of "secure border – safe haven" in Blunkett's thought is a way of defending the British national collectivity from the destructive effects of globalization and people's multilayered citizenships. The White Paper explicitly demands (p. 30) that in a world of multiple citizenships and belongings "the country of main residence can and should expect every individual to be committed to accept their responsibilities as well as embracing the rights which citizenship confers."

The British national collectivity

Endless books and television programs have been produced in recent years on the concept of Britishness. Rumor has it that, at the last count thirty-two books have recently been published on the subject. It has always been a subject of fascination, but especially so since Britain's turn from Empire to Europe, and the beginning of the UK devolution within the framework of the EU.

Enoch Powell was one of the British politicians who saw early and clearly that the days of the great British Empire were over. He called on the "Englishmen to come home" to reinforce and promote the "island race" at home (Barker 1981).

For Enoch Powell there was an identification between Englishness and Britishness. This enabled him to pursue his politics in Northern Ireland, after he was "exiled" from his central position in the Conservative Party, because Loyalism in Northern Ireland promotes there exactly such a cultural and political homogenization and identification. It also helped to hide the fact that the English could never have been constructed as an "island race" if the Welsh and Scots, let alone the Cornish, who reside along major parts of the British coasts, had not been incorporated into the boundaries of the nation. Powell, of course, was not alone in this hegemonic conflation. As Robert Miles commented in the early 1980s after he moved to live in Glasgow from Bristol, the equation between Englishness and Britishness, that was taken for granted in southern England, looked very different in Scotland (Miles 1982). Since devolution, and probably earlier, with the separation of the British national football teams in the European League, the automatic equation of Englishness and Britishness has been weakening in England as well.

While the construction of Englishness/Britishness in Powell's thought was assimilatory in terms of regional identities, "the marginal Celtish element" to use Hechter's expression (1975; see also Nairn 1977), it was completely exclusionary when it came to racialized British subjects who immigrated to Britain from the colonies (some, notably, brought directly by Powell as a minister in the Conservative government). He argued that "the West Indian does not, by being born in England, become an Englishman" (quoted in Gilroy 1987: 46).

In his "Rivers of Blood" speech, Powell argued that as West Indians do not belong to Britain, only disaster, mutual violence, and bloodshed could follow such an "unnatural" state of affairs. In this, Powell was a clear advocate of the doctrine Martin Barker (1981) has called "new racism" and Balibar has called *racisme différentialiste* (Balibar and Wallerstein,

1991). Le Pen in France and Haider in Austria are other clear examples of this doctrine, which does not construct an explicit racial hierarchy but rather an immutable fixed and organic belonging of specific people, territories, and states that in effect excludes and racializes all "Others."

In their publication *Freedom* (December 2001) the British National Party interpreted the riots in Northern England in 2001 as a vindication of the Powellian thesis. "Rivers of Blood" followed the entrenchment of "foreign" Asian Muslim communities in England and their mixing with "the natives."

Interestingly enough, however, the Cantle Report (2001) has come up with the opposite diagnosis. The cause of the riots, according to the Report, is not because there was too much mixing between the English and Asian communities but because there was not enough mixing. This was a result of the growing segregation of housing, schooling, and employment that has been developing during the previous twenty years, and which brought about a deterioration of any sense of social cohesion.

There is no space here to explore more fully the notion of social cohesion pursued in the Cantle Report (which modeled itself on the approach of Forrest and Kearns (2000) to community cohesion). This is a comprehensive and problematic approach (partly tautological) which includes, *inter alia*, common aims and objectives, common moral principles and support and participation in political institutions, absence of conflict, harmonious economic and social development, equal access to services and welfare benefits, a high degree of social interaction within communities and families and an intertwining of personal and place identity (Cantle 2001: 13).

The report is ambiguous about the relationship between the lack of a sense of social cohesion in the North of England and British multiculturalist policies. British multiculturalist policies have been to a great extent responsive to initiatives and demands from grassroots communities which have been incorporated into various local and national race-relations committees rather than via a centralized top-down structure (Modood and Werbner 1997). Indeed, one of the things the Cantle Report points to is the lack of any central guidance on the subject. The segregated structure found in the North of England is not evident in London or the South. What is important for our concern here is that the Cantle Report sees in such a segregation a direct cause of the riots, that cultural, religious, and identity differences and lack of contact, rather than racism, are being identified as the main cause of the riots. Most importantly of all, a direct link is being made by Blunkett between this, the need for national "social cohesion" and the new immigration policies. As Garry Young remarked in his article in *The Guardian* (February 9, 2002), such a construction does away with the achievement of the Stephen Lawrence Report (Macpherson *et al.* 1999)[2] that signaled the legitimate incorporation of black minority communities into the British national collectivity (see also Yuval-Davis 1999b). *CARF* (Campaign Against Racism and Fascism magazine) editorial (Feb./March 2002) goes even further and claims that no British Secretary of State has dared to make such a direct link for the last thirty years.

In between the Stephen Lawrence Report (Macpherson *et al.* 1999) and the Cantle Report (2001), the Runnymede Trust published a report, *Multi-Ethnic Britain,* coordinated by Bhikhu Parekh (2000). Unlike the other two reports, it did not have government sponsorship and included many more academic voices and community activists who have been active in antiracist struggles. Significantly, virtually none of them was asked to be involved in the Cantle Report.

Both the reports state firmly (and in complete contrast to the Powellian construction of the British national collectivity) that there is no inherent and/or homogenous ethnic construction of Britishness and suggest civic values, based on Human Rights conventions, as the basis for cohesive national collectivities. The Runnymede Report, however, focuses on British national regional, as well as ethnic, diversity and explores issues of institutional racism and exclusion in Britain, following the Stephen Lawrence Report. The White Paper (and the Cantle report) construct cultural diversity as a direct result of migration and thus link the need to contain it with the need to train immigrants in English and civic values. Racism is not even mentioned in the White Paper and hardly at all in the Cantle Report, and then only as an obstacle to social cohesion.

I do not want to create here the impression, however, that I wholeheartedly support the Runnymede Report, although it is clear that I am closer to it than to the government report. My main criticism of the Runnymede Report is that the British national collectivity is described in it as a "community of communities." This construction, in spite of some reservations in the report, reifies, homogenizes, and naturalizes communities and their boundaries in the old multicultural style (Anthias and Yuval-Davis 1992; May 1999; McLennan 2001). It does not relate to the fact that, on the one hand, the boundaries of these communities are not only contested but often cross British national borders. On the other hand, there are many people who are formally British citizens and who either belong to more than one community or do not feel themselves as belonging to any – including the British national one. The post-September 11,

2001 situation has only exacerbated some of the above issues, locally and globally.

Concluding ponderings

The magic solution to all the problems that the various reports point to is the concept and values of civic citizenship. Blunkett is aware of the fact that people are often citizens of more than one country (his attitude to asylum seekers suggests that he is less aware that often people do not even have citizenship rights in any state). As mentioned above, his White Paper argues that in this age of globalization it is the citizenship of the main country of residence that should get priority and loyalty.

Blunkett is trying hard not to be ethnocentric and to embrace the cultural and ethnic diversity of British citizens, although he constructs this diversity as a result of the immigration of outsiders and a basic unavoidable problematic that resulted from this. He calls, therefore, for two commonalities to unite all British citizens, to which they should all be committed. First, the English language, which he suggests making a mandatory condition for obtaining British citizenship; second, accepting the values of the European Human Rights Act that was adopted as British law in 1998. The latter is especially ironic, as Blunkett himself had already revoked part of this Act in the post-September 11 days and the "global war against terrorism." Moreover, adopting a European law just two years before the publication of the White Paper as the heart of Britishness might seem somewhat problematic, especially to the strong anti-European lobby in Britain.

But the question is of a more general nature. Indeed, in several settler states, such as Canada and the USA, where there is no common myth of origin except migration, civic nationalism has been pursued as the solution for a nonracialized civic nationalism, at least on the rhetorical level. However, even in such societies, this becomes problematic, once indigenous peoples find their voices and reject being incorporated into the nation as one more ethnic minority of the "imposing society" (to use an expression I heard from Australian Aboriginal peoples). In other societies, where the myth of origin of the majority of the population is indigenous to the place, the situation is even more complex. Often there are two or three regional and linguistic groupings that co-reside in the same territories that often used to be part of much larger empires, as well as other minority communities that immigrated to the country as a result of economic, political, religious, or social reasons.

It is here that we are returning to the problematics of the politics of belonging from the problematics of civic citizenship.

Michael Mann (2000) argues that murderous ethnic cleansing is a direct result of modernity and processes of democratic self-determination "of the people." Even before him, Michal Walzer, in his book *On Toleration* (1997), has argued that tolerance for pluralism was possible only in non-democratic imperial social and political orders.

If Mann and Walzer are right, we have a lot of rethinking to do and much to be afraid of. Balibar (1990) has argued that since the fall of the Soviet Union the concept of Europe has changed from an ideological (Western) into an identity one, in which there is a search for common cultural and religious denominators. It is in this context that "human rights" discourse, from being a resistance discourse, used in antiracist, antidiscrimination, and antiexclusion practices, can become a signifier of Western belonging in the "clash of civilizations" discourse on both sides. We have to be very wary of this. We have to think of ways in which this will not happen.

Let us hope we can succeed.

NOTES

1. Thanks to Richard Mowbray who drew my attention to this literature.
2. The Stephen Lawrence Report investigated the mishandling by the Metropolitan (London) Police of the murder of a black teenager, Stephen Lawrence, by a white racist gang. The Report found that the inept, bungled investigation, which resulted in no convictions, was indicative of wider institutional racism within the Metropolitan Police Force.

REFERENCES

Anderson, Benedict (1991 [1983]) *Imagined Communities*. London: Verso.
Anthias, Floya and Yuval-Davis, Nira (1992) *Racialized Boundaries*. London: Routledge.
Avineri, S. and A. Shalit (eds.) (1992) *Communitarianism & Individualism*. Oxford: Oxford University Press.
Balibar, Etienne (1990) "The nation form – history and ideology.' *New Left Review* 13 (3) (summer): 329–61.
Balibar, Etienne and Immanuel Wallerstein (1991) *Race, Nation, Class: Ambiguous Identities*. London: Verso.
Barker, Martin (1981) *The New Racism*. London: Junction Books.
Bell, Vikki (1999) "Performativity and belonging: an introduction." *Theory, Culture & Society: Special Issue on Performativity and Belonging* 16 (2) (September): 1–10.
Blunkett, David (2002) *Secure Borders, Safe Haven*. White Paper, Home Office.
Bowlby, J. (1969) *Attachment, Vol. 1 of Attachment and Loss*. London: Hogarth Press; New York: Basic Books.

228   *Nira Yuval-Davis*

(1973) *Separation, Anxiety & Anger. Vol. 2 of Attachment and Loss.* London: Hogarth Press; New York: Basic Books.

Brah, Avtar *et al.* (eds.) (1999) *Global Futures: Migration, Environment, Globalization.* London: Routledge.

Cantle, Ted (2001) *Community Cohesion: A Report of the Independent Review Team.* London: Home Office.

Castells, Manuel (1996–8) *The Information Age: Economy, Society, Culture.* 3 vols. Oxford: Blackwell.

Castles, Stephen and Mark J. Miller (1993) *The Age of Migration.* London: Macmillan.

Crowley, John (1999) "The politics of belonging: some theoretical consideration." In A. Geddes and A. Favell (eds.), *The Politics of Belonging: Migrants and Minorities in Contemporary Europe.* Aldershot: Ashgate, pp. 15–41.

Daly, Markate (1993) *Communitarianism: Belonging & Commitment in a Pluralist Democracy.* London: Wadworth Publishing Company.

Enloe, Cynthia (1990) "Womenandchildren: making feminist sense of the Persian Gulf Crisis." *The Village Voice,* September 25.

Favell, Adrian (1999) "To belong or not to belong: the postnational question." In A. Geddes and A. Favell (eds.), *The Politics of Belonging: Migrants and Minorities in Contemporary Europe.* Aldershot: Ashgate, pp. 209–27.

Fodor, N. (1949) *The Search for the Beloved.* New York: University Books.

Forrest, R. and A. Kearns (2000) "Social cohesion, social capital and the neighborhood." Paper presented in ESRC Cities Programme Neighbourhoods Colloquiu, Liverpool, June 5–6.

Fortier, Anne-Marie (2000) *Migrant Belongings: Memory, Space, Identities.* Oxford: Berg.

Fraser, Nancy and Axel Honneth (1998) *Redistribution or Recognition? A Philosophical Exchange.* London: Verso.

Giddens, Anthony (1991) *Modernity and Self Identity.* Cambridge: Polity Press.

Gilroy, Paul (1987) *There Ain't no Black in the Union Jack.* London: Hutchinson.

Hall, Stuart (1996) "Who needs 'identity?'." Introduction to S. Hall and P. du Gay (eds.), *Questions of Cultural Identity.* London: Sage.

Hall, Stuart and David Held (1989) "Citizens and citizenship." In Stuart Hall and Martin Jacques (eds.), *New Times.* London: Lawrence and Wishart.

Hechter, Michael (1975) *Internal Colonialism: The Celtish Fringe in British National Development.* London: Routledge & Kegan Paul.

Herzog, Lawrence A. (ed.) (1993) *Changing Boundaries in the Americas: New Perspectives on the US-Mexican, Central American and South American Borders.* San-Diego, CA: Centre for US-Mexican Studies, University of California.

Lake, Frank (1986 [1966]) *Clinical Theology.* London: Darton, Longman & Todd.

Macpherson *et al.* (1999) *The Stephen Lawrence Murder Inquiry Report.* London: HMSO.

Mann, Michael (2000) "COMPLETE." In M. Guibernault and J. Hutchinson (eds.), *Understanding Nationalism.* Cambridge: Polity Press.

Marshall, T. H. (1950) *Citizenship and Social Class.* Cambridge University Press, Cambridge.

(1975 [1965]) *Social Policy in the Twentieth Century.* Hutchinson, London.

(1981) *The Right to Welfare and Other Essays.* London: Heinemann Educational Books.

Marx, Karl (1975 [1844]) *Early Writings.* Harmondsworth: Penguin Books.

May, Stephen (ed.) (1999) *Critical Multiculturalism: Rethinking Multicultural and Antiracist Education.* London: Falmer Press.

McLennan, Gregor (2001) "Problematic multiculturalism." *Sociology* 35 (4): 985–89.

Miles, Robert (1982) "Racism and nationalism in Britain." In C. Husbands (ed.), *'Race' in Britain: Continuity and Change.* London: Hutchinson University Library, pp. 279–302.

Modood, Tariq and Pnina Werbner (eds.) (1997) *The Politics of Multiculturalism in the New Europe.* London: Zed Books.

Mott, F. J. (1948) *The Universal Design of Birth.* Philadephia: David McKay.

Nairn, Tom (1977) *The Break-up of Britain.* London: Verso.

Nugent, A. and P. Asiwaju (eds.) (1996) *African Boundaries: Barriers, Conduits and Opportunities.* London: Pinter.

Oldfield, Adrian (1990) *Citizenship and Community: Civic Republicanism and the Modern World.* London: Routledge.

Parekh, Bhikhu (ed.) (2000) *Multi-Ethnic Britain.* London: The Runnymede Trust.

Peled, Yoav (1992) "Ethnic democracy and the legal construction of citizenship: Arab citizens of the Jewish state." *American Political Science Review* 86 (2): 432–42.

Rank, Otto (1973 [1929]) *The Trauma of Birth.* London: Routledge & Kegan Paul.

Sahlins, Peter (1989) *Boundaries: The Making of France and Spain in the Pyrennees.* Berkley: University of California Press.

Stoetzler, Marcel and Nira Yuval-Davis (forthcoming), "Standpoint theory, situated knowledge and the situated imagination." *Feminist Theory.*

Stolcke, Verena (1995) "Talking culture: new boundaries, new rhetorics of exclusion in Europe." *Current Anthropology* 16 (1): 1–23.

Taylor, Charles (1994) "Examining the politics of recognition." In Amy Gutmann (ed.), *Multiculturalism.* Princeton: Princeton University Press, pp. 25–74.

Tönnies, Ferdinand (1940 [1935]) *Fundamental Concepts of Sociology (Gemeinschaft und Gesellschaft).* New York: American Book Company [English translation of the 1935 German edition].

Walzer, Michael (1997) *On Toleration.* Newhaven: Yale University Press.

Wilson, Thomas M. and Hastings Donnan (eds.) (1998) *Border Identities: Nation and State at International Frontiers.* Cambridge: Cambridge University Press.

Yuval-Davis, Nira (1991) "The citizenship debate: women, ethnic processes and the state." *Feminist Review* 39: 58–68.

(1997a) *Gender & Nation.* London: Sage.

(1997b) "National spaces and collective identities: borders, boundaries, citizenship and gender relations." London: Inaugural Lecture Series, The University of Greenwich.

(1999a) "Multilayered citizenship in the age of 'glocalization'." *International Feminist Journal of Politics* 1 (1).

(1999b) "Institutional racism, cultural diversity and citizenship: some reflections on reading the Stephen Lawrence Inquiry Report." *Sociological Review Online* (May).

Yuval-Davis, Nira and Pnina Werbner (eds.) (1999) *Women, Citizenship and Difference*. London: Zed Books.

11   Is it time to be postnational?

Craig Calhoun

In the wake of 1989, talk of globalization was often celebratory. This was true not only among anticommunist ideologues, corporate elites, and followers of Fukuyama's Hegelian announcement of the end of history. Enthusiasm for globalization was also prominent on the left. Even while an anticorporate movement gathered strength, many were eager to proclaim the rise of international civil society as a transcendence of the nation-state. Very few listened to reminders that national struggles in much of the world were among the few viable forms of resistance to capitalist globalization.[1]

Many embraced an ideal of cosmopolitan democracy. That is, they embraced not just cosmopolitan tastes for cultural diversity (which too often rendered culture an object of external consumption rather than internal meaning); not just the notion of hybridity with its emphasis on porous boundaries and capacious, complex identities; and not just cosmopolitan ethics emphasizing the obligations of each to all around the world. They embraced also the notion that the globe could readily be a polis, and humanity at large organized in democratic citizenship.[2] This is an attractive but very elusive ideal.

The discourse of globalization is gloomier early in the first decade of the twenty-first century than it was in the 1990s. Stock market bubbles burst, and even recovery has felt insecure; reviving equity prices have not been matched by creation of jobs. The world's one superpower has announced and implemented a doctrine of preemptive invasion of those it sees as threatening. Awareness of the global vitality of religion is growing, but intolerant fundamentalists seem to thrive disproportionately. Despite new doctrines of active intervention, a host of humanitarian emergencies and local or regional conflicts kill by the tens of thousands and impoverish by the millions. And the dark side of globalization includes diseases from SARS to AIDS and trafficking in women, drugs, and guns.

If 1989 symbolized (but only partly caused) the proglobal enthusiasms of the 1990s, 9/11 symbolizes (and also only partly caused) the reversal in mood. Some ask why we didn't see it coming. Focusing on 9/11 encourages the sense that simply a new event or malign movement defines the issue – as though, for example, terrorism were the fundamental underlying issue rather than a tactic made newly attractive by a combination of global organization and communications media on the one hand and local grievances and vulnerabilities on the other. We would do better to ask why we didn't see "it" – the dark side of globalization, or at least its Janus-faced duplicity – already there?

As globalization proceeded after 1989, shocks and enthusiasms alternated. The relative peacefulness of most postcommunist transitions – despite the dispossession and disruption they entailed – brought enthusiasm. Fighting among national groups in the former Soviet Union and Yugoslavia was a shock. There was an enthusiasm for global economic integration and the rapid development of Asian "tigers" and a shock with the currency crisis of 1997. There was an enthusiasm for information technology as the harbinger and vehicle of freer communication and new wealth and a series of shocks with the extent to which the Internet brought pornography and spam, then the dot.com bust, then a range of new surveillance regimes. There was enthusiasm for European integration and repeated shocks when wars erupted in Europe and the European Union could not achieve an effective common defense or foreign policy, and when immigration produced resurgent racism and nationalism. There was enthusiasm for global democracy and shock and disillusionment as war came even to highly touted new democracies like Ethiopia and Eritrea and intertwined political and economic meltdown in Argentina. There was enthusiasm for both human rights and humanitarian intervention and shock when the two came into conflict as the world failed to find an adequate way to address genocide and ethnic war in Central Africa.

Indeed, an explicit attack not only on nationalism but on the state was important to many of the enthusiasts. This was fueled not only by a growing confidence in global civil society (and potential supports for it, like the Internet). It was also driven by the tragic civil wars and ethnic slaughters of the era. Not only did these offer extreme examples of the evils associated with ethnicity and nationalism, they provided spectacles of possibly avertable tragedies in the face of which self-interested governments refused to act, sometimes citing notions of state sovereignty as rationale. So support grew for "humanitarian" interventions into crises, and also the belief that the crises were evidence of failed states and sovereignty only a distraction.[3]

For most of the 1990s, shocks failed to hold back enthusiasm. This was nowhere more evident than in the proliferation of cosmopolitan visions of globalization. These were (and are) internally heterogeneous. All, however, participated in a common contrast to overly strong politics of identity or claims to group solidarity. They extolled human rights and humanitarian interventions by "global society" into local messes. They praised hybridity and multiple, overlapping political memberships. Mostly produced from the political center and soft left, they shared with neoliberalism from the harder right a contempt for states which they understood mainly as authoritarian and dangerous. In this they reflected the libertarian side of 1960s conflicts, New Left disappointments in the welfare state, and a general antiauthoritarianism.[4] They focused not only on multilateral institutions but on the possibility that individuals might emancipate themselves from the sectionalism and restrictions of groups. Whether mainly ethical, political, sociopsychological, or cultural in their orientation, advocates of a more cosmopolitan world rejected nationalism, at least fundamentalism if not all religion, and most strong claims on behalf of ethnic groups. And so, the cosmopolitans suffered September 11 as an especially severe shock, and the continuing prominence of national security agendas and both religious and ethnic identities as a gloomy regression from what had seemed a clear progress.

To some extent this continues – in speeded-up form – a pattern common to the whole modern era. Enthusiasms for transcending old forms of political power have alternated since the Enlightenment – perhaps since the seventeenth century – with appeals for solidarity in the face of insecurity and state action to build better societies. "In a pattern of maniacal relapses and recoveries throughout European history, globalism keeps promising to arrive, always seems, in fact, to be just around the corner if not already here, but which continues to find its reality only in an unfulfilled desire against a backdrop of preparations for future war."[5]

There is much to feel gloomy about in the contemporary world, including the crisis of multilateral institutions, the prominence of reactionary political groups including but not limited to nationalists, and the assertion of military power as the solution to many of the problems of global inequality and instability. But this chapter is not about the dark side of globalization nor is it a challenge to the cosmopolitan ideal. Rather, it is an attempt to raise some sociological questions about what cosmopolitanism means as a project, rather than an ideal, and how it relates to nationalism. Perhaps most basically, I shall suggest cosmopolitanism and nationalism are mutually constitutive and to oppose them too sharply is misleading.[6] To conceptualize cosmopolitanism as the opposite to nationalism (and ethnicity and other solidarities) is not only a sociological confusion but an obstacle to achieving both greater democracy and better transnational institutions. And I shall suggest there are good reasons why nationalism survives – even though nationalist projects are certainly not all good – and good reasons to doubt whether we are entering a postnational era.

Beyond the nation-state?

Advocates for a cosmopolitan global order frequently present this as moving beyond the nation-state. Jürgen Habermas, for example, writes of a "post-national constellation."[7] Martin Köhler sees movement from "the national to the cosmopolitan public sphere," with "a world developing as a single whole thanks to the social activity and the deliberate will of a population sharing common values and interests, such as human rights, democratic participation, the rule of law and the preservation of the world's ecological heritage."[8] Köhler certainly recognizes that adequate structures of authority are not yet in place on a global scale; he is a moderate cosmopolitan who still sees a role for states. Ulrich Beck is more extreme. He describes a "politics of postnationalism" in which "the cosmopolitan project contradicts and replaces the nation-state project."[9]

Many other writers discuss the end of the Westphalian state system – by which they mean mostly an idea about sovereignty and the mutual recognition of states introduced at the end of the Thirty Years War.[10] The Treaty of Westphalia is perhaps a convenient marker for the transition to a global order of nation-states, and the development of an international approach to national sovereignty, but the image of Westphalia is usually evoked in a way that exaggerates the extent to which nation-states were already effective and discrete power containers in 1648, the basic units of international politics for the next three and a half centuries. In the first place, empires thrived for the next 300 years, though more as European projects abroad than on the continent of Europe itself. Second, the nation-state order was hardly put in place in 1648, even in Europe. It would be more accurate to say that after 1648 nation-state *projects* increasingly shaped history, both domestically in efforts to bring nation and state into closer relationship and internationally in the organization of conflict and peacemaking. Indeed, the very distinction of domestic from international is a product of these projects; it was minimally conceptualized in 1648 and for a very long time the interplay of nationalism and cosmopolitanism was not at all a simple opposition.[11]

The nation-state became relatively clearly formulated and increasingly dominant in Europe and the Americas during the nineteenth century. In much of the rest of the world, nationalism flourished more in the twentieth century and the project of trying to make states and nations line up plausibly remains very active in the twenty-first. Indeed, conflicts in central Asia, the Balkans, Central Africa, and South Asia reveal the extent to which nationalism and the nation-state project are current and not merely historical concerns. Moreover, these are not conflicts of a radically different sort from those that beset Europe in the era when modern states were first being consolidated there. Religion, culture, language, kin relations, demagogues, and economic opportunists mixed with the pursuit of political power, defensible borders, and state sovereignty in Europe as well. And Europeans complicated the matter further by pursuing overseas empires even while they consolidated national states at home. France – the paradigmatic nation of most theories of nationalism – was not only forged out of local wars and impositions of state power that unified the hexagon, even in its most revolutionary and nationalist moments it was also imperial. The First French Republic tried to repress Haitian independence just as the Fourth and Fifth Republics tried to repress Algerian independence.

The image of a Westphalian order thus marginalizes empire inappropriately, and deflects attention from the disorder and conflict wrought by attempts to make nation-states the dominant organizational units of sovereignty and monopolies of force. It flattens into legal abstraction an era that saw the world's most destructive wars and the development and recurrence of modern genocide, as well as the creation of a rich range of interstate institutions and agreements. The Peace of Westphalia certainly did not usher in a 350 year reign of peace, though arguably it inaugurated the cycle of philosophical and political declarations of plans for perpetual peace and wars to end all wars.[12]

And so it is unclear just what a "post-Westphalian" order signifies. For some, especially those for whom the European continent is the primary referent, it is more or less synonymous with "postnational constellation." And here too there are both domestic and international implications. The first is that cultural commonalities organized and mobilized in nationalism underwrote the necessary solidarities of citizens with states through most of the modern era, though now it is in some combination necessary and desirable to move beyond this. What lies beyond may be either solidarities based on the loyalties of citizens to specific political institutions, such as what Habermas has called "constitutional patriotism," or a move beyond particularistic solidarities altogether to some sort of ethical cosmopolitanism in which obligations to humanity as such supersede citizenship, community, and other more local bonds.[13] Second, internationally, the implication is simply that states cannot organize global politics or even the affairs once ostensibly contained in their own boundaries well enough to be considered the primary units of global order.

One of the problems with this discussion is that its empirical referents are unclear. Assertions are made like, "in the second age of modernity the relationship between the state, business, and a society of citizens must be redefined."[14] Which state (and for that matter what organization of business and society of citizens)? Discussion of whether the state is growing stronger, declining, or remains effective in international relations or for securing domestic welfare is quite frequently carried on without specification as to whether the state in question is, say, the United States of America or Chad. There is also an elision between discussions of a possible global "postnational constellation" or cosmopolitan democracy and debates over the integration of the European Union. The latter may be a model for what a postnational order might look like. Without going into that in any depth, however, it needs to be said (a) that it is not clear how well this is proceeding, and (b) that while European integration might be "post" the specific nation-state projects dominant for the last 300 years, it is not at all clear that it does not involve a new project of much the same kind, rather than a fundamentally different one.[15]

The last is an important point. The European Union is clearly an important innovation in many ways, and it clearly goes beyond anything imagined by the signatories of the Treaty of Westphalia. But one could focus on continuity rather than novelty. One could see the European Union as potentially a further centralization of political power and integration of both state administration and civil society of much the same sort as that which made modern France or Germany out of once less unified and often warring smaller polities. Indeed, Habermas' idea of "constitutional patriotism" – the loyalty of citizens to their political institutions rather than to any preexisting ethnic nation – is itself a reworking of the idea of civic nationalism.[16]

Many discussions of globalization and cosmopolitan governance proceed as though it were obvious that the specific states that have claimed sovereignty in the language of Westphalia define a determinate scale of social organization, as though "nation" must refer to the cultural solidarities and identities organized at the level of those states. But what we see all over the world is that the scale of national projects varies and is hotly contested – precisely because there are no "natural" nations and there is no naturally best scale for a state. It was an illusion of Romantic nationalism and the "Springtime of Peoples" in the first half of the nineteenth century that there could somehow be an autonomous state for every nation.

A post-Westphalian Europe does not in itself invalidate the projects of sovereignty and self-determination in countries of Asia or Africa. Nor does it necessarily mean in all senses a postnational Europe (though it may mean transcending the limits of existing European nation-states). As David Held says, "globalization is best understood as a spatial phenomenon, lying on a continuum with 'the local' at one end and 'the global' at the other. It denotes a shift in the spatial form of human organization and activity to transcontinental or interregional patterns of activity, interaction and the exercise of power."[17] But this "shift" is not neutral. It advantages some and disadvantages others. And that is in fact a crucial reason for the continuing reproduction of nationalism, and a reason why caution is warranted before suggesting that nationalist projects are inherently regressive and cosmopolitan projects progressive. And it is especially problematic to suggest that, from a standpoint of apparent academic neutrality that in fact coincides with the centers of current global political and economic power or former colonial power. The liberal state is not neutral. Cosmopolitan civil society is not neutral. Even the English language is not neutral. This doesn't mean that any of the three is bad, only that they are not equally accessible to everyone and do not equally express the interests of everyone.

Transformations in scale and struggles for equity

Globalization doesn't just happen. It is to a large extent imposed. This is misrecognized, though, when globalization is presented as simply the course of history, the mandate of necessity to which individuals and states must adapt or perish. Fortunately, as Kymlicka has noted, "globalization, far from encouraging political apathy, is itself one of the things which seems to mobilize otherwise apathetic people."[18]

One of the dominant patterns in modern history is the organization of power and capital on ever larger scales, and with new intensity. This precipitates a race in which popular forces and solidarities are always running behind. It is a race to achieve social integration, to structure the connections among people, and to organize the world. Capital and political power are out in front – sometimes in collusion and sometimes in contention with each other. Workers and ordinary citizens are always in the position of trying to catch up. As they get organized on local levels, capital and power integrate on larger scales.

The formation of modern states was both a matter of expansion, as smaller states gave way in the process of establishing centralized rule over large, contiguous territories, and of intensification, as administrative capacity was increased and intermediate powers weakened. Likewise, the growth of capitalism involved increases in both long-distance and local trade, the development of both larger and more effectively administered enterprises, the extension of trade into financial markets and production relations, and the subjection of more and more dimensions of social life to market relations. State formation and capitalism coincided in empires and sometimes imperialism without formal empire. Postcolonies, even where they did constitute more or less integrated nation-states, could seldom achieve the autonomy promised by nationalist ideology precisely because they confronted global capitalist markets and unequal terms of trade.

Certainly there have long been and still are outright rejections of capitalist globalization, including communitarian efforts to defend small islands of self-sufficiency and larger-scale socialist projects of autochthonous development. And there are certainly rejections of governmental power, whether articulately anarchist or simply resistant. But for the most part, popular struggles have demanded neither an end to economic expansion nor the elimination of political power but a much greater fairness in the structure of economy and polity. They have sought, in other words, that integration come with equity and opportunity (the latter commonly or problematically identified with growth). This is the primary concern of trade unions in advanced capitalist countries. It is the primary concern of minority groups in multicultural polities (and nearly all polities are multicultural). And it is the primary concern of people in the world's poorer and less powerful states – if not necessarily of those running the states. Indeed, an important dimension of nationalism is rooted in popular demands for equity. Though cosmopolitan thought often rejects nationalism as some combination of manipulation by the central state, ancient ethnic loyalty, or desire to benefit at the expense of others – all phenomena that are real – it commonly misses the extent to which nationalism not only expresses solidarity or belonging but provides a rhetoric for demanding equity and growth.

The demand that states operate for the benefit of nations comes in part from "below" as ordinary people insist on some level of participation and commonwealth as a condition of treating rulers as legitimate. But the integration of nation-states is an ambivalent step. On the one hand, state power is a force in its own right – not least in colonialism but also domestically – and represents a flow of organizing capacity away from local communities. On the other hand, democracy at a national level constitutes the greatest success that ordinary people have had in catching up to capital and power.

Ordinary people in many countries have achieved a modicum of democracy, and a number of other gains, but they did not choose the "race" in which electoral democracy is one of their partial victories. This was for the most part imposed by the development of more centralized states and the integration of capitalist markets. Most ordinary people experienced a loss of collective self-determination before the eventual gains of nineteenth and twentieth-century democratization. They experienced this loss as the communities and institutions they had created were overrun and undermined by state and market forces. This does not mean that workers two generations later were not in many ways materially better off, or that life chances in the advanced industrial countries were not generally better than in those that did not go through similar transformations. It does not mean that many workers would not have preferred the chance to be owners. It does mean that many of those who lived through the transformations lost – and bitterly resented losing – both what has recently been called "social capital" and the chance to choose ways of life based on their own values and manner of understanding the world. And there are threats of similar loss today if neoliberal ideology leads to both the "extensification" and the "intensification" of market economies and capitalist production without provision of greater equity.

Struggles against colonial rule have often reflected similar issues and paradoxes. Dominated peoples have simultaneously sought to resist foreign rule and to forge nations by drawing disparate "traditional" groups together.[19] A claim to common "traditional" culture underwrites both nationalism and sectional or "communal" resistance to it (each of which is a project of groups placed differently in a larger field, not simply a reflection of preexisting identity – though never unrelated to ongoing cultural reproduction). Nations appear simultaneously as always already-there cultural commonalities, as new projects occasioned by colonialism and independence struggles, and as impositions of certain constructions of the national culture over others' identities and cultural projects within the ostensible nation. The situation of struggle against external colonial power makes larger categories of "indigenous" solidarity useful, but the achievement of these is always a redistribution of power and resources – usually away from more or less autonomous local communities, subordinated cultures, and other groups. The sociologist Pierre Bourdieu describes one version of this, as true he argues for early twenty-first-century neoliberal globalization as it was for the French colonization of Algeria:

As I was able to observe in Algeria, the unification of the economic field tends, especially through monetary unification and the generalization of monetary exchanges that follows, to hurl all social agents into an economic game for which they are not equally prepared and equipped, culturally and economically. It tends by the same token to submit them to standards objectively imposed by competition from more efficient productive forces and modes of production, as can readily be seen with small rural producers who are more and more completely torn away from self-sufficiency. In short, *unification benefits the dominant*.[20]

Those who resist such market incursions or the similar centralizations of state power are commonly described as "traditional" in contrast to modern. Their defense of community, craft, religion, and kinship is seen as somehow irrational. It is indeed often backward-looking, though not always and not for this reason incapable of generating social innovation and sometimes truly radical visions of a better society. But to look backward is not inherently irrational – especially when there is no guarantee that the future amounts to progress – or that what some deem progress will advance the values ordinary people hold dearest.

Moreover, the communities and institutions that are defended by those who resist the incursions of expanding and intensifying capitalist markets and state administrations are not simply dead forms inherited from the past. They are social achievements, collectively created often in the face of considerable opposition. They provide some level of capacity for ordinary people to organize their own lives – imperfectly, no doubt, but with potential for improvement and some level of autonomy from outside forces. As Bourdieu remarks, their defense is rendered all the more rational by the extent to which unification benefits the dominant. And as I shall argue here, extremely rapid changes in social organization may especially benefit the dominant, disrupt life more, and reduce chances for social struggle to win compromises and create alternative paths of development.

The same is true, at least potentially, for the project of unifying the working class in order to fight better against more centralized capitalism. The Marxist notion of a progress from local struggles through trade union consciousness to class struggle is an account of "modern" unification in the pursuit of more effective struggle (based, according to the theory, on recognition of true underlying interests in solidarity). But even if unification is necessary to contest impositions of power from "outside" it is not necessarily egalitarian in its "internal" organization. Class unification can only come about if nonclass goals and identities are subordinate. Marxists often discuss nationalist or ethnic struggles as though these are merely diversions from the "correct" solidarity necessarily based on class.[21] But all such unifying solidarities – class and nation alike – are achieved in struggle and at the expense of others. This makes them neither artificial nor erroneous, but products of history.

Products of history may nonetheless be constitutive for personal identity, social relationships, and a sense of location in the world. In other words, it is a mistake to leap from the historical character of national and other solidarities to an account of "the invention of tradition" which implies that national traditions are mere artifice and readily swept away. Among other things, this misrepresents what is at stake in discussion of "tradition." Too often, to be sure, scholars take at face value (and perhaps have their own investments in) traditionalists' accounts of respect for ancient ways of life. But it is equally erroneous to imagine that demonstrating a point of origin sometime more recent that the primordial mists of ancient history debunks national culture. It is not antiquity that defines tradition. Rather, tradition is better grasped as a mode of reproduction of culture and social practices that depends on understandings produced and reproduced in practical experience and interpersonal relations, rather than rendered entirely abstract, as a set of rules or more formal textual communication. So tradition is not simply a set of contents, but a mode of reproduction of such contents. It works for people when it successfully organizes projects in their lives.

As a kind of ubiquitous involvement in culture, often incorporated prereflectively as *habitus*, tradition works best where change is gradual so that there can be continual adaptation embedded in the ordinary processes of reproduction. But it is misleading to approach "tradition" as the opposite of progress, as referring to simple continuity of the past, or as simple backwardness. Tradition is partly backward looking, a project of preserving and passing on wisdom and right action. But as a project, it is also forward looking. Traditions must be reconstructed – sometimes purified and sometimes enhanced – whether this is explicitly announced or not. Moderns have tended to look on changes to a story or a statement of values as necessarily falling into three categories: deceptions, errors, or clearly announced revisions. But in fact the constant revision of living traditions works differently. It is not as though there is simply a "true" or authoritative version at time one, against which the "changes" are to be judged. Rather, the tradition is always in the process of production and reproduction simultaneously. Usually the latter predominates enormously over the former – and thus there is continuity from the past. But this is achieved not merely by reverence but by action. People put the culture they have absorbed (or that has been inculcated into them) to work every time they take an action. But they also adapt it, mobilize the parts of it that fit the occasion and indeed their strategy. They do this commonly without any conscious decision and certainly without the intent of acting on the tradition. Put another way, tradition is medium and condition of their action, not its object, even though their actions will (collectively and cumulatively) have implications for tradition. Language is a good example, as people use it to accomplish innumerable ends, and shape it through the ways in which they use it, but only very exceptionally through an intention to do so.

It is misleading, thus, to equate tradition simply with antiquity of cultural contents. Max Weber is often cited for such a view, but this is an incomplete reading. Like most thinkers since the Enlightenment, Weber opposed mere unconscious reflex or unexamined inheritance to rationality as conscious and sensible action. He saw traditional action as "determined by ingrained habituation," and thought that it lay very close to the borderline of what could be called meaningfully oriented action.[22] I would suggest that we see this account as a forerunner – albeit problematic and limited – of Bourdieu's deeper development of the idea of *habitus*. The latter reaches beyond mere habituation and is less deterministic. Above all, it situates action in a field of social relations, not as the decontextualized expression or choice or even interaction of individuals.[23] Bourdieu reveals *habitus* to matter more in modern societies than Weber thought traditional action did; indeed, in important ways Bourdieu deconstructs the opposition of traditional to modern, showing for example how much reproduction there is within ostensibly progressive modernity. The crucial point, however, is that Weber approached tradition through its medium of reproduction – ingrained habituation. He may have grasped that too narrowly, but the approach was sound.

What Weber defined by its backward-looking character was not so much tradition as traditional*ism*. This was what Weber described as "piety for what actually, allegedly, or presumably has always existed."[24] Here too there is an echo in Bourdieu, who in his studies of colonial Algeria made much of the difference between "traditional" Berber society, which he was as much obliged to reconstruct as he was able to observe it in his fieldwork in Kabylia, and the traditionalism that was deployed by various indigenous interpreters of Berber culture in the context of rapid social change and destabilization of old ways of life. Both in the countryside and among labor-migrants to Algerian cities, Bourdieu observed self-declared cultural leaders who proffered their accounts of true and ancient traditions. But these accounts were already codifications – whether formally written down or not – at least one step removed from the ubiquitous reproduction of social life and culture in constant interaction.[25] We could think of traditionalism as the mobilization of specific contents of older culture as valuable in themselves, even if now disconnected from their previous modes of reproduction and ways of life.

This excursus on tradition is important because cosmopolitans are apt to see traditional culture as a set of contents, possibly erroneous, rather than a basic underpinning for many people's practical orientation to the world. They are apt to approach it with an eye to sorting its good from its bad elements – keep that folk art perhaps but lose that patriarchy. They are apt to regard it as a kind of possession, a good to which people have a right so long as it doesn't conflict with other more basic goods. This not only misses the extent to which culture is constitutive.[26] It also misses the extent to which rapid social change is not merely disorienting but disempowering. And finally, it misses the extent to which roots in traditional culture and communal social relations are basic to the capacity for collective resistance to inequitable social change – like that brought by global capitalism and perhaps exacerbated by some of the ways in which the United States uses its state power. Last but not least, absorbing the typical modern orientation to tradition as simply backward looking leads many cosmopolitans to miss the extent to which new forward looking projects are built – perhaps "grown" would be a better word – on traditional roots. I refer both to the extent to which self-conscious projects for a better society draw on themes in traditional culture – seeking not simply to resist change but to achieve in new ways things traditionally thought good – and to the extent to which even without self-conscious projects tradition offers a medium for bringing diverse people together in a common culture. Indeed, much of the actually existing cosmopolitan bridging of ethnic boundaries depends not on abstract universalism but on the commingling of older traditions and the production of new ones in informal relationships and local contexts.

Both roots and the need for roots are asymmetrically distributed. It is often precisely those lacking wealth, elite connections, and ease of movement who find their membership in solidaristic social groups most important as an asset. This is so whether the groups are communities, crafts, ethnicities, nations, or religions. Different groups of people struggle both to maintain some realms of autonomy and to gain some voice in (if not control over) the processes of larger-scale integration. The idea that there are clearly progressive and clearly reactionary positions in these struggles is misleading. So is the idea that there is a neutral position offering a cosmopolitan view that is not itself produced in part through tradition.

Philosophers have long proposed both ideal social orders and ethical precepts for individual action based on the assumption that individuals could helpfully be abstracted from their concrete social contexts, at least for the purposes of theory. The motivations for such arguments have been honorable: that existing social contexts endow much that is both evil and mutable with the force and justification of apparent necessity, and that any starting point for understanding persons other than their radical equality in essential humanness and freedom opens the door to treating people as fundamentally unequal. Such theories, grounded in the abstract universality of individual human persons, may provide insights. They are, however, fundamentally unsound as guides to the world in which human beings must take action. They lead not only to a tyranny of the abstract ought over real moral possibilities, and to deep misunderstandings of both human life and social inequality, but also to political programs which, however benign and egalitarian their intentions, tend to reproduce problematic power relations.

Among the instances of these problems is the overeager expectation that the world could happily be remade through ethical, political, sociopsychological, and cultural orientations in which individual freedom and appropriations of the larger world would require no strong commitment to intervening solidarities. This reveals a certain blindness in cosmopolitan theory, blindness toward the sociological conditions for cosmopolitanism itself and toward the reasons why national, ethnic, and other groups remain important to most of the world's people. It is about the ways in which cosmopolitanism – however attractive in some ways – is compromised by its formulation in liberal individualist terms that block appreciation of the importance of social solidarity. Nussbaum, for example, discerns two opposing traditions in thinking about political community and the good citizen. "One is based upon the emotions; the other urges their removal."[27] While each in its own way pursues freedom and equality, the first relies too much on compassion for her taste. "The former aims at equal support for basic needs and hopes through this to promote equal opportunities for free choice and self-realization; the other starts from the fact of internal freedom – a fact that no misfortune can remove – and finds in this fact a source of political equality." But surely this is a false opposition. Instead of adjudicating between the two sides in this debate, perhaps we should ask how to escape from it.

The social bases of cosmopolitanism

"To belong or not to belong," asks Ulrich Beck, "that is the cosmopolitan question."[28] Indeed perhaps it is, but if so, one of the most crucial things it reveals about cosmopolitanism is that some people are empowered to ask the question with much more freedom and confidence than others. Another is the extent to which cosmopolitanism is conceptualized as the absence of particularism rather than a positive form of belonging.

Oddly, Beck asks the question in a paper devoted to "the analysis of global inequality." His agenda is to focus our attention on the "big inequalities" between rich and poor nations. These, he suggests, dwarf inequalities within nations. There is much to this, though it oversimplifies empirical patterns of inequality. Beck is certainly right that "It is surprising how the big inequalities which are suffered by humanity can be continuously legitimized through a silent complicity between the state authority and the state-obsessed social sciences by means of a form of organized nonperception."[29] But what he doesn't consider is the extent to which participation in a superficially multinational cosmopolitan elite is basic to the reproduction of that nonperception. The elites of "poor" countries who participate in global civil society, multilateral agencies, and transnational business corporations not only make money their compatriots can barely imagine but make possible the cosmopolitan illusion of elites from rich countries. This is the illusion that their relationships with fellow cosmopolitans truly transcend nation and culture and place. Cosmopolitan elites too often misrecognize transnational class formation as the escape from belonging.

Elsewhere, I have analyzed the "class consciousness of frequent travelers" that underwrites this misrecognition.[30] I mean to call attention not just to the elite occupational status of those who form the archetypal image of the cosmopolitans, but to the grounding certain material privileges give to the intellectual position. "Good" passports and easy access to visa, international credit cards, and membership in airline clubs, invitations from conference organizers and organizational contacts all facilitate a kind of inhabitation (if not necessarily citizenship) of the world as an apparent whole. To be sure, diasporas provide for other circuits of international connectivity, drawing on ethnic and kin connections rather than the more bureaucratically formalized ones of businesspeople, academics, and aid workers. But though these are real, they face significantly different contextual pressures.

Post 9/11 restrictions on visas – let alone immigration – reveal the differences between those bearing European and American passports and most others in the world. The former hardly notice the change and move nearly as freely as before. The latter find their international mobility sharply impeded and sometimes blocked. Or else they find it to be forced – as, for example, thousands who have made lives and put down roots in America are deported each year, sometimes, especially children born in the US, to "homes" they barely know or even have never inhabited. European intellectuals like Georgi Agamben might cancel lecture engagements to protest the exercise of "biopower" by a US administration eager to print, scan, and type any visitor. But his cosmopolitan challenge to a regrettable national regime – however legitimate – is altogether different from the unchosen circumstances of those who migrated to make a better life, did so, and had it snatched from them.[31]

The global border control regime thus encourages a sense of natural cosmopolitanism for some and reminds others of their nationality (and often of religion and ethnicity as well). However cosmopolitan their initial intentions or self-understandings, these Asians, Africans, and Latin Americans are reminded by the ascriptions and restrictions with which they are confronted that at least certain sorts of cosmopolitanism are not for them. Normative cosmopolitans can (and do) assert that this is not the way the world should be, and that borders should be more open. But they need also to take care not to deny the legitimacy of any anticosmopolitan responses people may have to this regime of borders, including not just resentment but renewed identification with nations and even projects of national development which hold out the prospect of enabling them to join the ranks of those with good passports.

The point is not simply privilege. It is that a sense of connection to the world as a whole, and of being a competent actor on the scale of "global citizenship" is not merely a matter of the absence of more local ties. It has its own material and social conditions. Moreover, the cosmopolitan elites are hardly culture-free; they do not simply reflect the rational obligations of humanity in the abstract (even if their theories try to).

To some extent, the cosmopolitan elite culture is a product of Western dominance and the kinds of intellectual orientations it has produced. It reflects "modernity" which has its own historical provenance. "This revenant late liberalism reveals, in a more exaggerated form, a struggle at the heart of liberal theory, where a genuine desire for equality as a universal norm is tethered to a tenacious ethnocentric provincialism in matters of cultural judgment and recognition."[32] But the cultural particularity is not simply inheritance, and not simply a reflection of (mainly) Western modernity. It is also constructed out of the concrete conditions of cosmopolitan mobility, education, and participation in certain versions of news and other media flows. It is the culture of those who attend Harvard and the London School of Economics, who read *The Economist* and *Le Monde*, who recognize Mozart's music as universal, and who can discuss the relative merits of Australian, French, and Chilean wines. It is also a culture in which secularism seems natural and religion odd, and in which respect for human rights is assumed but the notion of fundamental economic redistribution is radical and controversial. This culture has many good qualities, as well as blindspots, but nonetheless it is culture and not its absence.

Martha Nussbaum and some other "extreme" cosmopolitans, present cosmopolitanism first and foremost as a kind of virtuous deracination, a liberation from the possibly illegitimate and in any case blinkering attachments of locality, ethnicity, religion, and nationality.[33] But like secularism, cosmopolitanism is a presence not an absence, an occupation of particular positions in the world, not a view from nowhere or everywhere. All actually existing cosmopolitanisms, to be more precise, reflect influences of social location and cultural tradition. The ways in which any one opens to understanding or valuing of others are specific and never exhaust all the possible ways. Secularism is again instructive. The parameters of specific religious traditions shape the contours of what is considered not

religious, or not the domain of specific religions. The not specifically religious, thus, is never a simple embodiment of neutrality. What is "secular"
in relation to multiple Christian denominations may not be exactly equivalent to what is secular in the context of Hindu or Muslim traditions (let
alone of their intermingling and competition). So too, cosmopolitan transcendence of localism and parochialism is not well understood as simple
neutrality toward or tolerance of all particularisms. It is participation in a
particular, if potentially broad, process of cultural production and social
interconnection that spans boundaries.

To say that the cosmopolitanism of most theories reflects the experience of business, academic, government, and civil society elites, thus, is
not merely to point to some reasons why others may not so readily share
it but also to suggest sources of its particular character. It is neither freedom from culture nor a matter of pure individual choice, but a cultural
position constructed on particular social bases and a choice made possible by both that culture and those bases. It is accordingly different from
the transcendence of localism on other cultural and social bases. Cosmopolitanism has particular rather than solely universal content, thus, so
its advocates sometimes fail to recognize this. Moreover, the content and
the misrecognition are connected to social bases of relative privilege.

Much thinking about ethnicity and the legitimacy of local or other particularistic attachments by self-declared cosmopolitans reflects their tacit
presumption of their own more or less elite position. I do not mean simply
that they act to benefit themselves, or in other ways from bad motives.
Rather, I mean that their construction of genuine benevolence is prej-
udiced against ethnic and other attachments because of the primacy of
the perspective of elites. Any prejudice by elites in favor of others in their
own ethnic groups or communities would amount to favoring the already
privileged (a very anti-Rawlsian position). So the cosmopolitans are keen
to rule out such self-benefiting particularism. But ethnic solidarity is not
always a matter of exclusion by the powerful; it is often a resource for
effective collective action and mutual support among the less powerful.
While it is true, in other words, that in-group solidarity by those in positions of power and influence usually amounts to discrimination against
less powerful or privileged others, it is also true that solidarity serves to
strengthen the weak. Indeed, those who are excluded from or allowed only
weak access to dominant structures of power and discourse have especially great need to band together in order to be effective. Of course, elites
also band together to protect privilege (and as Weber emphasized, exclu-
sivity is a prominent elite weapon against the inclusive strategies of mass
activists).[34] And elites manipulate solidarities to pursue their own advantages rather than considering equally the interests of all. Nonetheless,

elites are typically empowered as individuals in ways nonelites are not. In short, when cosmopolitan appeals to humanity as a whole are presented in individualistic terms, they are apt to privilege those with the most capacity to get what they want by individual action. However well intentioned, they typically devalue the ways in which other people depend on ethnic, national, and communal solidarities – among others – to solve practical problems in their lives. And they typically neglect the extent to which asserting that cultural difference should be valued only as a matter of individual taste undermines any attempt to redistribute benefits in the social order across culturally defined groups. They can extol multiculturalism, in other words, so long as this is defined as a harmonious arrangement in which all cultures are seen as attractive parts of a mosaic, but not when members of one cultural group organize to demand that the mosaic be altered.[35]

Cosmopolitanism, liberalism, and belonging[36]

As political theory, cosmopolitanism responds crucially to the focus of traditional liberalism on the relationship of individual persons to individual states (and sometimes to markets). Ideas of citizenship and rights both reflect the attempt to construct the proper relationship between liberal subjects and sovereign states. The cosmopolitan theorists of the 1990s recognized problems both in how this constituted international relations as relations among such states, neglecting the many other ways in which individuals participated in transnational or indeed nonnationally transstate activities, and in the difficulty of accounting for why specific populations of individuals belonged in specific states.

Earlier liberals had often relied at least tacitly on the idea of "nation" to give an account of why particular people belong together as the "people" of a particular state. So long as the fiction of a perfect match between nations and states was plausible, this was relatively unproblematic, though it meant liberal theory was sociologically impoverished. To their credit, the various theorists of a new cosmopolitan liberalism recognized that it was no longer tenable to rely so uncritically on the idea of nation.

The prioritization of the individual society came to seem increasingly untenable. It began to seem fundamental and not contingent that markets and other social relations extend across nation-state borders, that migration and cultural flows challenge nationalist notions of the integral character of cultures and political communities, that states are not able to organize or control many of the main influences on the lives of their citizens, and that the most salient inequalities are intersocietally global and thus not addressed by intrasocietal measures. Accordingly, an important project for liberals was to work out how to extend their theories of justice and political legitimacy to a global scale.

A cosmopolitan attitude appeared both as a timeless good and as a specific response to current historical circumstances. The extension of markets, media, and migration has, advocates of a new cosmopolitan liberalism argue, reduced both the efficacy of states and the adequacy of moral and political analysis that approaches one "society" at a time. At the same time, "identity politics" and multiculturalism have in the eyes of many liberals been excessive and become sources of domestic divisions and illiberal appeals to special rights for different groups. Accordingly, cosmopolitan theorists argue that the "first principles" of ethical obligation and political community should stress the allegiance of each to all at the scale of humanity.

The new cosmopolitans retain, however, one of the weaknesses of older forms of liberalism. They offer no strong account of social solidarity or of the role of culture in constituting human life. For the most part, they start theorizing from putatively autonomous, discrete, and cultureless individuals. Reliance on the assumption that nations were naturally given prepolitical bases for states had helped older liberals to paper over the difficulty of explaining why the individuals of their theories belonged in particular states (or conversely could rightly be excluded from them). The new cosmopolitanism is generally antinationalist, seeing nations as part of the fading order of political life divided on lines of states. Its advocates rightly refuse to rely on this tacit nationalism. But as they offer no new account of solidarity save the obligations of each human being to all others, they give little weight to "belonging," to the notion that social relationships might be as basic as individuals, or that individuals exist only in cultural milieux – even if usually in several at the same time.

Indeed, much of the new liberal cosmopolitan thought proceeds as though belonging is a matter of social constraints from which individuals ideally ought to escape, or temptations to favoritism they ought to resist. Claims of special loyalty or responsibility to nations, communities, or ethnic groups, thus, are subordinated or fall under a suspicion of illegitimacy. To claim that one's self-definition, even one's specific version of loyalty to humanity, comes through membership of some such more particular solidarity is, in Martha Nussbaum's words, a "morally questionable move of self-definition by a morally irrelevant characteristic."[37]

The individualism the new cosmopolitanism inherits from earlier liberalism is attractive partly because of its emphasis on freedom, which encourages suspicion of arguments in favor of ethnicity, communities, or nations. These, many suggest, can be legitimate only as the choices of free individuals – and to the extent they are inherited rather than chosen they should be scrutinized carefully, denied any privileged standing, and possibly rejected.[38]

Nonetheless, it is impossible not to belong to social groups, relations, or culture. The idea of individuals abstract enough to be able to choose all their "identifications" is deeply misleading. Versions of this idea are, however, widespread in liberal cosmopolitanism. They reflect the attractive illusion of escaping from social determinations into a realm of greater freedom, and from cultural particularity into greater universalism. But they are remarkably unrealistic, and so abstract as to provide little purchase on what the next steps of actual social action might be for real people who are necessarily situated in particular webs of belonging, with access to particular others but not to humanity in general. Treating ethnicity as *essentially* (rather than partially) a choice of identifications, they neglect the omnipresence of ascription (and discrimination) as determinations of social identities. And they neglect the extent to which people are implicated in social actions which they are not entirely free to choose (as, for example, I remain an American and share responsibility for the invasion of Iraq despite my opposition to it and distaste for the US administration that carried it out). Whether blame or benefit follow from such implications, they are not altogether optional.

Efforts to transcend the limits of belonging to specific webs of relationships do not involve freedom from social determinations, but transformations of social organization and relationships. Sometimes transcendence of particular solidarities involves no neat larger whole but a patchwork quilt of new connections, like those mediated historically by trading cities and still today by diasporas. But transcending local solidarities has also been paradigmatically how the growth of nationalism has proceeded, sometimes complementing but often transforming or marginalizing more local or sectional solidarities (village, province, caste, class, or tribe). Nations usually work by presenting more encompassing identities into which various sectional ones can fit. And in this it is crucial to recognize that nations have much the same relationship to pan-national or global governance projects that localities and minorities had to the growth of national states.

Will Kymlicka has argued that it is important "to view minority rights, not as a deviation from ethnocultural neutrality, but as a response to majority nationbuilding."[39] In the same sense, I have suggested that it is a mistake to treat nationalism as a deviation from cosmopolitan neutrality. In the first place, cosmopolitanism is not neutral – though cosmopolitans can try to make both global institutions and global discourse more open and more fair. In the second place, national projects respond to global projects. They are not mere inheritances from the past, but ways – certainly very often, problematic ways – of taking hold of current predicaments.

The analogy between nations faced with globalization and minorities within nation-states – both immigrants and so-called national minorities – is strong. And we can learn from Kymlicka's injunction, "Fairness therefore requires an ongoing, systematic exploration of our common institutions to see whether their rules, structures and symbols disadvantage immigrants."[40] Cosmopolitanism at its best is a fight for just such fairness in the continued development of global institutions. But the analogy is not perfect, and it is not perfect precisely because most immigrants (and national minorities) make only modest claims to sovereignty. Strong Westphalian doctrines of sovereignty may always have been problematic and may now be out of date. But just as it would be hasty to imagine we are embarking on a postnational era – when all the empirical indicators are that nationalism is resurgent precisely because of asymmetrical globalization – so it would be hasty to forget the strong claims to collective autonomy and self-determination of those who have been denied both, and the need for solidarity among those who are least empowered to realize their projects as individuals. Solidarity need not always be national, and need not always develop from traditional roots. But for many of those treated most unfairly in the world, nations and traditions are potentially important resources.

Conclusion

I have argued that there are good reasons to think we are not entering very abruptly into a postnational era. It is not at all clear, for example, that the European Union is a "postnational" project rather than a continuation of the same trend that produced national unification in France and Germany and subordinated Scottish, Irish, Welsh, and indeed English identities in the British state. Nor is it clear that the projects of broadening and deepening national solidarities and trying to join them to popular states are without value for people in most of the world's developing – or *un*developing – countries.

Fairness in global integration is not just a matter of achieving the "best" abstract design of global institutions. It necessarily also includes allowing people inhabiting diverse locations in the world, diverse traditions, and diverse social relationships opportunities to choose the institutions in and through which they will integrate.

I have suggested that most cosmopolitan theories are individualistic in ways that obscure the basic importance of social relationships and culture. I have defended tradition, thus, and urged thinking of it as a mode of reproduction of culture and practical orientations to action, not as a bundle of contents. On this basis I have suggested that when globalization causes abrupt social transformations it is typically disempowering, but that tradition importantly underpins popular resistance to asymmetrical globalization. Projects grounded in tradition can be forward-looking; they are not always captured by demagogic traditionalists extolling stasis or a return to some idealized past.

No one lives outside particularistic solidarities. Some cosmopolitan theorists may believe they do, but this is an illusion made possible by positions of relative privilege and the dominant place of some cultural orientations in the world at large. The illusion is not a simple mistake, but a misrecognition tied to what Pierre Bourdieu called the *"illusio"* of all social games, the commitment to their structure that shapes the engagement of every player and makes possible effective play.[41] In other words, cosmopolitans do not simply fail to see the cultural particularity and social supports of their cosmopolitanism, but cannot fully and accurately recognize these without introducing a tension between themselves and their social world. And here I would include myself and probably all of us. Whether we theorize cosmopolitanism or not, we are embedded in social fields and practical projects in which we have little choice but to make use of some of the notions basic to cosmopolitanism and thereby reproduce it. We have the option of being self-critical as we do so, but not of entirely abandoning cosmopolitanism because we cannot act effectively without it. Nor should we want to abandon it, since it enshrines many important ideas like the equal worth of all human beings and – at least potentially – the value of cultural and social diversity. But we should want to transform it, not least because as usually constructed, especially in its most individualistic forms, it systematically inhibits attention to the range of solidarities on which people depend, and to the special role of such solidarities in the struggles of the less privileged and those displaced or challenged by capitalist globalization.

NOTES

1. But see Timothy Brennan, *At Home in the World: Cosmopolitanism Now*, Cambridge, MA: Harvard University Press, 1997.
2. The most important theorist specifically of cosmopolitan democracy was David Held, *Democracy and Global Order*, Cambridge: Polity, 1995. Held drew on the more general theory of Jürgen Habermas who himself developed a similar idea of postnational solidarity, e.g. *The Postnational Constellation*. Cambridge, MA: MIT Press, 2001. And a wide variety of approaches shared much of the same vision if not the same specifics. Anthologies

representing diverse approaches include Daniele Archibugi and David Held (eds.), *Cosmopolitan Democracy*, Cambridge: Polity, 1995; Daniele Archibugi, David Held, and Martin Kohler (eds.), *Re-Imagining Political Community*, Cambridge: Polity, 1988; Pheng Cheah and Bruce Robbins (eds.), *Cosmopolitics: Thinking and Feeling Beyond the Nation*, Minneapolis: University of Minnesota Press, 1998; Daniele Archibugi (ed.), *Debating Cosmopolitics*, London: Verso, 2003; and Steven Vertovec and Robin Cohen (eds.), *Conceiving Cosmopolitanism*, Oxford: Oxford University Press, 2002. The last two of those anthologies include my own less optimistic assessments.

3. That there are only a handful of clear successes – say, Mozambique – seems not to dim enthusiasm for humanitarian intervention. This is renewed as part of a broader social imaginary and ethical stance more than simply a utilitarian calculation. See Calhoun, "The emergency imaginary," in D. Gaonkar and T. McCarthy (eds.), *Modernity and Social Imaginaries: Essays in Honor of Charles Taylor*, Minneapolis: University of Minnesota Press, forthcoming.

4. This produced a disabling coincidence of attacks on the state from the Hayekian right and the cosmopolitan left, a coincidence that greatly weakened defense of the welfare state when its dismantling began. Hostility to the state was redoubled by desire to achieve distance from any association with the Soviet model. As Timothy Brennan suggests, "attacks on the viability of the nation-state have been the contemporary form that an attack on socialism takes. For, apart from ethnic purists and right-wing nationalists, socialists are the only ones who still defend national sovereignty in the age of the global subaltern . . ." (1997: 301).

5. Brennan, *At Home in the World*, pp. 139–40.

6. As Friedrich Meinecke argued "The current view . . . sees cosmopolitanism and national feeling as two modes of thought that mutually exclude each other, that do battle with each other, and that supplant each other. Such a view cannot satisfy the historical mind that has a deeper awareness of circumstances . . . ," *Cosmopolitanism and the National State*, Princeton: Princeton University Press, 1970, p. 21.

7. Habermas, *The Postnational Constellation*.

8. Köhler, "From the national to the cosmopolitan public sphere," in Archibugi, Held, and Köhler (eds.), *Re-Imagining Political Community*, p. 231.

9. Beck, "Sociology in the second age of modernity," in Vertovec and Cohen (eds.), *Conceiving Cosmopolitanism*, Oxford: Oxford University Press, 2002.

10. See, e.g. Andrew Linklater, "Citizenship and sovereignty in the post-Westphalian European state," in Archibugi, Held, and Köhler (eds.), *Re-Imagining Political Community*.

11. Micheline Ishay, *The Betrayal of Nationalism*, Minneapolis: University of Minnesota Press, 1995; Meinecke, *Cosmopolitanism and the National State*.

12. See the excellent anthology revisiting Kant's classic cosmopolitan essay on perpetual peace: James Bohman and Matthias Lutz-Bachmann, (eds.), *Perpetual Peace: Essays on Kant's Cosmopolitan Ideal*, Cambridge, MA: MIT Press, 1997. Also see Hans Joas, *War and Modernity*, Cambridge, MA: Blackwell, 2002.

13. Jürgen Habermas, *Inclusion of the Other*, Cambridge, MA: MIT Press, 1998; Martha Nussbaum, *For Love of Country*, Boston: Beacon, 1996. See also the essays in Daniele Archibugi (ed.), *Debating Cosmopolitics* and my own discussion of these and other variants of cosmopolitanism in "Belonging in the cosmopolitan imaginary," *Ethnicities* 4 (2003): 531–53.
14. Beck, "Sociology in the second age of modernity," p. 77.
15. See M. Berezin and M. Schain (eds.), *Europe without Borders: Re-Mapping Territory, Citizenship and Identity in a Transnational Age*, Baltimore: Johns Hopkins University Press, which includes my "The democratic integration of Europe: interests, identity, and the public sphere," pp. 243–74.
16. Habermas, *The Inclusion of the Other*. See also Friedrich Meinecke, *Nationalism and Cosmopolitanism*, Princeton: Princeton University Press, 1970, and Hans Kohn, *The Idea of Nationalism*, New York: Macmillan, 1944, on the classic traditions of German thought that try to reclaim civic nationalism from the notion that Germans are essentially ethnic nationalists. As Meinecke wrote in 1928, "the best German national feeling also includes the cosmopolitan ideal of a humanity beyond nationality and that it is 'un-German to be merely German'" (p. 21).
17. Held, "Democracy and globalization," in Archibugi, Held, and Köhler (eds.), *Re-Imagining Political Community*, p. 13. See also Hans Kohn's words from sixty years ago: "Important periods of history are characterized by the circumference within which the sympathy of man extends. These limits are neither fixed nor permanent, and changes in them are accompanied by great crises in history," *The Idea of Nationalism*, p. 21.
18. Will Kymlicka, *Politics in the Vernacular*, Oxford: Oxford University Press, 2001, p. 322.
19. The work of Partha Chatterjee is particularly informative on this issue. See *Nationalist Thought and the Colonial World: A Derivative Discourse?* London: Zed Books, 1986 and *The Nation and its Fragments*, Princeton: Princeton University Press, 1994. See also Calhoun, *Nationalism*, Minneapolis: University of Minnesota Press, 1997.
20. Pierre Bourdieu, "Unifying to better dominate," in *Firing Back*. New York: New Press, 2002.
21. Eric Hobsbawm, *Nations and Nationalism Since 1780: Programme, Myth, Reality*, Cambridge: Cambridge University Press, 1990 is paradigmatic, but the tendency is widespread.
22. Ibid., p. 25.
23. See Bourdieu's discussion in *The Field of Cultural Production*, New York: Columbia University Press, 1993, esp. the title essay.
24. Weber, "The social psychology of world religions," in *From Max Weber*, H. H. Gerth and C. Wright Mills (eds.), London: Routledge and Kegan Paul, 1948, p. 296.
25. These are themes Bourdieu addressed in several works; see notably *Algérie 60: Structures économiques et structures temporelles*, Paris: Minuit 1977 and Bourdieu and Abdelmalek Sayad, *Le déracinement: La crise d'agriculture traditionelle en Algérie*, Paris: Minuit, 1964. See also the useful discussion in Laurent Addi, *Sociologie et anthropologie chez Pierre Bourdieu: Le paradigme*

anthropologique kabyle et ses conséquences théoriques, Paris: Decouverte, 2003.

26. See Charles Taylor, *Modern Social Imaginaries*, Duke: Duke University Press, 2004.

27. *Upheavals of Thought*, 2001: 367.

28. Ulrich Beck, "The analysis of global inequality: from national to cosmopolitan perspective," Mary Kaldor, Helmut Anheier, and Marlies Glasius (eds.), *Global Civil Society 2003*, Oxford: Oxford University Press, 2003, p. 45.

29. Ibid., 50.

30. Calhoun, "The class consciousness of frequent travelers." *South Atlantic Quarterly* 101 (4) (2000): 869–97.

31. James Clifford, "Traveling cultures," in Lawrence Grossberg, Cary Nelson, and Paula Treichler (eds.), *Cultural Studies*, New York: Routledge, 1992 and Timothy Brennan, *At Home in the World*, pp. 16–17, both rightly raise the problems posed by using the metaphor of "travel" to think about migrant labor and displacement, a habit that has hardly disappeared, rooted perhaps in the situation of intellectuals but disturbingly inapt for many others.

32. Sheldon Pollock, Homi Bhabha, Carol Breckenridge, and Dipesh Chakrabharty, "Cosmopolitanisms," *Public Culture* 12 (3) (2000): 581.

33. See Calhoun, "Belonging in the cosmopolitan imaginary," for the distinction of different varieties of cosmopolitans, including extreme from moderate. See also Samuel Scheffler, *Boundaries and Allegiances: Problems of Justice and Responsibility in Liberal Thought*, Oxford: Oxford University Press, 2001.

34. Max Weber, *Economy and Society*, Berkeley: University of California Press, 1978 [1922].

35. See Jon Okamura's analysis of Hawaii's myth of a multicultural paradise. Whatever reality this may reflect, it also enshrines an existing distribution of power and resources. It not only encourages the idea that individuals from each cultural group should be treated equally (as against, say, affirmative action). It especially inhibits self-organization by members of any group traditionally on the losing end – say native Hawaiians – to alter the terms of the distributive game. Such organization can only appear as hostile to the idealized multicultural harmony. Jonathan Okamura, "The illusion of paradise: privileging multiculturalism in Hawai'i," in D. C. Gladney (ed.), *Making Majorities: Constituting the Nation in Japan, Korea, China, Malaysia, Fiji, Turkey, and the United States*, Stanford: Stanford University Press, 1998, 264–84.

36. The arguments taken up in this section are made at more length in Calhoun, "Constitutional patriotism and the public sphere: interests, identity, and solidarity in the integration of Europe," in Pablo De Greiff and Ciaran Cronin (eds.), *Global Ethics and Transnational Politics*, Cambridge, MA: MIT Press, 2002, 275–312 and Calhoun, "Belonging in the cosmopolitan imaginary." *Ethnicities* 4 (2003): 531–53.

37. *For Love of Country*, p. 5.

38. See Calhoun, "Belonging in the cosmopolitan imaginary"; Rogers Brubaker, "Neither individualism nor 'groupism': a reply to Craig Calhoun," *Ethnicities* 4 (2003): 554–7; Calhoun, "Variability of belonging: a reply to Rogers

Brubaker," *Ethnicities* 4 (2003): 558–68. See also Rogers Brubaker, "Ethnicity without groups," *Archives européennes de sociologie* 43 (2) (2002): 163–89 and Rogers Brubaker and Frederick Cooper, "Beyond 'identity'," *Theory and Society* 29 (2000): 1–47.

39. *Politics in the Vernacular*, p. 38.
40. *Ibid.*, p. 162.
41. Pierre Bourdieu, *The Logic of Practice*, Stanford: Stanford University Press, 1990.

Index

Lightning Source UK Ltd.
Milton Keynes UK
UKHW04f0030200818
327495UK00001B/71/P